# Financing Community Colleges

# The Association of Community College Trustees and Rowman & Littlefield Publishers

## The Futures Series on Community Colleges

Sponsored by the Association of Community College Trustees and Rowman & Littlefield Publishers, *The Futures Series on Community Colleges* is designed to produce and deliver books that strike to the heart of issues that will shape the future of community colleges. *Futures* books examine emerging structures, systems and business models, and stretch prevailing assumptions about leadership and management by reaching beyond the limits of convention and tradition.

Topics addressed in the *Series* are those that are vital to community colleges, but have yet to receive meaningful attention in literature, research and analysis. *Futures* books are written by scholars and practitioners who deliver a unique perspective on a topic or issue— a president or higher education consultant bringing expert and practical understanding to a topic, a policy analyst breaking down a complex problem into component parts, an academic or think tank scholar conducting incisive research, or a researcher and a practitioner working together to examine an issue through different lenses.

*Futures* books are developed on the premise that disruptive innovation and industry transformation are, and will be, an ongoing challenge. Gradual improvement is, understandably, a natural preference of leaders. It will not be enough, however, to position our colleges for the future. The future will be about transformation and, to perform optimally, our colleges will need to become capable of large-scale change. As leaders come face-to-face with digital forces and rapidly changing social, economic and public policy conditions, they will have no choice but to get ahead of change or relinquish market position to competitors. *Futures* books are a vehicle through which leaders can learn about and prepare for what's ahead. Whether it's through analysis of what big data will mean in the next generation of colleges, or which business models will become the new normal, *Futures* books are a resource for practitioners who realize that the ideas of out-of-the-box thinkers and the innovative practices of high-performing organizations can be invaluable for answering big questions and solving complex problems.

Richard L. Alfred, Series Co-Editor
Emeritus Professor of Higher Education
University of Michigan

Debbie Sydow, Series Co-editor
President
Richard Bland College of the College
of William and Mary

## Forthcoming Books in *The Futures Series on Community Colleges*

*Unrelenting Change, Disruptive Innovation, and Risk: Forging the Next Generation of Community Colleges*
By Daniel J. Phelan

In this book, thirty-five-year veteran Dan Phelan shares key insights from his personal and professional journey as a transformational, entrepreneurial community college leader.

The book's wisdom and insights are amplified by observations gleaned from interviews and visits with dozens of leading practitioners. Drawing upon his sailing experiences, Phelan argues that leaders should stop playing it safe in the harbor because the real gains driving institutional and student success are found in uncharted waters. *Unrelenting Change, Disruptive Innovation, and Risk* dares community college leaders to innovate and provides them with a toolkit for understanding changing conditions, assessing risk and successfully navigating change.

*The Urgency of Now: Equity and Excellence*
By Marcus M. Kolb, Samuel D. Cargile, et al

*The Urgency of Now* asserts that in addition to being granted access to the community college, all twenty-first-century students need uncompromised support to succeed. Success means demonstrating relevant learning for transfer and employment, and timely completion of credentials. Looking to the future, the authors contend that community colleges, both by their past successes and future challenges, are at the epicenter for determining the essential ingredients of a new student-centered system that guarantees equity and excellence.

*The Completion Agenda in Community Colleges: What It Is, Why It Matters, and Where It's Going*
By Chris Baldwin

Community colleges in many states are facing intensifying pressure from policymakers for improved student outcomes overtly manifested in aggressive performance-based funding formulas. In this book, Chris Baldwin asks and answers an overarching question: Are community colleges, government agencies, foundations and other entities aware of the unintended consequences of actions related to the completion agenda? The book explores the potential benefit of increased educational attainment and credentials versus the possible sacrifice of quality and the labor market value of the credentials awarded.

*Institutional Analytics: Building a Culture of Evidence*
By Karen Stout

*Institutional Analytics* paints a clear picture of the challenges involved in cultural change and building a team capable of using analytics to gain a competitive advantage for the future. Revealing that community colleges pretend to be more data driven than they actually are, Stout challenges leadership teams to set clear goals, define what success looks like, and ask the right questions to get there. By adopting new tools, abandoning legacy systems and relationships, and boldly adopting open source solutions, colleges can turn large quantities of data into business intelligence that drives transformation.

# Previously Published Books in *The Series on Community Colleges*

*Minding the Dream: The Process and Practice of the American Community College, Second Edition*
By Gail O. Mellow and Cynthia M. Heelan

*First in the World: Community Colleges and America's Future*
By J. Noah Brown

*Community College Student Success: From Boardrooms to Classrooms*
By Banessa Smith Morest

*Re-visioning Community Colleges*
By Debbie Sydow and Richard Alfred

*Community Colleges on the Horizon: Challenge, Choice, or Abundance*
By Richard Alfred, Christopher Shults, Ozan Jaquette, and Shelley Strickland

# Financing Community Colleges

## Where We Are, Where We're Going

Richard M. Romano
and James C. Palmer

with Richard L. Alfred and
Debbie L. Sydow

ROWMAN & LITTLEFIELD
Lanham • Boulder • New York • London

Published by Rowman & Littlefield
A wholly owned subsidiary of The Rowman & Littlefield Publishing Group, Inc.
4501 Forbes Boulevard, Suite 200, Lanham, Maryland 20706
www.rowman.com

Unit A, Whitacre Mews, 26-34 Stannary Street, London SE11 4AB

British Library Cataloguing in Publication Information Available

**Library of Congress Cataloging-in-Publication Data**

Library of Congress Cataloging-in-Publication Data Available

ISBN 978-1-4758-1062-2 (cloth : alk. paper)
ISBN 978-1-4758-1063-9 (pbk. : alk. paper)
ISBN 978-1-4758-1064-6 (electronic)

♾™ The paper used in this publication meets the minimum requirements of American National Standard for Information Sciences—Permanence of Paper for Printed Library Materials, ANSI/NISO Z39.48-1992.

Printed in the United States of America

# Contents

# Acknowledgments

This book draws its major intellectual approach from the seminal study by Breneman and Nelson published by the Brookings Institution in 1981 and entitled *Financing community colleges: An economic perspective.* We owe a great debt of gratitude to their pioneering work and hope that ours will qualify to sit on the same shelf. More immediately we would like to thank Richard Alfred and Debbie Sydow for inviting us to write this book and for guiding us through the approval and publishing process.

Over the years, others have helped to shape our ideas on the mission and financing community colleges, most notably, Arthur M. Cohen and George B. Vaughan. During the research and writing process we have also benefited from the comments of a number of people who read portions of the book, provided us with valuable information or participated in either structured or unstructured interviews. Some of them wished to remain anonymous. Others include: Ronald Ehrenberg (Cornell University); D. Bruce Johnstone (State University of New York [SUNY] Buffalo); Cliff Harbour (University of Wyoming); Thomas Bailey (Columbia University); Nate Johnson (Postsecondary Analytics); Rita Kirshstein (American Institutes for Research); Ozan Jaquette (University of Arizona); Sue Kater (Maricopa Community College District); Williard Hom (WestEd); Lynn Neault (San Diego Community College District); Gary Hendricks (Texas State Technical College); Christopher Mullin (State University System of Florida); Donald A. Dellow (University of South Florida); Alicia Dowd (University of Southern California); Joseph Hankin (SUNY Westchester Community College); Carl Haynes (SUNY Tompkins/Cortland Community College); Kevin Drumm, Regina Losinger, Douglas Lukasik, and Ben Kasper (SUNY Broome Community College); and George Anker and Jay Quaintance (SUNY Central).

ix

To all of them we appreciate the time they spent on our behalf and we absolve them of any responsibility for our views. Special thanks go out to Donna Desrochers at the American Institutes for Research who contributed an important data analysis that appears in chapter 5.

And finally, we extend heartfelt thanks to our spouses, Ellen Romano, Dick's lifelong companion and chief editor and critic who, he says, makes him look a lot smarter than he really is, and Catherine Palmer, Jim's personal librarian and chief supporter whose insights are invariably on target.

# Introduction

According to a report issued in 2013, more than 40 percent of community college presidents in the United States are likely to retire in the next few years. The report, entitled *Crisis and Opportunity: Aligning the Community College Presidency with Student Success*, was produced by the Aspen Institute and Achieving the Dream. It predicted that a mass exit from the presidency will result in a leadership gap because current pathways to the top position are not sufficient to develop a corps of leaders to replace those who are leaving. The report found critical deficiencies among prospective leaders in the area of budget and finance. "In short supply were fund raising skills and an ability to align resources with efforts toward improving student success" (Aspen Institute, 2013, p. 17).

Surveys of community college presidents and students in the graduate pipeline have added to concerns about the resource management skills of current and future leaders. Duree (2007), for instance, surveyed presidents to determine the extent to which they believed their graduate education had prepared them for critical leadership competencies identified by the American Association of Community Colleges ([AACC], 2006).

The respondents (n = 415) indicated that taking "an entrepreneurial stance in seeking ethical alternative funding sources" was among the skills for which they were least prepared (p. 82). Concern about fiscal competencies was also identified in a 2009 survey undertaken by the Institute for Community College Development at Cornell University involving graduate students in eighteen community college doctoral programs in thirteen states. Survey results revealed a lack of confidence in financial management.

Asked to assess their graduate curricula in terms of the AACC leadership competencies, students gave finance the lowest rating and indicated that resource management was much less of a concern than other leadership priorities; only community college advocacy was rated lower (Romano, Townsend, & Mamiseishvili, 2009).

It is possible that the lack of confidence expressed by future leaders in their ability to manage college finance can be explained by the academic disciplines from which presidents emerge. They are more likely to come from education, psychology, and student affairs than economics, finance, and management. Future leaders do not embark on a career trajectory with a discernible interest in finance.

Furthermore it is unlikely that graduate students will be able to make up this deficiency with a single course in finance as part of a graduate curriculum. Perhaps resource management and fund-raising are skills better learned through experience, networking, professional development, and personal reading and reflection.

This book is part of the learning process. It is directed to community college leaders, both current and prospective, who wish to acquire an understanding of where community colleges currently stand on financial issues and where they may be headed. As such, it is part of the process of learning how to think about the future.

## AN ECONOMIC PERSPECTIVE

Analysis of community college finance may proceed from a number of different perspectives. This book is grounded in an economic perspective, which is rooted in three fundamental observations about social reality that were nicely summarized some forty years ago by Stanford economist Victor Fuchs (1974).

The first observation is that our wants, as a society, exceed the resources we have to satisfy those wants at any given point in time. The second is that resources, both physical and human, have alternative uses. Colleges are built and financed at the expense of fewer tanks or fewer hospitals. Some resources are more flexible and mobile than others. It is easier, for instance, to divert steel from the construction of dormitories to the construction of tanks than it is to convert coal miners into computer programmers. The third observation is that people have different wants and needs.

As Fuchs observed, "the oft-heard statement, 'Health is the most important goal,' does not accurately describe human behavior" (p. 4). The same holds for education. Spending one's tuition money on a car may be short-sighted from an educator's perspective, but may reflect higher priorities, at the time, on the part of the student.

Given these observations, the fundamental economic problem is how to allocate scarce resources to best satisfy societal needs. This requires individuals, organizations, and society as a whole to make choices, and choices have costs. In order to allocate resources efficiently, for instance, society must strive to assure that the benefits of education, or any other public service or good, exceed as much as possible, the total costs of producing it. Accordingly economists approach analysis with a cost-benefit mentality, which is not the same thing as saying that all they are concerned about is money.

The economic point of view may be contrasted with what might be called the romantic and the mono-technic (industry-centric) points of view. Again, drawing on Fuchs:

> the romantic point of view fails to recognize the scarcity of resources relative to wants. The fact that we are constantly being confronted with the need to choose is attributed to capitalism, . . . the unions, war, unemployment or some other scapegoat. Because *some* of the barriers to greater output and want satisfaction are clearly man-made, the romantic is misled into confusing the real world with the Garden of Eden. (p. 5)

The mono-technic view is more defensible than the romantic, but still fails to recognize the diversity of human needs and preferences. This viewpoint is most often found among specialists and professionals in a particular field who are trained in a particular technology. For example, an engineer might want to build the best bridge technically possible or an educator the best schools. A position of this type is understandable from their point of view, but is not always an effective guide for social policy. As Fuchs put it, "the mono-technic person fails to recognize the claims of competing wants or the divergence of their priorities from those of other people. . . ." (Fuchs, p. 5).

Working within an economic perspective, the analysis presented in this book is mostly mono-technic in nature because it is addressed to college leaders and constituent groups interested in maximizing benefits from the resources given to them. The fact that those resources might be better used if given to secondary schools or to people in the form of tax cuts is something that is part of the political process and influenced through advocacy.

While occasionally we examine the broader implications of policy, we do not take a position on whether resources allocated to community colleges might be better spent elsewhere. Ultimately, however, in the words of Breneman and Nelson (1981), "the future of the community college will depend, in part, on how persuasively . . . [the] case [for the community college] is made to the public" (p. 111).

## RESEARCH ON COMMUNITY COLLEGE FINANCE

The community college literature pays relatively little attention to finance and fiscal issues. Occasional volumes in the New Directions for Community Colleges series have examined fiscal challenges (e.g., Alfred, 1978; Bers, Head, & Palmer, 2014; Katsinas & Palmer, 2005; Lombardi, 1973; Milliron, de los Santos, & Browning, 2003). But, as far as we know, this is only the second book devoted exclusively to community college finance since the seminal work of Breneman and Nelson in 1981 (The first, by Mullin, Baime, & Honeyman, 2015, was published just as our text was completed). In the chapters that follow, we have distilled—in the language of the practitioner— a vast number of studies that we and others have considered influential in advancing our understanding of community college finance and policy.

In reviewing thirty years of research, we find that they might be classified into three broad categories. The first—*Type-1 studies*—are those conducted by individual colleges and generally not available for public consumption because they are confidential internal documents.

It is important for colleges to conduct applied research, but the information generated is almost always descriptive and devoid of sophisticated analysis. This information may be useful for internal decision-making, but is of little interest to external audiences. Occasionally, campus institutional researchers present some of this research at academic meetings and it becomes incorporated into Type-2 studies (discussed below). Colleges also report some of their internal data to the Integrated Postsecondary Education Data System (IPEDS) and statewide data systems, and this information is used by researchers at a more sophisticated level of analysis.

*Type-2 studies* encompass the vast majority of published work on community college finance. These studies are sometimes descriptive but may employ advanced analytical techniques, often drawing on internal data reported by individual colleges. Studies of this type may show that correlations exist between variables, but rarely do they provide strong evidence of causation.

A problem with Type-2 studies is one of selection. For example, if the most academically able and motivated students are also more likely to go to college and be financially successful, how do we know that their positive outcomes later in life are due to the effects of going to college? In spite of our inability to control for all of the variables that might explain cause and effect, Type-2 research can be very suggestive and is often all we have available. In this volume we have drawn on the best of these studies, as determined by experts in the field

*Type-3 studies* represent the methodological gold standard. They consist of randomized, controlled trials where students are assigned to different groups on a random basis and then followed to determine if and how the treatment group differs from the control group. Even in this type of research a variety of variables about the participants must be known.

This type of research is most often conducted in the pure sciences and medicine, and is a better guide to what works and what does not work than Type-2 analyses. In education research, due in part to ethical and practical constraints, the experimental approach is comparatively rare but, when used, allows us a better claim to direct causal effects. Quasi-experimental studies are also included in our definition of Type-3 research. This kind of research employs methods such as regression discontinuity designs, propensity score matching, and difference-in-differences comparisons. (For a recent review of these methods with respect to higher education, see DesJardins & Flaster, 2013).

The chapters that follow draw on Type-2 and Type-3 studies supplemented by primary source data and by insights gleaned by the authors through informal interviews with administrators. Primary source data include information on college revenues, expenditures, and outcomes that is collected by the U.S. Department of Education through IPEDS and repackaged in a user-friendly form by the Delta Cost Project, the College Board, and other agencies with a focus on finance.

## CHAPTER ORGANIZATION

The first two chapters in this book provide background information for the chapters that follow. The introductory chapter describes fiscal challenges facing community colleges from a national perspective. Because local circumstances vary, campus leaders will need to interpret these issues in the context of information from their states or service regions. This is followed by principles of public finance that explain why public subsidies to higher education are justified on grounds of efficiency and equity. These principles provide an important framework for understanding the policy positions taken throughout the book.

The second chapter examines revenue and expenditure (cost) trends for community colleges over the last ten years for which we have the data. Throughout this chapter we look at revenue and expenditures from a national perspective, although it is worth noting that significant variation exists among states and across institutions. Because a portion of the tuition revenue received by colleges comes from state and federal financial aid, we present information on these sources. On the expenditure (cost) side of the budget, comparisons are made with public four-year colleges. The reader will note that community colleges have performed effectively in keeping costs under control although some will ask whether this has come at the expense of quality. The last part of this chapter addresses college affordability with respect to community colleges specifically.

Chapters 3 and 4 then examine productivity and outcomes. Chapter 3 delves into the technical aspects of measuring productivity and argues that an accurate measure is hampered by our inability to measure quality. Nevertheless, the accountability movement requires attention to the measures that colleges have. Cautions are issued about basing campus policy decisions on imperfect information and a narrow range of outcome indicators. Frequently used outcome measures such as credential production, student transfer, learning, and labor market success are necessary and important, but they do not depict the full range of college outcomes. A brief review of some of the best research in these areas is given, along with warnings about the difficulty of tying some outcomes to funding.

This leads to an extensive discussion of performance-based funding in chapter 5. After summarizing the early history of performance-for-pay strategies in different industries, we describe the early stage of performance-based funding for higher education, in which states provided small amounts of money as bonus payments above and beyond the operating budget. This phase ran from 1979 to 2002, when the recession of 2001–2002 diminished the capacity of states to provide colleges with additional revenues.

Next we describe recent iterations of performance-based funding, starting in 2008–2009 and continuing today. This latest phase is different from the first in that performance funding is tied directly to the operating budget in contrast to being added to the budget as a bonus payment.

Included in this chapter are the findings of an analysis completed specifically for this volume by Donna Desrochers of the Delta Cost Project at the American Institutes for Research. Desrochers explores the connection between the desired impact of performance-based funding in terms of student outcomes and what actually has been achieved.

Although the effect of performance-based funding on student outcomes remains inconclusive, and although there are serious concerns that funding tied to student performance might weaken academic standards and diminish quality, efforts to link funding to performance have gained momentum and they need to be taken seriously by community college leaders. We hope that our arguments will provide background information that will help leaders shape the future of this type of funding for community colleges.

The last two chapters provide an opportunity to step back and examine policy stances we have taken and to explore where current trends might take community colleges. In chapter 6 we examine emerging trends on the revenue side of the budget, including possible changes in the Pell and student loan programs that may find their way into reauthorization of the Higher Education Act. We also focus on the cost side of the budget, describing a model for costing out degree programs and discussing activity-based accounting procedures, both of which can provide leaders with effective approaches to resource allocation.

The final chapter explores possible scenarios over the next decade and beyond. Included are the fiscal implications of trends in credentialing and enrollment, institutional mission, and declining state support and growing reliance on tuition. The implications of the continuing tension between demands to do more with less and the need to increase costly support services for at-risk students are also examined, along with the continuing push to tie funding to student outcomes. In addition, we review potential disruptive influences that may have a bearing on the fiscal support of community colleges in the years to come.

It is not our intention to paint a gloomy picture. Rather, our hope is that this book will help college leaders make sense of the challenges they face in securing and managing resources to carry out the community college mission.

If an army travels on its stomach, then a college travels on its budget. It has become increasingly urgent for community college leaders to understand that the battles they are fighting will require money and responsible resource management. Leaders will be better at winning these battles if they know enough about finance to anticipate the future and mitigate forces that could impose conditions incompatible with the values of higher education and the goal of student success.

*Chapter 1*

# Public Finance and Community Colleges

As this book goes to press, President Obama's plan to provide students a tuition-free community college education has attracted a great deal of media attention and has helped to remind the public of the positive role that two-year colleges play in postsecondary education. It's not that the media ignored higher education before the president's 2015 State of the Union address, but most of the earlier attention focused on some of the negative aspects of going to college, such as the rising cost of tuition and the growing student loan debt.

While the problems of rising cost and student debt have been related mostly to four-year colleges and universities, just below the surface one also finds criticisms of the community college. Most of these critiques have not reached the general public but do resonate in public policy circles. The most common are the low graduation rates and the inability of remedial programs to produce positive results. Some critics also worry about the quality of the community college and the wisdom of "putting so many eggs in the flimsy community college basket" (Butler, 2015, para. 8).

All of this points to growing public scrutiny of the funding, expenditures, and outcomes of community colleges—topics that are at the heart of this book. Many of the fiscal problems faced by community college leaders are faced by higher education leaders in general, but some are unique to the community college and require solutions that may not apply to four-year colleges.

At the present time, community college leaders are under pressure to educate more students and produce more degrees and other workforce credentials, especially in the so-called STEM fields (science, technology, engineering, and mathematics). This, combined with the decrease in state support for higher education (which we discuss in the next chapter), means that colleges are being asked to do more with less and to document their progress to key constituents, including those who control the public purse as well as the students and parents who are paying an increasing share of the bills.

Some of the issues and challenges covered in our scan of the current financial environment include:

- paying for the increasing number of students entering community colleges in most states, and expanding institutional capacity, both human and capital, to accommodate these students;
- determining, on campuses where enrollments are falling, how to reach beyond college service regions to attract more students or engineer a controlled downsizing of existing efforts without disrupting the educational process and damaging the reputation and quality of the institution;
- responding to and funding societal demands for increased student completion rates in programs, but particularly in high-cost, high-demand programs (such as those in the health sciences) and in remedial programs;
- prioritizing the use of campus resources among multiple demands in a way that considers the costs and benefits, both measured and unmeasured, of their use;
- coping with the instability of state funding, which remains vulnerable to the ups and downs of the business cycle and during economic downturns leaves community colleges underfunded at precisely the time that enrollments spike;
- dealing with the desire to keep tuition down through cost control while at the same time paying bills and maintaining quality;
- responding to the political shift from what we will call trust-based funding (i.e., unrestricted appropriations), to funding based on outcomes;
- furthering important goals of the open-access mission (e.g., helping students test the waters, gage their interests in a low-cost environment or regroup after a failed university experience) that are undervalued in the contemporary completion agenda and not recognized in performance-funding schemes;
- resisting threats to access and quality posed by performance-based funding schemes (e.g., sustaining academic quality and standards, as well as access for underrepresented and underprepared students, in the face of growing attempts to tie funding to outcomes);
- providing the funding and flexibility needed to test new campus initiatives that meet current and future needs; and
- increasing external funding (grants and gifts) in a competitive environment that favors four-year public and private colleges with a larger and wealthier donor base.

All of these challenges factor into fiscal decision-making processes, not only on the campus level, but also on the state and national levels where campus leaders have an important advocacy role to play. This book will touch on and examine all of these issues and provide campus leaders with a constructive way to think about the future.

In order to respond to fiscal issues on both the campus level and beyond, it is useful to understand key financial trends and to have a framework for thinking about where we are going and where we might want to go. This chapter and the next will do just that.

The next chapter will provide some basic information about the revenue and expenditure patterns of community colleges from a national perspective. Decision makers will need to interpret these in context with information from their own states, as considerable variations can occur across the nation. The remainder of this chapter provides a few theoretical principles that guide our thinking about national revenue and expenditure trends and help leaders assess relevant public policy measures.

## PRINCIPLES OF FINANCE

As stated earlier, our approach to analyzing the fiscal challenges presented above draws primarily on the principles of public finance developed by economists. Exploring these principles is not an empty academic exercise, but can provide a framework for informing decisions on the campus level and engaging the broader environment within which community colleges operate.

Central to these ongoing decisions is the debate about the proper role of government in the higher education market, and determining how we should answer the age-old questions of who benefits, who pays, and who should pay? On a policy level, these questions are critical because community colleges, like all other colleges, sell their product (service) at a price (tuition) below what it costs to produce. The difference is covered by a public subsidy paid for by taxpayers or from private sources contributed by alumni, friends, foundations, etc.

College leaders making the case for government fiscal support for their institutions must answer a fundamental question: In a society that seems to favor private spending over public, what justification can we give for the public subsidy of higher education?

Economists weigh their answers to this question against the principles of *efficiency* and *equity*. Some understanding of these concepts, which provide the theoretical framework used to select the topics and policy recommendations addressed throughout this book, gives practitioners a logical framework for responding to constituents and shaping policy beyond the campus level.

In the pages that follow, we briefly introduce these constructs and apply them by way of illustration to the community college systems of California and New York. Admittedly, this economic approach takes us only so far and does not lead to an optimal level of public subsidy. It leaves plenty of room for uncertainty and ambiguity as to the proper mix of private and public funds in financing community colleges—a mix that is as much a product of political wrangling as it is a product of fiscal analysis. But the principles offered here do provide college leaders with a framework for explaining and justifying requests for public subsidies to various constituencies.

## EFFICIENCY

Operating efficient public enterprises is important to the public because it is a sign that their tax dollars are not being wasted. However, from a broader perspective, efficiency is not solely concerned with producing a good or service at the lowest possible cost (often referred to as *technical efficiency*), but is also a measure of how well society's scarce resources are allocated in accord with consumer choices, which balance the costs of producing a good or service against its presumed benefits (often referred to as *allocative efficiency*).

It is possible to produce something at a low cost that would not be highly valued by the society, once all of the costs and benefits were known. In this case we would have technical but not allocative efficiency (Breneman & Nelson, 1981). Community college leaders have a good deal of influence over technical efficiency, but their influence over allocative efficiency is more limited and is linked to their advocacy role. Thus leaders can seek to run an efficient organization with the resources given to them, but must compete in the political arena to get those resources, which have alternative uses.

### Technical Efficiency

Technical efficiency has to do with producing a given level and quality of output at the lowest possible cost. The corollary of this is that more output of a given quality can be produced with the same or fewer resources. With respect to higher education, this is reflected in statements such as "Let's educate the same students at lower cost," or "Let's educate more students at the same or lower costs," or "Colleges are being forced to do more with less."

All of these propositions are part of the rhetoric over the rising cost of higher education and what, if anything, is happening to the quality of post-secondary education—an issue reflecting policymaker demands for evidence that investment in higher education yields positive benefits to students and society in general.

Economists can show that technical efficiency is promoted by competition among producers in an industry where both producers and consumers have perfect knowledge and in which entry and exit into the industry are relatively easy. But it can be forcefully argued that none of these conditions exist in the higher education industry and, despite arguments to the contrary, might not be possible within such an industry.

What we are left with is an imperfectly competitive industry that, under the right conditions, might face sufficient pressure to warrant minimizing its costs. While college administrators will argue that they are squeezing as much (technical) inefficiency out of the system as they can, some studies show that even community colleges are "falling short of their productivity potential" (Harris & Goldrick-Rab, 2010, p. 41).

The next chapter will look at the issue of college costs in greater detail and provide simple comparisons between community colleges and other sectors of public higher education. One of the problems in dealing with the issue of technical efficiency and the related concept of productivity is that we do not have a good measure of the quality of service colleges are providing. In fact, we will argue in chapter 4 that we don't even have an agreed-upon measure of the outputs that the different sectors of higher education produce, and this is especially true with respect to community colleges. For now we will leave this topic to a more detailed discussion in the chapters that follow.

## Allocative Efficiency

It is often argued that higher education would be under-produced in a strictly private market economy—one in which there are no public tax subsidies—because individuals would only recognize the benefits that occur to them individually, such as a better job and higher incomes, and not the benefits to society that occur as spillovers to others in the form of a more educated citizenry, lower crime rates, lower social welfare expenditures, shared values, etc. In this framework, total social benefits equal the sum of private benefits plus spillover benefits.

If individuals only consider private benefits when they purchase higher education, then they undervalue the total benefits and the industry will be allocatively inefficient because it will under-produce this service. This justifies a public subsidy, which drives the price (tuition) down to where, at least theoretically, more of the service is consumed and produced, resulting in greater allocative efficiency.

Unfortunately, the calculation of private and, especially, spillover benefits, is imprecise. If we could measure them more precisely, efficiency would be improved if the spillover effects were paid for by society through taxes (since taxpayers are the ones who benefit) and the private benefits would be paid for by the individual. Thus the proper mix between payments by students (tuition) and public subsidy cannot be specified.

The question of the type of education that generates the most spillovers (also called positive externalities) is also a matter of concern. For instance, Nobel prizewinning economist Milton Friedman felt that "vocational and professional education did not have the [positive externalities] . . . attributed to general education" (Friedman, 1962, pp. 100–101).

For higher education as a whole and for community colleges in particular, if the costs of educating students exceed the benefits, that would be a sign that the industry is allocatively inefficient. However, this is not the case, as evidence continually reveals that benefits, both to students and taxpayers, exceed costs. This indicates that higher education is under-produced and that society would benefit if more resources were shifted into its production.

The fact that the concept of allocative efficiency is infrequently found in discussions of financing community colleges does not mean that it is irrelevant but, rather, that it is widely accepted and understood as a basis for justifying public subsidies. It also can serve as a guide for policy decisions in the future. For instance, Breneman and Nelson (1981) used the concept of allocative efficiency in arguing for full funding of remedial programs, because the benefits were largely external, and against funding for avocational courses because the benefits were largely private.

Allocative efficiency is hard to achieve in higher education because of imperfect information and imperfect capital markets. When markets work imperfectly we refer to it as a *market failure*. As we stated above, markets work best when competition is present, when consumers (in this case students and parents) have perfect information about what they are buying, when these students are perfectly mobile (i.e., are not limited by financial constraints and are not tied down to one geographic location and therefore limited to colleges within that area).

Clearly, none of these conditions holds in the education market, and we therefore see a variety of government interventions in the market to correct for imperfections. For instance, we find the government pushing colleges to disclose outcomes, or to provide better information on the net price of attendance, both of which help students and their parents fill in the information gap about college attendance. This is especially true for low-income students who are more likely to under-consume higher education due to a lack of information. These and similar topics will come up in the chapters that follow.

Another example of a market failure applied to higher education is that of the imperfect capital (financial) market, which brings us to the topic of student loans. Student loans are an important and necessary part of financing higher education for a growing number of students. The media storm over rising student debt and loan defaults masks the reality that without the availability of loans (capital), higher education would be under-produced and therefore allocatively inefficient. Students would not be able to raise the necessary money to finance their education on the promise that future income will be high enough to pay off a loan. Private markets would not be willing to take such a risk without adequate collateral.

As with other types of market failures, the government can step in to correct this failure by supplying the capital. This is not to say that government fixes are always the best choice or work in the desired direction. We can and do have government failures, and government policies often yield unintended consequences. For example, in periods of stagnant or falling personal incomes, the need to pay off loans may limit the capacity of college graduates to buy homes, start businesses, or enter low-paying but beneficial social service professions, thereby further reducing economic growth and the higher incomes needed to pay for education. But despite the problems noted above, federal actions to correct for imperfections in the capital market have been largely positive.

## EQUITY

If community college leaders only had to worry about running efficient organizations and producing favorable outcomes, things would be a lot easier for them. Simply shrink the enrollment, admit students who are most likely to succeed, and screen out those who are struggling. But things are not that simple because the mission of the community college is to open access and to help underrepresented and underprepared students succeed. In short, the goal of equity stands alongside that of efficiency and at times may conflict with it.

While the concept of efficiency is well developed within the policy literature, the concept of equity is much more subjective. Equity means different things to different people but often refers to the impact of different policies on different income groups. Not only do we have to consider who benefits from a particular policy, but also who pays for it. Thus we can argue over whether a particular type of financial aid benefits lower- or higher-income students and which income groups the money comes from to finance aid. The financial aid issue will be addressed in subsequent chapters, but at this point we can indicate that state need-based, as opposed to merit-based, financial aid advances the goal of equity and that federal grants (such as Pell) also serve that goal.

Aside from looking at the costs and benefits from the perspective of different income groups, we might also consider how college impacts various ethnic and racial groups (Bragg & Durham, 2012). Prominent among the research focused on equity concerns is the work of the Center for Urban Education at the University of Southern California. Its Equity Scorecard ™ is used by a number of colleges to isolate inequalities in access and outcomes (Bensimon & Malcom, 2012; Dowd, 2008).

Equity from this perspective would mean that students from different racial/ethnic and income groups would have an equal opportunity to attend college and would achieve outcomes equal to their ability. Although campus-level data on measures of equity are not generally available to researchers, national data at the macro level would strongly suggest that we have a long way to go in achieving this kind of equity.

Looking behind the concept of equity we find two overarching theories. The first is called *horizontal equity*, the second *vertical equity*. Horizontal equity means treating students with similar or equal needs, equally. For instance, considering only those who benefit and not those who pay, states promote horizontal equity when they provide equal appropriations to students in different sectors of higher education. A variation of this idea is that if a given student went to a public community college for the first two years of a bachelor's degree instead of a public master's-level college, he or she would be provided with the same subsidy for the first two years. Our analysis of college expenditures and affordability in the next chapter suggests that we may be closer to achieving this type of equity than we are to achieving vertical equity.

Vertical equity means treating unequal students unequally. Again looking only at the benefit side, this theory would argue for a disproportionate level of funding for students who enter college with deficiencies. Pell and other need-based grants are examples, as are remedial education and supportive services for students who need them. If students at the bottom end of the income distribution have greater deficiencies (needs) and those at the top are taxed to pay for it, we are promoting vertical equity.

This conception of equity is more controversial since it is a direct attempt to redistribute income in society as a means of creating a more equitable distribution of outcomes (See Dowd & Shieh, 2013, for a more complete discussion of these ideas). In subsequent chapters we will argue that the community college is underfunded given the job that it is asked to do. That job is, at least in part, to promote vertical equity.

As a start toward assessing campus equity, colleges should begin to disaggregate enrollment and outcomes data by ethnic and racial groups and, if possible, by income groups. Here, again, we enter the world of politics and subjective judgments over which groups to favor. The political preference of the authors of this volume is to favor solutions that benefit the least advantaged segments of the population. Such a policy stance is particularly important for the community college and its open-admissions policy.

## EQUITY AND EFFICIENCY: NEW YORK VERSUS CALIFORNIA

In 2003, Romano conducted a detailed assessment of the funding of selected state public community colleges using the principles of efficiency and equity as formulated by Breneman and Nelson (1981). He found New York to be a more efficient and equitable system than California, a conclusion that still applies today. Appendices A and B to this chapter briefly describe the current situation with respect to the financing of community colleges in California and the State University of New York (SUNY) system. Both illustrate the concepts of efficiency and equity within the context of important states for postsecondary education delivery.

In examining these large system case studies, remember that efficiency recognizes that many of the benefits from education are private and flow to the individual. Efficiency dictates that those who benefit should pay, other things being equal. This line of thinking argues against a no- or low-tuition policy for community colleges.

On the other hand, a completely privatized system would result in an underproduction of higher education (allocative inefficiency) and would not recognize the public benefits derived from higher education. The benefits of higher education justify some public subsidy, although the exact percentage coming from tuition and public support cannot be specified in any precise way (Romano, 2005). Allocative efficiency would require, under most conditions, that colleges be allowed to expand as the demand for their services increases. As the discussion in Appendix A argues, California is particularly deficient on this score.

In addition to allocative efficiency, we also have the question of technical efficiency, which is improved when colleges have an incentive to use the resources given to them in a cost-effective manner, both currently and with an eye toward the future. It is likely that technical efficiency would be improved, for instance, if colleges had more control over their budgets and were able to keep their tuition revenue. Based on these criteria, New York is judged to have a more efficient system of financing its community colleges than does California.

All of these judgments based on efficiency are mediated by concerns over equity. For instance, a high-tuition policy should be accompanied by a high need-based, as opposed to merit-based, financial aid policy to accommodate equity concerns. A "free" or low-tuition policy that provides an across-the-board subsidy to all students redistributes income in the wrong direction because a significant proportion of students who attend the community college are not from the poorest segments of society. A "free" or low-tuition policy, however, does have political appeal.

Proponents of low tuition argue that by expanding the benefits of low tuition to a larger universe of families, voters are more likely to approve of the policy. History shows, however, that the political argument for universality has not worked, because state policymakers have a history of cutting appropriations for higher education to cover budget shortfalls or to favor higher budget priorities. Thus, even for the community college, it would be better (i.e., it would require less public revenue and be more equitable) to charge a higher tuition to all and to target financial aid to those least able to afford it.

For this reason, we judge New York to be more equitable than California even though California is a high-aid state. In addition, the inability of California community colleges to expand with student demand greatly reduces access for low-income students. This failure is a direct result of the method used to fund community colleges and not necessarily because the state will not increase their budgets.

One additional equity concern centers on the role of local funding. Both California and New York use local taxes to support community colleges. This might be justified on efficiency grounds because local districts benefit from the presence of a community college in their region and because graduates are more likely to live and work locally than students who attend four-year colleges. However, from an equity perspective, local funds are generally raised by regressive property and sales taxes; so local funding for colleges would be obtained from taxes that come disproportionately from lower-income groups who are less likely to attend college than higher-income groups.

This argument against local funding has weakened over time, as an increasing share of high school graduates enter college. Still, to the extent that local taxes used to support community colleges are paid by lower-income families who do not participate in higher education to the extent that higher-income families do, there is a redistribution of income from lower- to higher-income groups. The same may apply to the use of state taxes in states that do not have a progressive income tax and that rely on regressive sales taxes.

Local funding, where it is used, also mirrors regional income differences. In fact, work done by Dowd and Grant (2006) showed that the presence of local funding exacerbates intrastate differences in funding between community college districts and further redistributes income in the wrong direction. For this reason, state support, which in most states is collected in a more progressive way, might be preferred to local support. To offset the regressive impact of local funding from both an income and a racial/ethnic perspective, it is desirable, as some states now do, to equalize intrastate funding by providing additional public dollars to poor districts that have a low tax base.


## WHAT IS THE PROPER BALANCE?


No definitive judgments can be made about the most desirable balance between tuition, state, and local funding for community colleges. No ideal formula exists that can be applied to all states, because funding patterns tend to follow the history, governance, and mission assigned to community colleges in a particular state.

What we can say is that from an economic perspective, a justification for some money from all three sources can be made on efficiency grounds. And from an equity perspective, a high-tuition, high-aid policy is best. But for the high-aid policy to work better than it does today, students and families will need to recognize what the net price of attending college is; that is, the price after need-based financial aid has been factored in. This remains an important problem requiring a solution.

Of key interest to students and policymakers alike is the question of what proportion of a college operating budget should come from tuition. Garms (1977) suggested 50 percent; Breneman and Nelson (1981) settled on one-third. McMahon (2009) attempted to calculate the social and private benefits from higher education and suggested a 40 percent contribution from tuition. We have found no way to improve on these estimates and settle on an amount somewhere between 30 and 50 percent.

On this score, New York has about reached its limit, but California has a long way to go. Even New York, however, is below this percentage for low-income students when federal and state need-based aid dollars are factored in. Again, it is important to note that the high-tuition model must be accompanied by a high financial aid policy if equity concerns are to be addressed.

In addition to tuition, the balance of a college operating budget would ideally be covered by state appropriations, especially when they derive from progressive income taxes rather than regressive sales taxes. In states where local funds are not used to support community colleges, an argument can be made for local tax contributions if they could be employed to offset tuition for local, low-income students, or if they could be used to expand programs (e.g., tutoring, on-campus childcare, etc.) that benefit these students.

Targeting local funds to benefit low-income students helps to redress the imbalance in equity that comes from using local support to fund the general operating budget. It also provides evidence that local support is going directly to needy students, which will reduce the need for social welfare spending in the future. Local governments may be more reluctant to cut spending for specific services to local students than they are to cut spending for the general operating budget that benefits all students.

In the end, a key fiscal challenge facing community colleges lies not simply in the competition for additional federal, state, and local dollars, but in securing a mix of revenue streams that maximizes the yield of desired private and social benefits accrued through the education provided by community colleges while at the same time assuring that low-income and less-advantaged populations are not excluded from those benefits.

We will never achieve a definitively optimal balance. But keeping these goals in mind may at least move fiscal policy in a positive direction, helping to avoid unintended consequences, such as in California where a well-intended but ultimately counterproductive low-tuition policy has, along with other factors, reduced access to community colleges.

## APPENDIX A

### California: A Low-Tuition, High-Aid State

California has the largest system of public higher education in the United States with 112 community colleges and more than 2.1 million students, enrolling in about 25 percent of all community college students in the nation. This means that statistics from California have a strong influence on national data, which would not be a problem if the state was not such an outlier in many respects.

California community colleges did not charge state residents any tuition (legally referred to as fees) until 1984–1985 when it began to impose a per-unit enrollment fee for all students. Initially, the fee was $5 per unit up to a maximum of $50 per semester. This has increased to $46 *per unit* in 2013–2014. To offset college costs for low-income students, California has the most generous need-based student aid program in the nation. In contrast to New York, which is a high-tuition, high-aid state, California is a low-tuition, high-aid state.

Community college tuition is set by the state legislature and not by local elected boards. State allocations to colleges and districts are calculated from a formula based primarily on enrollment, per-capita income, and projections of state revenues. The total amount distributed is subject to state-level budget negotiations every year and is often not finalized until well into the academic year.

The state determines how much revenue is due to each district and the revenue bucket for the operating budget is then filled, first by local property tax revenue. Next into the bucket are enrollment fees (tuition), with the balance coming from the state. Enrollment fees are used to offset state support, so if tuition revenues go up, the state reduces its share.

Since tuition revenue reduces the state share, there is no incentive for colleges or districts to support fee increases, and additional students do not bring in additional revenue. Colleges are allowed to carry over operating funds from one year to the next, but these funds are normally kept at the district and not at the campus level.

For California community colleges, the proportion of revenue coming from the state in 2012–2013 was roughly 65 percent, with the balance coming largely from local property taxes. Slight variations exist among colleges depending on the amount of property tax revenue collected. The 7 percent that might have come from tuition is included in the state share figure because it goes directly into the state coffers to offset state apportionment. Community colleges therefore receive a negligible amount from tuition to support their operating budgets.

On the surface, California appears to have an accessible and equitable community college system. Low tuition reduces financial barriers and financial aid pays for the tuition and additional college expenses of low-income students. The number of students on Pell grants (20 percent) is lower than one would expect, given the student demographics. The reason for this is that state grants (Cal grants) and tuition waivers (Board of Governors fee waivers), which do not require filling out the federal FAFSA form, are generous enough to drive the net price of attending college into the negative range.

In fact, approximately 40 percent of California community college students receive tuition waivers, which make this program the most important source of financial aid for students. The ease with which waivers are granted has been criticized by some because minimal guidelines exist for their use, and colleges have little incentive to limit the waivers given because they do not get to keep tuition revenue (Finney et al., 2014).

Despite generous financial aid, when Heller (2005) examined the system of public higher education in California from an equity perspective, he found it wanting, noting, for example, that Latino students benefited from a share of state fiscal support for higher education that was smaller than their representation in the higher education system itself.

In California the number of students that can be served is heavily dependent on state funding. During periods of recession when enrollment expands, state support is cut, and community colleges are forced to cut class sections and limit the number of students they admit. As economists point out, when prices are fixed (i.e., when tuition and/or revenue do not rise) and demand is high, available spaces must be rationed.

The failure to fund rising enrollments has reportedly left 500,000 students without a place to go and has pushed up enrollments in the expensive for-profit college sector (California Community Colleges Chancellor's Office, 2014). In this case, the low-tuition policy, combined with the lack of control over tuition revenue, has resulted in reduced access. In contrast, SUNY colleges get to keep the tuition revenue, and students bring enough with them to allow colleges to expand the number of classes offered and even rent space to allow them to accommodate the bulge in enrollments during periods of economic downturn and/or enrollment growth (Romano, 2003).

We find that the California community college system is inefficient because with its low tuition levels it fails to recognize the private benefits derived from going to college. Combined with the lack of control over tuition revenues, the system is allocatively inefficient because it results in the underproduction of higher education. The lack of control over tuition revenue and the limited ability to carry over fund balances also leads to technical inefficiencies because it gives colleges fewer incentives to use their budgets wisely. Over time, these policies have reduced access and equity, rapidly driving California into the category of a low-tuition, low-access state.

## APPENDIX B

### New York: A High-Tuition, High-Aid State

New York State has two community college systems, the State University of New York (SUNY) and the City University of New York (CUNY). In his 2003 survey of state funding systems, Romano only examined the SUNY system of thirty colleges, determining that it ranked very high (and California very low) when measured against the goals of efficiency and equity. SUNY is a high-tuition, high-aid system with state funding linked directly to enrollment. The balance between the state, local, and tuition shares of the operating budget varies with each of the thirty community colleges.

In 2011–2012, the average state share was 24.8 percent, the local share was 30.3 percent, and the share made up of tuition and fees was 44.9 percent. Tuition is set by local boards within parameters established by the State University system, with tuition caps that have proven to be flexible. Colleges get to keep all tuition and fee revenue and are allowed to carry surpluses forward in a reserve fund to offset difficult budget years. State University policy recommends that the reserve account balance be maintained at a level equal to 5–15 percent of operating costs.

To offset its high tuition charge, New York has one of the most generous need-based tuition assistance programs (TAP) in the nation. In 2011–2012, only Washington ($1,077) and New Jersey ($1,061) had a higher-average need-based grant per full-time-equivalent (FTE) undergraduate than New York ($1,024). Currently the top grant is $5,000 per year, which can be used at public or private colleges in the state. TAP is simple to administer and is high enough to cover the full cost of community college tuition for low-income students.

The state portion of funding to the community colleges comes through a stipend given to the college per FTE student based on the prior year's enrollment. Local funding varies depending on the college but averages around 30 percent of the operating budget (in 2011–2012, the range was 10–44 percent). The local share is generally not based on enrollment but is a negotiated fixed amount with maintenance-of-effort provisions built-in by the state. The percentage of the operating budget covered by the local share has been declining slowly over the past twenty years.

Within SUNY, community colleges develop a five-year enrollment plan, with incentives built-in to "get it right." A state stipend per FTE student based on this plan becomes part of state budget deliberations and goes up and down with the business cycle. In years when a college's enrollment is growing, the state will pay the highest stipend allowed so that colleges not only get the additional tuition revenue from new students, but also additional state revenue tied to expanding enrollment. Thus, colleges acquire additional revenue when they need it and are able to expand the number of class sections along with student demand. In years when enrollment falls, the state cushions the fall in revenue by allowing the colleges to set the state stipend based on prior year enrollment or, if greater, on a three-year weighted average of enrollments.

All of the features mentioned above are deemed desirable from both an efficiency and equity standpoint. However, other features of the state funding system are deemed less desirable. In the 1990s, for instance, the state discontinued bonus stipends for technical and business programs, part-time and disadvantaged students, core operations, equipment, and full-time faculty.

Reduced stipends for programs provide an incentive to substitute lower-cost alternatives. Less-expensive degree programs, for instance, might be favored over more-expensive, but highly desirable, vocational programs. Performance funding measures have not been used in the past, but a modest amount ($3 million), with metrics developed after the fact, was included in both the 2013–2014 and the 2014–2015 state budgets. The amount distributed in 2013–2014 was a bonus over and above the state stipend per FTE student. More on this can be found in chapter 5.

*Chapter 2*

# Revenue, Expenditures, and Affordability

Analyses of community college revenue streams, as well as expenditures, are constrained by the limitations of available data. The Department of Education's Integrated Postsecondary Education Database (IPEDS) is the most comprehensive data set, detailing revenue and expenditure data from colleges and universities nationwide. Yet changes in IPEDS reporting guidelines, notably revised accounting standards implemented in the early 2000s, complicate long-term trend analyses. So, too, does the shifting number of institutions falling under the community college umbrella as two-year colleges initiate bachelor's degree programs.

In addition, there is a considerable time lag in the publication of IPEDS data, an understandable result of the difficulty involved in collecting and vetting data from thousands of institutions. As of this writing, the most recent reliable fiscal data available extend only to 2011.

The Delta Cost Project overseen by the American Institutes for Research has analyzed IPEDS data, controlling for inflation, drawing community college data from carefully selected sets of associate degree–granting institutions, and making adjustments to "harmonize and standardize the data to the extent possible in order to account for changes in accounting standards and . . . reporting formats" (Desrochers & Hurlburt, 2014, p. 6). The analyses that follow draw on the Delta Cost Project IPEDS data whenever possible.

This chapter starts with an examination of revenue trends by source, detailing the challenges faced by community colleges in sustaining fiscal support in the face of recurring economic recessions, and notes how financial aid disbursements mesh with government appropriations in community college revenue streams. Looking at the other side of the operating budget, the patterns and trends of college expenditures are explored.

Here we use the words *college costs* and *expenditures* interchangeably because we are interested in the cost of educating students and, from the college perspective, this is measured through the medium of expenditures. When we shift to the student/parent perspective we are interested in the *price of attendance* (tuition and fees), which is quite a bit lower than the actual costs of educating them. Once we enter the realm of the student, the price, or cost of going to college, turns out to be a complex construct which we treat under the general heading of *affordability*.

At the outset, it must be acknowledged that the national trends reported here mask variations across states. For example, local tax monies are used to support community colleges in only twenty-seven states, and reliance on tuition and fees varies considerably—from only $1,000 per full-time-equivalent (FTE) student in California in 2011–2012 to $7,176 per FTE student in New Hampshire (Dowd & Shieh, 2013). In addition, within-state variations across institutions can be considerable.

In Illinois, for example, the proportion of total funding accounted for in local tax revenues in 2009–2010 ranged from 4 percent to 47 percent across the state's 39 community college districts; the proportion derived from state sources ranged from 6 percent to 31 percent, and the proportion derived from tuition and fees ranged from 19 percent to 36 percent (Illinois Board of Higher Education, n.d.). These variations reflect the relative autonomy of community colleges in Illinois to set tuition rates (in contrast to California, for example, where tuition is set at the state level) as well as uneven levels of property tax wealth across districts. But from a fiscal management standpoint, they serve as a reminder that individual colleges face unique patterns of revenue dependency.

Leaders of colleges that rely on local revenues, for example, must occasionally appeal to voters in tax-hike referenda, while leaders of colleges that do not rely on local tax support (e.g., Connecticut or Florida) must be all the more savvy in understanding and influencing state budgeting processes.

Our examination of national trends in revenue also masks the variations in the methods that states use to allocate funds to community colleges in each budget cycle. Although a few states have no funding formula, most do, with enrollments being the primary factor in determining yearly allocations. Aside from enrollment, some formulas also consider the cost of programs or include an equalization component designed to help poorer districts, among other things. It is not our purpose here to review funding formulas, but in chapter 5 we will consider the most recent addition to state allocation mechanisms, performance-based funding.

## COLLEGE REVENUE

Data in Table 2.1 detail, by source, average community college revenues nationwide per FTE student in constant 2011 dollars. These figures underscore how dependent community colleges are on state and local tax appropriations, which accounted for almost half (46 percent) of total operating revenues in 2011. In contrast, these appropriations accounted for only 33 percent of total revenues at public bachelor's institutions, 31 percent of revenues at public masters degree institutions, and 20 percent of total revenues at public research universities (Desrochers & Hurlburt, 2014).

Tuition and fees constituted the next largest revenue source for community colleges (28 percent of operating revenue per FTE student in 2011), followed by federal appropriations and government contracts (approximately 15 percent in 2011), and miscellaneous sources (approximately 11 percent in 2011) derived from numerous *auxiliary, independent,* or *other* sources such as contracted education programs, bookstore sales, or athletic programs. Only 1 percent of total revenues per FTE student derived from private gifts, investments, and endowments, reflecting the limited capacity of most community colleges, especially in less-affluent rural districts, to generate income through private fund-raising.

A key trend highlighted in Table 2.1 is the striking shift in revenue streams from state and local taxes on the one hand to tuition and fees on the other. The 23 percent decline in tax appropriations per FTE student between 2001 and 2011 coincided with a 42 percent increase in net tuition, signaling greater reliance on students themselves to shoulder the burden of paying for college.

This trend, depicted in the timeline in Figure 2.1, reflects the well-documented vulnerability of state fiscal support for higher education to periodic recessions (e.g., Hodel, Laffey, & Lingenfelter, 2006; Palmer, 2013; Zumeta, 2004). Each recession reduces state tax revenues and therefore diminishes state capacity to increase higher education funding. Higher education's vulnerability to fiscal downturns is further exacerbated by intensifying competition from agencies lined up at the state trough (e.g., health care, K-12 education, and corrections), as well as by its standing as a discretionary rather than mandatory item in state budgets. This discretionary standing, as well as the availability of tuition as an alternative revenue source makes it easier for legislators to cut higher education funding during tough economic times or, at a minimum, forgo funding increases.

As a result, higher education is used as a "balance wheel" by state governments (Hovey, 1999, p. 19), during recessions. Funding declines at a level disproportionate to reductions in other agencies and, although funding levels are later increased during good times, they do not return to their previous levels (Delaney & Doyle, 2011). This results in a secular trend of reduced public funding and rising tuition at both two- and four-year public colleges. By this we mean that although state funding has gone up and down over time, as the economy moves in and out of recessions, it has decreased overall in the long term.

**Table 2.1   Average Revenues per Full-Time-Equivalent (FTE) Student at Community Colleges for Selected Years, 2001–2011**

| | 2001 (%)[a] | 2003 (%)[a] | 2006 (%)[a] | 2007 (%)[a] | 2009 (%)[a] | 2010 (%)[a] | 2011 (%)[a] | % change, 2001–2011 |
|---|---|---|---|---|---|---|---|---|
| Net tuition | 2,410 (19%) | 2,630 (21%) | 2,964 (23%) | 3,053 (22%) | 3,176 (24%) | 3,321 (27%) | 3,424 (28%) | 42% |
| State and local appropriations | 7,320 (56%) | 6,458 (52%) | 6,829 (53%) | 7,140 (53%) | 6,849 (51%) | 5,837 (47%) | 5,638 (46%) | –23% |
| Federal appropriations and federal state and local grants and contracts | 1,807 (14%) | 1,840 (15%) | 1,803 (14%) | 1,867 (14%) | 1,984 (15%) | 1,860 (15%) | 1,782 (15%) | –1% |
| Auxiliary enterprises, hospitals, independent operations, and other sources | 1,330 (10%) | 1,317 (11%) | 1,253 (10%) | 1,274 (9%) | 1,279 (10%) | 1,331 (11%) | 1,314 (11%) | –1% |
| Private and affiliated gifts, grants, contracts, investment returns, and endowment income (PIE) | 215 (2%) | 190 (2%) | 299 (2%) | 382 (3%) | 179 (1%) | 158 (1%) | 149 (1%) | –31% |
| Total operating revenue | 12,986 | 12,370 | 13,003 | 13,573 | 13,345 | 12,394 | 12,195 | –6% |

*Note:* Data are from page 17 of Desrochers and Hurlburt (2014), who explain that "data may not sum to totals because revenues were summed at the institution level before calculating aggregate . . . averages" for the community college sector.

[a]Percentages refer to the percent of total operating revenue in the respective column.

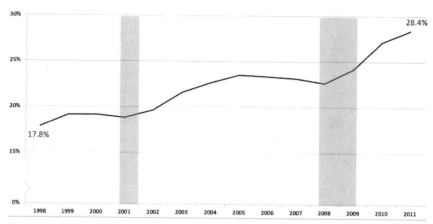

**Figure 2.1** **Net tuition per FTE student as a percent of total operating revenues per FTE student, 1998–2011, in constant 2011 dollars.** Revenue data for 1998 are from Desrochers, Lenihan, and Wellman (2010). Data for 1999 and 2000 are from Desrochers and Wellman (2011). Data for 2001 through 2011 are from Desrochers and Hurlburt (2014). Shaded areas represent periods of economic recession.

In addition, tuition increases instituted with each recession to compensate for attenuated government funding are rarely rescinded as the economy improves, resulting in a long-term increase in tuition rates as well. The increase in tuition revenue per FTE student at community colleges from 2001 through 2011, as detailed in Table 2.1, is substantial although well below that registered at public four-year colleges. Delta Project data show that state and local government appropriations per FTE student declined between 2001 and 2011 by 28 percent, 26 percent, and 25 percent at public research, public master's, and public bachelor's degree institutions, respectively—only slightly higher than the 23 percent decline experienced by community colleges. Yet tuition and fee rates per FTE student at these institutions rose at much higher rates— 64 percent, 59 percent, and 62 percent, respectively—than the 42 percent increase at community colleges (Desrochers & Hurlburt, 2014).

An unanswered question is the extent to which local tax monies (which are combined with state tax appropriations in the revenue data reported by the Delta Cost Project) have been affected by economic downturns. The Rockefeller Institute of Government has noted that property taxes, on which local funding largely depends, "remained relatively strong during and immediately after the Great Recession," but that falling housing prices may ultimately have a depressing impact on property tax collections in the long term (Dadayan, 2012, p. 1).

Another question concerns prospects for continued economic recovery from the last recession (December 2007–June 2009) and the impact of that recovery on higher education funding. While our analysis draws on data that extend only to 2011, economic growth in subsequent years may have restored some portion of state funding and decelerated the growth in tuition rates.

The annual *Grapevine* compilation of data on total state fiscal support for higher education (which unfortunately no longer provides breakdowns between two-year and four-year colleges) shows that after declining nation-wide by 8.8 percent from fiscal year (FY) 2009 to FY 2013, state funding for higher education—in current rather than constant dollars—increased by 6.1 percent from FY13 to FY14, the first increase registered since the reces-sion, and by 5.2 percent from FY14 to FY15 (Palmer, 2015). Should the economy continue to improve, state support for community colleges may increase accordingly, although (as noted above) past trends suggest that a full recovery to pre-recessionary levels is unlikely.

Among the factors that will impinge on the ability of many state and local governments to fund higher education, in the near term, are the overhang of underfunded public pension funds and the rising cost of Medicaid. In fact, current efforts to shore up pension funds can distort data on state higher edu-cation appropriations because, in some states, payments to pension funds are included in these appropriations figures.

For instance, the most recent state higher education finance report issued by the State Higher Education Executive Officers (SHEEO) shows that Illinois increased its per-student appropriations to higher education by almost 50 percent from 2009 to 2014. This was much larger than the increase in any other state. However, almost all of the increase was accounted for by payments to the state's pension fund for retired college and university personnel. "Retirement appropriations now make up 43.2 percent of the total [state] funding provided [to higher education in Illinois] while in 2007 they comprised just 3.1 percent" (SHEEO, 2015, p. 37). Once the pension appro-priations were taken out of the calculation, the funding to support college operating budgets actually declined.

While Illinois is an extreme example, it does illustrate how underfunded pensions can, at least in the short run, limit the ability of state and local gov-ernments to increase funding for higher education and stem the growth of tuition as a percentage of total revenue. Combined with the increasing cost of Medicaid, meeting these obligations will further restrict the ability of the public sector to support higher education and reinforce the tendency to rely on increases in tuition to fund operating budgets.

## Enrollment and the Business Cycle

The fiscal challenges faced by community colleges during economic down-turns are compounded by the tendency of rising unemployment to increase college enrollment. The surge in enrollments during economic downturns occurs as state and local appropriations decline, causing a funding problem for community colleges in most states. While enrollments move with the cycle (unemployment up, enrollment up), funding moves in the opposite direction (unemployment up, funding down).

This pattern of competing cycles is depicted in the schematic below (Figure 2.2), which shows the typical pattern of state and local funding along with unemployment and enrollments over an idealized business cycle. No attempt has been made to precisely align the curves with actual data. However, the connections and movement of the curves are based on well-documented studies using national and local data. In the upper UE (unemployment and enrollment) curve we show the positive relationship between unemployment and enrollment.

While admittedly our simple UE curve omits separations between the two variables at different times and does not show time lags, it does reflect what all of the studies of this connection have documented—that unemployment and enrollment are closely related and move in the same direction. In a multiyear study (1969–1985), Betts and McFarland (1995) estimated that a 1 percent rise in the regional unemployment rate resulted in about a 4 percent increase in full-time enrollment. Their study used institutional-level enrollment data from every region of the nation and concluded that "community college enrollments rise and fall remarkably in phase with the ups and downs of unemployment" (p. 749).

In addition to charting the link between unemployment and enrollment, Betts and McFarland also showed the pro-cyclical behavior of public

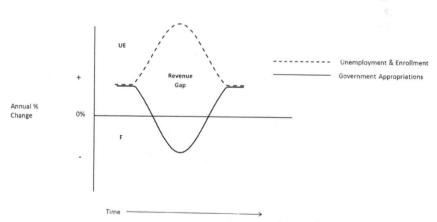

**Figure 2.2** Conceptual diagram of the counter-cyclical nature of annual percent changes in unemployment and enrollment (UE) on the one hand and annual percent changes in government appropriations (F) on the other.

funding depicted in our bottom curve labeled F. Public funding for community colleges is reduced during recessions as state tax revenues decline and transfer payments increase. This creates a cyclical revenue gap because public funding declines when community colleges need it the most. Because budgets must be balanced, the gap between revenues and expenditures must be closed so colleges cut costs, increase tuition and, in some states, restrict enrollments. It would be better public policy if funding and enrollment were to move in the same direction.

A more recent study by Hillman and Orians (2013) verifies and updates the connection between local unemployment rates and community college enrollment during business cycles over a twenty-year period, 1990 through 2009. They reported that a 1 percent increase in the unemployment rate is associated with an average increase in enrollments of about 2.4 percent, with full-time students increasing by 3.3 percent and part-time students increasing by 1.1 percent to 1.6 percent.

Unlike the study by Betts and McFarland, Hillman and Orians did not examine the pattern of public funding associated with these enrollment changes. But, as noted above, other studies have shown how state governments balance their budgets during economic downturns through disproportionately large cuts in higher education subsidies.

The challenge for public policy, and for open-access community colleges, is to find a revenue stream that will expand during recessions and contract when enrollment demand falls back to its normal level. History has demonstrated that we cannot expect the public sector to behave in this manner. Therefore, the only solution may be to require students to provide sufficient revenue through tuition and fees to allow colleges to expand the number of classes offered and to hire adjunct instructors to teach them.

A necessary condition for this to work would be to set tuition at a level high enough to generate the required short-term revenue and allow colleges to keep it. This may require a departure from the historical trend of minimizing tuition increases for community colleges in comparison to relatively large increases at public four-year colleges. In addition, grant aid, discussed below, must be available for low-income students to cover these rising tuition costs. Our cyclical enrollment and funding model supports the high-tuition, high-aid policy promoted in chapter 1 and advances the twin goals of efficiency and equity.

## Financial Aid, Tuition Revenue, and Student Debt

The importance of federal programs in helping students finance the costs of higher education is well understood. In 2010–2011, federal loans were the most important source of undergraduate support, totaling $70 billion.

This was followed by federal grants, including Pell, totaling $47.8 billion (College Board, 2011). Considering community college students alone, however, the importance of these two sources of aid is reversed. Federal grant aid, especially Pell grants, is the most important form of financial aid that community college students receive, but the number of loans is small. In 2007–2008, federal grants, mostly in the form of Pell grants, made up 66 percent of all grant aid to full-time students at community colleges. The remaining 34 percent consisted of state, institutional, and other grants (Baum, Little, & Payea, 2011).

Data in Table 2.2 highlight the importance of federal grants as opposed to loans for community college students. Although the proportion of community college students receiving federal grants (including Pell grants) is approximately the same as the proportion of all undergraduates receiving this aid, the proportion of community college students taking out federal loans is much lower. And although community college students are less likely to receive institutional and state grants compared to undergraduate students in general, the grants they receive are more likely to leave lower-income students with net tuition and fee rates of zero or below.

Since the 2007–2009 recession, the importance of Pell grants in financing the education of community college students has grown. For instance, from 2000–2001 to 2006–2007 Pell money going to community college students increased by 48 percent, but from 2008–2009 to 2010–2011 it increased by 102 percent from approximately $5.6 billion to more than $11.3 billion (Baime & Mullin, 2011).

In addition to the economic impact of the recession on the income of students and their families, some of the recent increase in Pell money is due to higher enrollments, enhanced student services in applying for grants, and reverse transfer of students from four-year colleges where there is greater awareness of the Pell application process among students and parents. In any case, it is clear that anything that affects eligibility for Pell grants, the amount and level of grants awarded, or the way they are distributed to students will have an impact on college revenue.

The fact that grants make up such an important source of financial aid for community college students brings up the question of how much of the tuition and fee money paid to colleges is covered by grant-based aid and how much comes out of the pockets of students or parents.

We do not have the data to answer the question precisely. Data on Pell grants are readily available but that for state grant aid is more difficult to obtain, because of the numerous state programs from which these monies emanate. The most frequently used data are from the annual surveys of the National Association of State Student Grant and Aid Programs (NASSGAP). Analyzing data available through NASSGAP's online Annual Survey Query

Table 2.2  Proportion of Public Two-Year College Students and All Undergraduates Receiving Financial Aid, by Type of Aid, and Total Tuition and Fees Minus Total Grant Aid, 2012

|  | Public two-year college students (%) | All undergraduates (%) |
|---|---|---|
| Pell grants |  |  |
| 0 | 62.3 | 58.7 |
| $100–1,999 | 11.6 | 10.1 |
| $2,000–2,999 | 10.7 | 10.4 |
| $3,200–4,499 | 8.8 | 9.5 |
| $4,500–5,550 | 6.5 | 11.2 |
| Total federal grants |  |  |
| 0 | 62.1 | 58.5 |
| $100–1,999 | 11.7 | 10 |
| $2,000–3,299 | 11.1 | 10.7 |
| $3,300–5,499 | 8.5 | 9.2 |
| $5,500–29,600 | 6.6 | 11.5 |
| State grants |  |  |
| 0 | 88.3 | 85.1 |
| $100–899 | 4.4 | 3.7 |
| $900–1,899 | 4 | 3.8 |
| $1,900–3,699 | 2.5 | 3.6 |
| $3,700 or more | 0.7 | 3.8 |
| Institutional grants |  |  |
| 0 | 86.7 | 79.9 |
| $100–899 | 7.9 | 5 |
| $900–2,699 | 4.7 | 5 |
| $2,700–8,999 | 0.6 | 4.9 |
| $9,000 or more | 0.1 | 5.2 |
| Tuition and fees minus all grants |  |  |
| 0 | 38.4 | 26.5 |
| $1–999 | 33 | 18.5 |
| $1,000–2,999 | 22.7 | 18.7 |
| $3,000–7,599 | 5.7 | 18 |
| $7,600 or more | 0.2 | 18.4 |
| Total federal loans (excludes Direct PLUS Loans to parents) |  |  |
| 0 | 83.3 | 59.8 |
| $100–4,099 | 8.3 | 10.1 |
| $4,100–6,199 | 4.2 | 9.9 |
| $6,200–8,899 | 1.9 | 10.2 |
| $8,900 or more | 2.3 | 10 |

Note: Data are from tables generated on the QuickStats website of the National Center for Education Statistics, http://nces.ed.gov/datalab/quickstats/default.aspx.

Tool (http://www.nassgap.org/customquery/CQB01ListQueries.aspx), as well as other sources leads to the following back-of-the-envelope calculations.

Roughly 40 percent of community college students in 2011 received a total of $11.3 billion in Pell grants. In addition, the amount awarded to community college students in 2011 from the states' primary need-based grant programs (e.g., California's Cal Grants, Illinois's Monetary Award Program, and New York's Tuition Assistance Program) was approximately $800 million out of the total of $5.4 billion that went to all undergraduates.

Using conservative assumptions, let's say that one half of all tuition and fee money, nationally, for the community college students receiving Pell grants is paid by some form of federal and state grant aid. Looking at Table 2.1 we can see that in 2011 tuition and fee revenue was $3,424 per FTE student. Using conservative assumptions, and converting all aid figures to FTE levels, would mean that at least $1,000 of the revenue collected by colleges per FTE student came from need-based aid.

The reader is reminded that the net tuition revenue shown in Table 2.1 includes money from grant aid sources. It also includes money obtained from student loans, but, as we will note below, this amount is quite small. Table 2.1 shows that in 2011, 28.4 percent of the total operating revenue of community colleges came from tuition and fees. If we count only the portion that actually comes out of the pocket of students and parents, the percentage falls to 20.1 percent. The real percentage is probably lower because of our conservative assumptions.

For instance, in our state grant aid estimate we have not counted merit-based grants or grants earmarked for specific student groups (such as National Guard enlistees or students pursuing career training in nursing and other high-demand fields). And by using only Pell grants, we have not counted federal grants to veterans and others with special needs, nor have we counted any education tax credits. In addition, the assumption that only one half of tuition and fee costs are paid from grant money is low, since data presented later in this chapter show that for those with a full Pell grant the net price is negative. Nevertheless, we feel comfortable with our estimate that at least $1,000 out of the average $3,424 paid to colleges in tuition comes out of major sources of grant money.

Grant aid does not have to be paid back, but student loans do. While federally sponsored loans are the most important source of undergraduate student support, they are less important for community college students than for students at public four-year colleges. Studies show that only one of five (20 percent) community college students took out a federal loan in 2011–2012 (Cochrane & Szabo-Kubitz, 2014). This is because, as we will illustrate below, the net price of attending a community college is much less, and even below zero for the lowest-income students.

Even for full-time students, there is less need to borrow at the community college level because they can reduce expenditures by living at home and because two years of college costs less than four years. In fact, in 2007–2008, 62 percent of students who graduated with an associate's degree

(70 percent for those who completed certificates) had no debt at all, and another 23 percent of those who took out loans were less than $10,000 in debt. This contrasts with students graduating from public four-year colleges with a bachelor's degree, where only 38 percent finished with no debt (Baum, Little, & Payea, 2011).

One is tempted to argue that student debt is not a problem for community college students and, under the right circumstances, could become an important contributor to student success in the future. With a program of income-based repayment, student loans could help students attend college full time rather than work excess hours to cover their expenses. We will examine this idea further in chapter 6.

### Stabilizing Revenue

Thus far we have highlighted four important sources of revenue for community colleges: tuition (and fees); state appropriations; federal money (mostly in the form of Pell grants); and local appropriations. Of these sources, tuition revenue and federal money have been the most stable and have fluctuated the least with respect to the business cycle. State appropriations are the least stable. Tuition, as long as enrollment is stable or growing, and federal money help to stabilize community college revenues during economic downturns. Tuition revenue goes up and down in most states as students move in and out.

The free tuition plan proposed by President Obama in his 2015 State of the Union Address would federalize a greater share of the operating budgets of the average community college and make revenues fluctuate less than the current reliance on state appropriations because federal budgets don't have to be balanced and state budgets do. The free tuition plan is worthy of consideration, but a greater federal role in funding the budget is highly unlikely. Beyond that, the policy would subsidize students who can afford to pay and it would distort student choice by diverting students from four-year to two-year colleges.

### Conclusions on Revenue

Community colleges, more than other public postsecondary institutions, rely heavily on state and local government appropriations. But these funding streams have diminished over time in the wake of recurring economic recessions that have increased institutional dependence on tuition and fees. And although most community colleges now engage in private fund-raising, the dollars raised have been small and highly vulnerable to economic downturns.

Over time, private dollars have declined (as detailed in Table 2.1) at a higher rate than the decline registered for state and local appropriations. Absent political decisions to federalize the funding of community colleges or for the states to substantially raise taxes or increase community college appropriations with monies cut from the budgets of other government entities, the capacity of community colleges to fulfill their mission will ultimately depend on policies that enable colleges to raise tuition, especially during economic downturns when enrollment increases, while at the same time ensuring adequate financial aid for low-income students.

## COLLEGE EXPENDITURES (COSTS)

No higher education issue has attracted more attention in recent years than cost: Why is the price of going to college so high? and Can students afford it? The simple answer to the first question is that, as we have shown, tuition and fees at public institutions have gone up rapidly because state and local subsidies to these institutions have declined. And yet, even if we ignore this factor, we can find continuing forces that push up the cost of educating students. This section considers those forces, examines the expenditure patterns of community colleges and compares those patterns with other sectors of public higher education.

### What Drives College Expenditures

Economists have postulated two distinct theories of college cost. The first was suggested by William Baumol and William Bowen (Baumol, 1967; Baumol & Blackman, 1995; Baumol & Bowen, 1966) and might be labeled the *low-productivity theory of cost* or the "cost disease" explanation. This theory suggests that education belongs to a class of service industries in which productivity is difficult to increase without reducing quality—an industry in which producers are forced to pay competitive wages and prices to attract qualified personnel for production. Medicine, restaurants, and symphony orchestras fit this category. In these industries, productivity growth is slower than that in the overall economy causing costs to rise faster than the general rate of inflation. So, holding down the cost of educating students means increasing productivity, assuming quality is not compromised.

The second theory of costs is the *revenue theory*. According to this theory, put forth by Howard Bowen (1980), colleges raise all the money they can and spend all of the revenue they raise. So, holding down costs essentially means holding down revenue.

A recent examination of higher education costs by Archibald and Feldman (2011) argues that the low-productivity theory is the dominant one, although it is not clear whether it applies to community colleges, which do not compete on the national market for high-priced faculty to the extent that four-year colleges do. In addition, over the course of the business cycle, expenditures (costs) tend to track revenues rather closely.

Accordingly, it would seem that the revenue theory would hold, at least over the short term, but over longer periods of time productivity would have a major impact on the secular trend of costs. If we were to increase productivity dramatically, it would reduce costs and perhaps sticker prices. We will take a closer look at the connection between productivity, costs, and price in higher education in the next chapter. For now, we turn to the question of what drives costs.

**Cost (expenditure) pushers.** Without productivity increases, the cost of educating students will increase at a steady pace as long as the cost of the inputs that colleges employ continue to rise. With close to 70 percent of the typical community college budget going to salaries and benefits, it would be expected that the cost of personnel would be a primary cost pusher. But evidence suggests that this is not the case. Although labor costs are the main college expenditure, recent data show that they are not rising at a rapid rate, and total expenditures per FTE student for this input have actually fallen for community colleges over the last several years.

Figures compiled by the Delta Cost Project show that the compensation per FTE employee at community colleges increased at a yearly average of 1.5 percent from 2002 to 2010. Benefits were the main driver of these cost increases (up 4.3 percent), but when the minimal increase in salary outlays and the rise in enrollment are figured in, community colleges were the only sector of higher education, public or private, to see a decrease (–0.9% per year) in total employee compensation per FTE student (Desrochers & Kirshstein, 2014). Community colleges have clearly performed most ably among higher education institutions in keeping compensation costs under control. If they continue to do so they will be able to control cost per student, but this might come at the expense of quality.

Looking at cost from a different perspective, Ehrenberg (2000) and others have identified a number of other factors that push the expenditures per student up at four-year colleges. These include the "rising cost of technology, student services, and institutional financial aid" (Ehrenberg & Rizzo, 2004, para. 3). Additional factors pushing expenditures up include "unrelenting competition to be the best in every dimension of an institution's activities, and, at research universities, the increased instructional costs of scientific research" (Ehrenberg & Rizzo, 2004, para. 3).

How can we relate these underlying cost factors to community colleges? Two factors that have limited relevance to community college budgets are the rising cost of research and increases in institutional aid. Community colleges have none of the first and relatively little of the second. But the rising cost of student services is important to community college budgets.

Data in Table 2.3 (below) show that the cost of student services is one of the few expenditures that has increased as a share of the budget from 2001 to 2011 (9.7 percent to 10.1 percent), even though it has decreased in absolute terms. One could easily argue that the cost of student services is still too low because students entering the community college often need more of these services to succeed than students at four-year colleges. Webber (2011) and Webber and Ehrenberg (2010) have suggested that expenditures on student services, especially for those from disadvantaged backgrounds, lead to higher persistence and graduation rates. Because cuts in this function will negatively impact student outcomes, student services will probably continue to be a cost pusher.

Finally, the rising cost of technology would seem to affect community college budgets in a manner similar to four-year colleges. In traditional manufacturing industries, improvement in technology has lowered costs, but in higher education the addition of more technology to the classroom, for instance, has probably raised costs, although it may have also improved quality (Archibald & Feldman, 2011, pp. 67–69).

Colleges have certainly used technology to reduce some costs, such as putting the college catalog online and automating payrolls, financial records, and registration, but these savings are less important than technological advances that might reduce instructional cost. As we look toward the future, many hope that technology in the form of online instruction will lower instructional costs.

In their current form, however, online courses at the community college create a higher cost for the institution, though not necessarily for the student, than face-to-face instruction and result in lower course completion rates (Instructional Technology Council, 2011; Xu & Jaggars, 2011). Reviewing the research on this topic, Jaggars (2011) advanced a series of recommendations that might improve student completion rates in online courses, but acknowledged that they "will require a substantial investment of new resources in online learning" (p. 3).

Colleges might be able to deliver full online degree programs at a lower cost, but they will need to break loose from the traditional classroom seat time credit model in a manner that would disrupt current college organizational structures (Christensen et al., 2011; Ehrenberg, 2011). The business model needed to bring about macro or "disruptive" innovation will confront quality issues, especially in the teaching of remedial students, which has yet to yield to the influence of technology. Efforts in this area to date have largely been a failure, and success in improving its quality will likely come with a higher cost per student (Bailey, Jeong, & Cho, 2010).

In examining the role of technology as a cost pusher, Romano (2012) concluded that with current institutional structures, modern technology will be a factor that will push costs up rather than pull them down. No college wants to be seen as being behind the technological curve, and students expect wireless campuses and an array of computer and online services that they have become accustomed to. After all, not keeping up with students' technological expectations would have a negative impact on enrollments.

**Mission creep.** At many four-year colleges, especially research universities, the relentless pursuit of "being the best" is a cost pusher. This translates into competition for the best faculty members, provision of premium services and amenities, and more selective admission policies. Most of these factors are not issues for community colleges, however, a corollary of "be-the-best" is that community colleges push for recognition and for greater service to local communities. They continue to harbor an inferiority complex with regard to their place in American higher education and in many localities seek the recognition and prestige of their four-year counterparts. This often translates into a desire to be all things to all people and the pursuit of opportunities beyond their reach. If leaders see an educational void in their communities, they look for ways to fill it. This mission creep can push costs up and have a negative impact on outcomes if colleges take on tasks that exceed their capacity.

In many states community colleges are looking more and more like four-year public colleges. A growing number of colleges have dropped the word "community" in their name. One in five (21 percent) now offer on-campus living facilities and almost half of the states (twenty-two) have authorized community colleges to offer the bachelor's degree, although as of 2014, only seventeen states have actually done so.

Of course, not all colleges will opt to build on-campus housing as a means of increasing enrollments, on a belief that costs (and problems) associated with residence halls will not be worth the benefits. In addition, the pressure to increase enrollments is less pressing in areas where enrollments are already growing rapidly. But in other areas of the country, such as the northeast and midwest, increased competition for students will provide an incentive to build residence halls, which, in turn, can become a cost pusher, especially if they operate below capacity. As residential campuses expand, the expense for increased security and counseling services will also push costs up. Additionally, when students chose to live away from home, they invariably borrow to finance their education.

The pressure to offer the bachelor's degree will also become a cost pusher. California recently joined the band wagon, authorizing a pilot program for fifteen colleges to offer the bachelor's degree in selected areas (Koseff, 2014). The move toward the bachelor's degree will certainly raise average costs per FTE student at community colleges, since it costs more to educate upper-division than lower-division students. Furthermore, if the diversion of students to community colleges causes four-year colleges to become more selective, and shrinks their size, their average costs could also rise.

When the long-time president of a large Florida community college was asked by a local reporter if he could see the day that his college would offer graduate degrees (it currently offers twenty-three bachelor's degree programs), he replied that this would be determined on the basis of need ("In Step with Edwin Massey," 2013). Some call this mission creep, while others welcome it as fulfilling a local, regional, or state need that existing public colleges refuse to fill. In any case, an expanded role for community colleges will likely push the average cost per student up, even though community colleges may still be able to educate upper-division students at a lower cost than existing public four-year colleges.

**Political and regulatory environment.** Beyond the cost pushers mentioned thus far, the political system that community colleges operate in imposes costly regulatory demands on colleges and creates uncertain funding patterns. The unrelenting drive for accountability is an example. The increased administrative costs of documenting and reporting student progress, often in conjunction with performance funding formulas, will continue to push costs up. So too will state budgeting processes that make it impossible for colleges to know what their budgets will be until late in the game. This makes planning difficult and creates inefficiencies at the campus level.

Additional cost pushers can be identified when we consider the circumstances of college operation in particular states. As we argued in the last chapter via rough comparisons between California and New York, inefficiencies are built into the way states handle their subsidies to colleges. Most of these inefficiencies are easy to spot but hard to remedy given the historical circumstances and political climate in states.

**The challenge of fiscal solvency.** With all of the underlying factors that push costs up, how is it that community colleges have been able to reduce their expenditures by more than $1,000 per FTE student from 2001 to 2011 (as detailed in Table 2.3, below)? It could be that technical efficiency has increased, but, such a large jump is highly unlikely. Rather, reduced expenditures have come almost exclusively from cuts in faculty and administrative expenditures, which have probably reduced quality, especially for the most disadvantaged students.

In the face of rising input costs and an uncertain economic and political environment, effective management is necessary to sustain quality while keeping colleges financially solvent. Mission creep in an uncertain fiscal environment exposes community colleges to potential financial risks. Internal and state budget audits and accreditation requirements are not enough of a check on financial stability.

The sudden collapse of the for-profit Corinthian Colleges in 2014 and the troubles at the City College of San Francisco could be a wakeup call even for public community colleges. Current trip wires such as the student loan default rate may come too late in the game. States or state systems of higher education will need to take the lead in this area. Perhaps a stress test for college finances is overdue. Clearly some balance must be found between signaling questionable finances and allowing colleges the flexibility to shift resources around as they respond to local and state needs.

## Community College Costs

The cost of educating students, in contrast to posted tuition and fee prices, can be measured by looking at expenditures in the operating budget. Examining the way colleges spend their money also gives us an idea of what their priorities are. Table 2.3 below provides a national picture of how community colleges spend their money, detailing expenditures per FTE student (adjusted for inflation) for the most recent years data are available, 2001–2011. Figures are taken from the Delta Project database, which, as noted in the previous chapter, uses adjusted IPEDS data that facilitate multiyear comparisons.

Aside from the standard IPEDS expenditure categories (e.g., instruction, student services, etc.), the bottom half of Table 2.3 lists the expenditures that come closest to representing the cost of educating each student—*education and related* (E&R) expenses (per FTE student and adjusted for inflation). This measure includes spending on instruction, student services, and administrative and maintenance costs associated with instruction. E&R expenditures make up over 80 percent of the typical community college budget and are often used by researchers as "a proxy for the full cost of educating students" (Desrochers, Lenihan, & Wellman, 2010, p. 18).

Another figure of interest in Table 2.3 is the total *education and general* expenditure category, which includes all expenditures aside from those incurred by auxiliary enterprises (e.g., book stores and other operations that are largely self-supporting). This expenditure category varies with the business cycle.

**Table 2.3 Average Community College Operating Expenditures per Full-Time-Equivalent Student, 2001–2011, for Selected Years (with Selected Shares In Percentages), in 2011 Dollars**

| IPEDS category[a] | 2001 ($) | (%) | 2006 ($) | 2008 ($) | 2009 ($) | 2010 ($) | 2011 ($) | (%) |
|---|---|---|---|---|---|---|---|---|
| Education and general (E&G) expenditures | | | | | | | | |
| Instruction | 5,514 | (42.5) | 5,120 | 5,408 | 5,241 | 4,894 | 4,843 | (41.9) |
| Research | 41 | (0.3) | 69 | 44 | 72 | 59 | 64 | (0.6) |
| Public service | 447 | (3.4) | 377 | 372 | 357 | 327 | 310 | (2.7) |
| Academic support | 1,113 | (8.6) | 983 | 1,043 | 1,012 | 933 | 919 | (7.9) |
| Student services | 1,259 | (9.7) | 1,236 | 1,297 | 1,292 | 1,207 | 1,172 | (10.1) |
| Instructional support | 1,910 | (14.7) | 1,804 | 1,947 | 1,889 | 1,714 | 1,716 | (14.8) |
| Operation and maintenance (O&M) | 1,191 | (9.2) | 1,228 | 1,278 | 1,247 | 1,061 | 1,029 | (8.9) |
| Net scholarships[b] | 1,710 | (13.2) | 979 | 1,031 | 1,188 | 1,645 | 1,766 | (15.3) |
| Total education & general | 12,987 | (100) | 11,542 | 12,173 | 12,016 | 11,577 | 11,560 | (100) |
| Auxiliary enterprises and other | 922 | | 1,087 | 1,270 | 1,370 | 1,392 | 1,422 | |
| Total operational expenditures | 13,822 | | 12,573 | 13,385 | 13,322 | 12,915 | 12,918 | |
| Grouped expenditures | | | | | | | | |
| Education and related | 10,805 | (83.2) | 10,216 | 10,812 | 10,518 | 9,676 | 9,550 | (82.6) |
| Research and related | 64 | (0.49) | | | | | 97 | (0.84) |
| Public service and related | 703 | (5.4) | | | | | 484 | (4.2) |
| Net scholarships[b] | 1,401 | (11.5)[c] | | | | | 1,766 | (15.3) |
| Total education and general | 12,987 | (100) | | | | | 11,560 | (100) |
| Auxiliary enterprises and other | 922 | | | | | | 1,422 | |
| Total operating expenses | 13,822 | | | | | | 12,918 | |

*Note:* Adapted from Delta Cost Project IPEDS database, 11-year matched set (Desrochers & Hurlburt, 2014).
Data may not sum to totals because expenditures were summed at the institution level before calculating aggregate category averages. May not add to 100% due to rounding.
See http://nces.ed.gov/ipeds/deltacostproject/ for a link to the definition of categories.
[a] IPEDS = Integrated Postsecondary Education Data System. [b] Prior to 2002 colleges reported gross and not net scholarships making 2002 a more accurate number for comparisons with following years (Desrochers & Hurlburt , 2014, p. 20). [c] For 2002.

In the aftermath of the recession in 2001, expenditures fell over the next four years (2002–2005) as state and local appropriations per FTE student declined. During the next upswing in economic activity, public appropriations increased, as did spending through 2006–2008. But, as Table 2.3 shows, neither total education and general spending, nor E&R spending, nor total operating expenditures returned to their 2001 levels.

After the 2008–2009 recession and the slow economic growth that followed, college revenues and expenditures fell rapidly. Thus, we see again that not only revenues, but expenditures, as well, move with the business cycle. As revenues fall, colleges reallocate resources to support institutional priorities. These adjustments are a healthy sign within an environment of scarce resources. Over the ten-year period from 2001 to 2011, all categories of expenditures were reduced except for a small increase in net scholarships. The largest cuts in dollar terms came in the area of instruction, which constitutes about 42 percent of the operating budget, falling from $5,514 per FTE student in 2001 to $4,843 in 2011. This is a drop of 12.2 percent. Education and related spending fell by 11.6 percent. This indicates that spending fell faster than the rise in the rate of inflation.

## Comparative Costs

It is worth noting that spending per FTE student for the major expense categories we have highlighted rose for all sectors of public higher education except community colleges over this same period. The relative thriftiness of the community college is reflected in the data from Table 2.4, which shows national revenue and cost comparisons between community colleges and other sectors of public higher education.

From 2001 to 2011, state and local appropriations were reduced for public research and public master's colleges to a more significant extent than they were for public community colleges, both in real dollar terms and percentage change over that period. In response, all three sectors increased their tuition, with the lowest increases recorded for community colleges. But not only did public four-year colleges increase tuition and fees, they also increased education and related spending per FTE student.

One would assume the objective was to maintain quality, but because quality measures are not available, we cannot be certain of this. The increase in public four-year college tuition revenue made up for the cut in public appropriations. The story was different for the community colleges. Community colleges have an incentive to keep tuition down, and they responded to the decline in public appropriations by not only cutting spending, but by cutting it below the level necessary to keep comparative costs from increasing.

**Table 2.4  Average Tuition and Fees (Sticker Price), State and Local Appropriations, and Education and Related Expenditures, by Sector, 2001–2011 (per FTE Student in 2011 dollars)**

| Sector | 2001 | 2011 | $ Change | % Change |
|---|---|---|---|---|
| Public research universities | | | | |
| Tuition and fees | $4,639 | 7,939 | 3,300 | +71.1% |
| State and local appropriations | $10,983 | 7,902 | –3,081 | –28.1% |
| Education and related expenditures | $15,295 | 16,009 | 714 | +4.7% |
| Public Master's | | | | |
| Tuition and fees | $3,904 | 6,425 | 2,521 | +64.6% |
| State and local appropriations | $7,883 | 5,823 | –2,060 | –26.1% |
| Education and related expenditures | $12,030 | 12,554 | 524 | +04.4% |
| Community Colleges | | | | |
| Tuition and fees | $1,845 | 2,718 | 873 | +47.3% |
| State and local appropriations | $7,320 | 5,638 | –1,682 | –23.0% |
| Education and related expenditures | $10,805 | 9,550 | –1,255 | –11.6% |

Note: Adapted from Desrochers and Hurlburt (2014) and authors' calculations. Tuition and fees represent the average sticker price for in-state undergraduates for four-year colleges and the in-district price for community colleges. This is not the same as the tuition and fee revenue used in Table 2.5, below , which represents average tuition revenue from all students less institutional aid and discounts.

As Tables 2.3 and 2.4 show, community colleges are great cost cutters compared to their four-year public counterparts. They have accomplished this principally by substituting lower-cost part-time faculty for full-time instructors and by increasing class sizes, including cutting back on low-enrollment classes. National figures indicate that the percentage of part-time faculty in community colleges increased from 66.5 percent in 2003–2004 to 70 percent in Fall 2011. In contrast, only 34 percent of the faculty in public four-year colleges were employed part-time (Snyder & Dillow, 2013, Table 286). Likewise student/faculty ratios are lower at public four-year colleges (15.1 percent) than at public two-year colleges (21.1 percent) for Fall 2011 (Snyder & Dillow, 2013, Table 288).

A real difference can also be seen in the ratio of FTE students per FTE staff (other than faculty). In community colleges the ratio stood at 10:1, but was a hefty 4.6:1 at public four-year colleges (Snyder & Dillow, 2013, Table 288). The most recent analysis of hiring and expenditure patterns across all sectors of higher education indicates that community colleges cut more deeply than their four-year counterparts in all categories of expenditures, including full-time faculty and administration between 2000 and 2012 (Desrochers & Kirshstein, 2014).

The cost-cutting efforts illustrated in these figures have clearly worked to hold down the sticker price of attending a community college. They have also held the necessity for public subsidies in check. This might be seen as an increase in technical efficiency, but if it came at the expense of quality or other measures of student outcomes, such as degree production, then we cannot call it an increase in productivity.

## Student Enrollment Patterns and Cost of Education

If more students enrolled in community colleges rather than public four-year colleges, would the cost of educating them go down? It appears that this would be the case given the costs data we have presented. The average education and general expenditure (cost) per FTE student at public research universities in 2011 was $28,339, at public master's-level colleges it was $15,349, and at public community colleges it was $11,560.

These figures are often used to argue that community colleges are underfunded since expenditure figures also represent the resources that colleges have to spend on each student (Century Foundation Task Force, 2013; Mellow & Heelan, 2008). But the comparison is questionable because the figures for public four-year colleges include spending on higher-cost upper-division and graduate students.

The comparison with public research universities is especially problematic since their mission is different from that of community colleges. Furthermore, if students are diverted from four-year to two-year colleges, they are least likely to come from research universities. A more appropriate comparison can be made between public two-year and master's-level colleges where the flow of students in both directions (diversion and transfer) is heavier.

Yet, even here calculating the cost of educating upper-division and graduate students presents some difficulty. It would be better if we could compare the cost of educating lower-division students in four-year colleges with those at community colleges. Precise data for making this comparison are not available, but several reasonable attempts have been made at estimating them.

A widely cited early study of this issue was conducted by James (1978). Looking at data from California and other selected colleges, she found that "community college students cost more, pay less, and hence receive a greater annual financial subsidy than do lower division university students" (James, 1978, p. 178). In their seminal study of community college finance, Breneman and Nelson (1981) reviewed the relevant research on comparative costs and concluded that "in general, the level of resources and subsidies spent on community college students does not differ widely from that spent on their lower division counterparts at senior public institutions" (p. 118).

Another study of the cost difference between community colleges and public four-year colleges was conducted by Rouse (1998) using 1992–1993 data from the National Center for Education Statistics (NCES) on mean costs per FTE student. Excluding capital costs, she estimated that, on the surface, costs appeared to be almost twice as high at the public four-year college than at the public two-year college (a $3,117 difference in 1994 dollars).

However, after adjusting four-year college costs to take into account more expensive upper-division courses and the small number of graduate students at public non-research universities, the cost advantage of community colleges was reduced to $935 per FTE student. Since tuition at community colleges is usually lower than at four-year colleges, she surmised that the public subsidy to community colleges per FTE student might be greater. Aware of data limitations, however, Rouse concluded that conservative estimates suggest that it more likely costs the public sector "about the same or less" to educate a student for the first two years at a community college (Rouse, 1998, p. 614).

And finally, the most recent study of comparative costs was completed by Baum and Kurose (2013). Using a different technique for making cost comparisons, they concluded that lower-division undergraduates enrolled in public master's-level colleges "do not appear to benefit from significantly more public funding than they would have in two-year institutions" (p. 97). They also noted that "students bear a smaller share of the cost of their education at community colleges than in any other sector" (p. 91).

Our own examination of the cost differences between two-year and four-year colleges is a modification of the approach used by Rouse (1998) and by Romano and Djajalaksana (2011). Tracking average cost figures from 1987 to 2005, Romano and Djajalaksana found that the cost of educating lower-division students at public master's-level colleges was lower than at the community college, and that after 1997 the public subsidy required was also lower at four-year colleges. An updated and modified version of this analysis for the year 2011 is presented in Table 2.5.

Column 1 in Table 2.5 shows the education and general expenditures per student in master's-level public colleges and community colleges. Using these numbers we can see that in 2011 community colleges had $3,789 less to spend on each FTE student than did public four-year colleges. But when we adjust the master's-level college's spending to include only what is spent on lower-division students we get the opposite result; community colleges had $1,462 more to spend per FTE student.

The adjustment is based on data that indicate that at master's-level colleges, 87.6 percent are undergraduate students and 12.4 percent are graduate students. Of the total undergraduate students, 40 percent are upper-division students and 60 percent are lower-division students. The cost per FTE is weighted as follows: graduate students, 3.75; upper-division undergraduates, 1.50; lower-division undergraduates, 1.00; and unclassified students 1.00 (see Breneman & Nelson, 1981; James, 1978; and Romano & Djajalaksana, 2011 for a list of the studies that support these estimates).

*Chapter 2*

Table 2.5    Average Expenditures, Tuition and Fee Revenue, and Subsidies (in $1,000s) per Full-time-Equivalent (FTE) Student at Public Two- and Four-Year Colleges, 2011

| | Education and general expenditures per FTE student | | | | |
| | Total | Minus research and public service | Tuition and fee revenue | Public subsidy - 1 | Public subsidy - 2 |
| | *(1)* | *(2)* | *(3)* | *(4)* | *(5)* |
| Two-year colleges | 11,560 | 11,186 | 3,424 | 8,136 | 7,762 |
| Public master's colleges[a] | 15,349 | 14,379 | 6,681 | 8,668 | 7,698 |
| Public master's adjusted for lower division[b] | 10,098 | 9,460 | 6,681 | 3,417 | 2,779 |
| Difference: four-year minus two-year: | | | | | |
| 4-year unadjusted | 3,789 | 3,193 | 3,257 | 532 | (64) |
| 4-year adjusted | (1,462) | (1,726) | 3,257 | (4,719) | (4,983) |

*Note*: Data are derived from the Delta Cost Project IPEDS database (Desrochers & Hurlburt, 2014). Column 1 = operating costs (excludes capital costs); column 2 = column 1 minus research and public service; column 3 = revenue from tuition and fees less institutional grants and discounts; column 4 = column 1 minus column 3; column 5 = column 2 minus column 3.
[a]Excludes research universities. [b]Adjusted to approximate the costs of lower-division instruction using a divisor of 1.52. Other divisors containing reasonable assumptions provide similar results (see Romano & Djajalaksana, 2011, Appendix A).

If students were diverted from public master's colleges to community colleges it would be more accurate to estimate the impact on cost using a marginal cost calculation. Romano and Djajalaksana (2011) furnished examples of how this might be done, and for purposes of illustration, we include an updated version of one of these estimates in column 2 of Table 2.5. The data reveal that master's-level colleges have a $1,726 cost advantage over community colleges once expenditures are adjusted for lower-division students.

Column 3 presents a simplified picture of the tuition and fee revenue received by each type of college based on the assumption that tuition for upper-division students is the same as that for lower-division students. Reasonable estimates of the actual differences would not change our conclusion. On average, national figures show that students at community colleges pay $3,257 less per year than students at public master's-level colleges. The lower sticker price results in a higher public subsidy once we step away from the unadjusted figures in column 1.

Finally, columns 4 and 5 show two different estimates of the public subsidy provided to each type of college. The subsidy is about the same for each college type with a $532 disadvantage for the community college if we use column 4, but a $64 advantage if we use column 5. Trend data going back to 1987 show that from 1997 to the present, the public subsidy figure (column 4), based on unadjusted costs, varies, so that in some years community colleges received a larger subsidy than four-year colleges and in other years they did not, but the differences are very small. Once we adjust costs to account for lower-division students alone, we see that community colleges have a significant advantage—almost $5,000 more per FTE student coming from public subsidies compared to public master's-level colleges.

It is worth noting that in a number of states the public subsidy for community colleges comes from the local government as well as the state, whereas the master's colleges receive little, if any, local tax support. Accordingly it is possible to argue that in some states the state gives more to public four-year colleges than it does to community colleges, but once local funding is included, this changes.

This is an important point, because when we look at the latest published national figures available (2010–2011), about 40 percent of what is lumped together as state and local appropriations for community colleges comes from local sources (Snyder & Dillow, 2013, Table 401). In stark contrast to state appropriations, local funding has been a stable source of funding over the business cycle, rising in percentage terms when state funding is cut and falling when state funding is restored. Even so, over long periods of time, local funding has declined as a share of college operating budgets on a national scale (authors' calculations from Snyder & Dillow, 2013; Snyder, Dillow, & Hoffman, 2009). We also note that state and federal grants, such as Pell, are not included in public support data since grant dollars show up in tuition and fee revenue.

Our analysis thus far indicates that it is cheaper to educate students for the first two years of college at public master's-level colleges than it is at community colleges. So diverting students from public four-year colleges to community colleges will not save the public money and will probably cost more. But, a cautionary note is in order here. For diverted students, the cost advantage of public four-year colleges would disappear if students enrolled in less-expensive programs at community colleges. As we will see in chapter 6, some associate's degree programs cost more than bachelor's degree programs in four-year colleges. Thus, the advantage of public master's-level colleges varies depending on how students distribute themselves in community college programs.

Comparisons become even more complicated when we drill down into the details of college revenues and expenditures. For instance, compared to their four-year counterparts, community colleges maintain a larger continuing education effort. Revenues and expenditures for noncredit students are included in college operating budgets and reflected in the figures that we have reported. But noncredit students are not factored into enrollment data. This makes the FTE cost figures for credit students look higher than they actually are (Baum & Kurose, 2013). We could present numerous examples that reveal an upward or downward bias of two- and the four-year college cost figures.

## Which Is Cheaper?

Given the data available, it is difficult to determine which is cheaper—public four-year colleges or community colleges. We have illustrated that cost comparisons between the two- and four-year colleges are much more nuanced than the gross spending figures used to argue that community colleges are underfunded (i.e., for 2011, $28,339 per FTE student at public research universities, $15,349 at public master's-level colleges, and $11,560 for community colleges). Given the number of studies that have been conducted on this issue, it is reasonable to conclude that the expenditures for lower-division students at public master's-level college are probably lower than at community colleges, but not by much.

We can also indicate that advocates who believe that community colleges are underfunded, as we do, would be on firmer ground if they argued that more money is needed to educate the many low-income and at-risk students enrolled in community colleges, in much the same way as proponents of greater funding for disadvantaged students at the elementary and secondary levels. In essence, this is a political argument for the concept of vertical equity as described in chapter 1 (treating unequal students, unequally).

Disadvantaged and underprepared students in community colleges need a high-touch environment, and this is expensive. Just how much additional money would be needed to improve completion rates is a question we can't answer at this time. An understanding of increased cost might be achieved through analysis of student outcomes produced by New Community College opened in 2012 at the City University of New York. Renamed Guttman Community College, Guttman restricts the program choices that students have, requires and supports full-time study, and delivers more support services in comparison to peer institutions.

Thus far the results at Guttman look promising, but it is too early to know what the full costs and benefits of its approach will be. With an opening class of just 300 students in 2012, officials estimate that the cost per student will exceed $30,000, but as enrollments expand these costs will fall. A successful but less intensive program that is open only to a limited number of low-income students at six City University of New York (CUNY) community colleges—Accelerated Study in Associate Programs (ASAP)—operates at a cost of about $17,000 per FTE student, compared to a cost of about $10,000 per FTE student for the average student at CUNY community colleges (Perez-Pena, 2012).

An extensive Type-3 study of ASAP is underway and recent reports on the impact of this program indicate that it has been able to increase the graduation rate to 40 percent within three years compared to a graduation rate of just 22 percent for students in the control group. The ASAP program costs more per student (the City of New York kicked in an extra $35 million to run the program), but the cost is less per degree produced (Kirp, 2014; Fain, 2015b). The projected cost of educating disadvantaged students successfully in community colleges prompts us to consider whether the additional resources needed wouldn't be better spent further down the educational ladder. Providing extra help as far down as preschool is probably the best approach, but it may not be too late even at the high school level. Considering the New York City example above, experiments with smaller high schools seem to dramatically improve results.

In a Type-3 study using control groups, MDRC followed about 21,000 students through high school and into college. Their study showed that smaller high schools, with a more rigorous curriculum and a more personalized approach, greatly increased graduation and college entry rates among black and Hispanic students (Unterman, 2014). Although the cost per student was somewhat higher at smaller schools, the cost per graduate was lower than for a control group of students attending larger high schools. Generally speaking, the earlier that needed intervention services are provided, the lower the long-run costs to society.

## Conclusions on Expenditures

Data show that community colleges have not only controlled their costs over the last ten years, but have actually reduced their expenditures per FTE student when adjusted for inflation. This has not reduced the sticker price for college attendance because public appropriations have been cut. Expenditures have been reduced largely by substituting part-time for full-time faculty, increasing average class size, and reducing administrative and other expenses. Critics will claim that these measures will likely reduce quality but, as we will argue in the next chapter, we lack consensual measures of quality, so this is hard to prove. What is clear is that cost pushers will continue to challenge the ability of colleges to provide an avenue for social mobility for students in need of support.

In the next chapter, we will examine the connection between college expenditures, prices and quality. But before we do that, we will conclude this chapter with a different perspective of the price/expenditure connection and the question of affordability.

## AFFORDABILITY

From a student perspective, the cost of going to college is wrapped up in the question of affordability. In turn, the public perception of affordability is based almost exclusively on the rising posted price of a college education. But the real story is considerably more complicated than that.

In addition to the price posted by the college, which is often called the sticker price, we must consider the net price. This is the sticker price minus the grants that are received by students. Affordability also forces us to consider the ability of families to pay, which is determined by personal income and wealth. And finally, affordability is influenced by the expected value that the average student receives from investing in a college education. Let's take a closer look at each of these factors with respect to community colleges (The analysis in this section draws from the ideas found in Baum & Ma, 2014a).

## Sticker and Net Prices

As noted above, the sticker price is not the true price paid by most students, whose direct costs are often reduced through scholarships (i.e., discounts) and grants (such as Pell grants or state financial aid based on need or merit). In fact, the difference between sticker price and real (net) price is a problem in itself. The difficulty of estimating financial aid makes it harder for students and parents to base college entry decisions on the real price. This has led to calls for better information about prices and outcomes, including the introduction of net price calculators on college websites where students can estimate the financial aid and net price of the colleges they are interested in.

Drawing on data from the College Board (Baum & Ma, 2014a), Table 2.6 details average sticker and net prices for full-time students at community colleges and public four-year colleges over the past twenty years. As these data show, community colleges have become comparatively less expensive

Table 2.6  Published and Net Yearly Average Tuition and Fees for Public Community Colleges vs. Public Four-Year Colleges, 1993–1994 to 2013–2014, Adjusted for Inflation (2013 dollars)

|  | Community colleges | | Public 4-year colleges | |
| --- | --- | --- | --- | --- |
|  | Sticker prices | Net prices | Sticker prices | Net prices |
| 1993–1994 | $2,010 | $600 | $4,100 | $2,040 |
| 2003–2004 | $2,420 | –420 | 5,900 | 1,920 |
| 2013–2014 | $3,260 | –1,550 | 8,890 | 3,120 |
| 20 year $ change | $1,250 | –2,150 | +4,790 | 1,080 |
| 20 year % change | 62% | –358% | +116% | +53% |

Note: Published tuition and fees (sticker price) is for instate students. Net prices are calculated by subtracting from the sticker price the total grant aid from all sources and federal tax credits. (Adapted from Baum & Ma, 2014b)

over that time period, with a sticker price that has increased only 62 percent compared to a 116 percent increase for public four-year colleges.

When we factor in financial aid that does not have to be paid back, the relative price difference is even greater. This is because the net price for community colleges has fallen into negative territory—minus $1,550—for 2013–2014, down by 358 percent in twenty years, while that of the public four-year colleges has risen by 53 percent.[1] Of course, these are national figures and the circumstances will differ from state to state.

What's wrong with these figures? They are the best available national figures that we have, but the net prices only apply to those students who qualify for financial aid. For these students, generous Pell grants have been the primary factor driving the net price charged to the lowest-income groups into the negative range. However, even though Pell and other need-based grants are essentially free money, some of this money is left on the table since many eligible students fail to apply for these grants.Working with a federal financial aid data set, Kantrowitz (2009) estimated that, at community colleges, only 58 percent of Pell-eligible students filled out the Free Application for Federal Student Aid (FAFSA) form (compared to 99.5 percent of the Pell-eligible students at for-profit, two-year colleges).

Again, it is the lack of information and complexity of the application process that are the primary reasons for leaving money on the table. Chapter 6 has some suggestions for correcting this problem, but for now we can say that colleges should renew their efforts to smooth the process of applying for financial aid and should locate eligible students on their own campuses needing help through this process.

The need to do a better job of helping low-income students through the financial aid process notwithstanding, it should be recognized that even for students who pay the full sticker price, cost-cutting measures have given public two-year colleges a relative price advantage over public four-year colleges. Indeed, the falling relative price underscores Archibald and Feldman's (2011) conclusion that "public two-year institutions have become more affordable" for all segments of income distribution (p. 195).

If this net price advantage continues, and if community colleges are able to keep their sticker price down, more students will divert from public and private four-year colleges to community colleges. Reviewing public four-year college affordability over the period 1984 to 2011, Delaney (2014) analyzed trends in state appropriations, tuition and fees, student aid, and family income. She found that public four-year colleges are much less affordable now than they were twenty-five years ago. This means that the community college is comparatively less expensive and, given current trends, will probably continue to have an affordability advantage over its public four-year counterparts.

This affordability advantage is even greater when we factor in the cost of room and board. Most community college students live at home while most four-year college students do not. The calculation for financial aid usually includes an allowance for room and board. We are not recommending that these expenses be eliminated from the formula for calculating aid, but most of them are not an extra out-of-pocket expense of attending a community college.

As economists point out, most of these expenses would be incurred even if the student was not in college. Likewise the allocation allowed for housing is not usually an additional cost of going to college, but may be thought of as a subsidy that parents willingly provide to dependent children when they are studying. In short, living at home increases the cost advantage of the community college and this factor is not fully reflected in calculations used in determining federal and state financial aid.

## Ability to Pay

In addition to the importance of looking at the net price of attending college, the affordability question is strongly influenced by trends in the ability of students and parents to pay for college out of personal income. One trend is growing income inequality, which has the potential to affect the community college in a number of ways. Data on income show that the real mean income of the bottom 20 percent of families has fallen by 4 percent from 1970 to 2012 and that of the next 20 percent has increased by only 7 percent over the latest forty-year period for which we have data (see Figure 7.1 in chapter 7).

For students in the bottom 40 percent of the income distribution, who make up the largest share of the community college enrollments and who pay the full sticker price, stagnant family incomes have made the community college less affordable. Many, if not most, of these students should be receiving need-based financial aid, which means they would only be paying the net price. Low-income students who pay the net price of going to community colleges are devoting a lower share of their family income to paying for college in 2013 than they did in 1993, even after accounting for stagnant incomes.

The real gains in family income over the past forty years have come at the top end of the income distribution. This is an income group that is less likely to attend community colleges than lower-income groups, although precise figures on the income stratification within higher education are hard to come by and vary depending on the data that are used. Census data compiled by the College Board show that in 2011–2012, 36 percent of dependent students attending community colleges had family incomes of less than $65,000, while 22 percent had family incomes over $106,000 (Baum, Ma, & Payea, 2013).

An annual study by Sallie Mae (2014), *How America Pays for College*, indicated that in 2013–2014, 25 percent of community college students had incomes over $100,000 while 44 percent had incomes under $35,000. Another report from Georgetown University estimated that 42 percent of community college students were from the top half of the income distribution (Carnevale & Strohl, 2010).

Given the available data, we estimate that somewhere between 40 and 50 percent of community college students can afford to pay the full average national sticker price. A "no-or-low" tuition policy would represent a direct income transfer to these families and make the distribution of income even more unequal. It is the 38 percent of families with incomes below $29,000 (See Figure 7.1 in chapter 7) who are overrepresented in community colleges and who are the group of greatest concern.

Most of their incomes have remained stagnant, at best, over the past forty years, and as a consequence, even the net negative price of the community college still consumes a proportionately high share of the family budget for individuals in this income group when the opportunity cost (lost income) of attending college is included. One way that the federal government can redress the balance between the stagnant income of the bottom 40 percent of families and the cost of a community college education is to tie the repayment of student loans to future income. This point was made earlier and will be discussed further in chapter 6.

## Return on Investment

In considering the affordability question, it is important to note that we have only looked at the cost side of the decision to attend college: What is the price and can I afford it? A more balanced view would also consider the potential benefits that would be received. If we look only at the increase in lifetime incomes (private benefits), we can see that community college attendance clearly pays off—higher earnings outweigh the costs.

A simple way to look at the cost-benefit decision can be found in an annual report by the College Board entitled *Education Pays* (Baum, Ma, & Payea, 2013). The most recent edition of this publication presents various cost-benefit scenarios that estimate how long it would take a student to start realizing a gain from investing in a community college degree.

One scenario compares the lifetime income of a high school graduate with that of an associate degree recipient. Assuming the associate degree recipient completes her degree two years after leaving high school, does not work while in college, pays the full average sticker price, and borrows all of the money to attend, her "total earnings net of loan repayment will exceed the total earnings of high school graduates by age 34" (Baum, Ma, & Payea, 2013, p. 13).

After this break-even point, the earnings premium of a college degree continues. For students who attend part-time, work, have grant aid, or take longer than two years, the break-even point will be earlier or later depending on their unique circumstances (e.g., the student's field of study, employment history, etc.).

## Conclusions on Affordability

Considering both costs and the benefits, a community college education has become more affordable over the last 30–40 years in both an absolute and a relative sense for students, even after factoring in the stagnant incomes of those with the lowest incomes. However, this could easily change if Pell and other need-based grants are not expanded in the future and if qualified students are not encouraged to apply for these grants.

Although loans are not a major source of financing a community college education, they should, when necessary, be used by students, but only under the condition of a broad income-based repayment plan. This idea is explored in greater depth in chapter 6.

## NOTE

1. The net prices for 2014–2015 had not been released by the College Board in time for this publication but a draft copy of the document indicates that it had dropped by about $200 from the figure shown in Table 2.6. For a full-time student attending a community college, the average net price for an in-state student was minus $1,740 (Baum & Ma, 2014a, p. 22).

# Chapter 3

# Productivity and Quality

The concept of productivity may be viewed from both a technical and a practical (alternative) perspective. Both are important. The technical perspective is in keeping with the economic thrust of this book. Here productivity is linked to the cost of educating students as measured by college expenditures. This perspective requires examination of the linkage between productivity, cost, and quality, recognizing that the unit cost of educating students will go down only if productivity goes up and quality is not compromised. This is difficult to achieve as steps taken by colleges to lower costs can result in lower quality. Alternatively, if productivity gains are too slow, costs will rise and additional revenue will be needed to cover costs.

Because of our inability to come up with acceptable measures of quality in higher education, policy makers are forced to use alternative definitions of productivity that focus on the efficiency of producing some unit of output (e.g., degrees) without reference to costs or quality. Despite this limitation, alternative definitions of productivity can serve as acceptable measures of effectiveness. They are more readily understood by the coordinating bodies, which use words like "productivity" and "quality" to describe institutional performance.

Coordinating bodies and government agencies want greater productivity because it implies greater efficiency, which keeps costs and taxes down. They want quality because it implies that students will be better educated, get better and more satisfying jobs, and become better citizens. But rarely do they tie these constructs together, recognizing—as many policymakers do—the complex interaction between productivity, cost, and quality.

While it is not our intention to engage in an exhaustive examination of productivity and quality issues, the discussion that follows does provide an important extension to the previous chapter on revenues and costs, as well as a linkage to the following chapter on outcomes. Outcomes, in turn, are tied to one of the most important trends in community college finance— performance-based funding, which is the focus of chapter 5.

## PRODUCTIVITY

Productivity is not an abstract theoretical concept, but is a pervasive force impacting the United States and all economies. Rising productivity is alternatively seen as a cause of unemployment as machines replace labor; as an important source of economic growth; and as a key factor in controlling price inflation.

Productivity growth is also inextricably linked to the quality of the goods and services being produced. In many cases, rising productivity is accompanied by a rise in quality, such as in the automobile and computer industries. In other cases, rising productivity may come at the cost of lower quality. Many claim that this is the case in higher education and other labor-intensive service industries.

In this section, we will first examine productivity in the economy in general and higher education in particular, describing what it means, how it is measured, and how it might be linked to educational quality. We will then address alternative, more familiar measures of productivity currently in use in colleges and universities.

### Economy-Wide Productivity

From a technical point of view, productivity is more of an engineering concept than an economic one. It is defined as a measure of the quantity of output produced in relation to the quantity of inputs needed to produce that output, with both inputs and outputs adjusted for quality. Productivity is calculated as a ratio of outputs to inputs and is often expressed as a percentage change per year.

The Bureau of Labor Statistics calculates national productivity for the U.S. economy, adjusted for quality, both in terms of labor productivity and multi-factor productivity (which includes other inputs such as capital). The media tends to pick up on the first of these measures stating, for example, that labor productivity (the increase in output per unit of labor) increased by 3.3 percent in a given year.

Since productivity changes with the business cycle, figures for one year or one quarter are not as meaningful as figures over a longer range of time. Increases in productivity over a period of years reflect the fact that we have been able to produce more output with the same inputs or have been able to produce the same output with fewer inputs or some combination of both. In other words, productivity measures the efficiency with which inputs are used to produce a given amount of output, other things being equal.

According to the Bureau of Labor Statistics, productivity may be increased by "variations in the characteristics and efforts of the workforce, changes in managerial skill, changes in the organization of production, changes in the allocation of resources between sectors, direct and indirect effects of research and development, and new technology" (Bureau of Labor Statistics, 2014). On a national level, rising productivity is seen as a source of economic growth and competitiveness. Education is widely recognized as a key to technological progress and enhancement of worker skills, which are important contributors to the rise in economy-wide productivity. Rising productivity, in turn, fuels growth in output and income that provides operating capital for public agencies including colleges and universities.

National productivity measures are averages of the varying productivity rates across all sectors of the economy, and it is this variation that drives the reallocation of resources away from low-productivity sectors into higher-productivity sectors. This is what happened in the United States and other high-income countries as resources shifted from agriculture to manufacturing and finally to the service sector. During this process some workers became unemployed and, over time, were redirected to sectors of the economy where jobs were plentiful.

Over the past 200 years, this process of economic transformation has raised average incomes and greatly improved living standards. In the words of Nobel Prize winning economist Paul Krugman, "productivity isn't everything, but in the long run it is almost everything. A country's ability to improve its standard of living over time depends almost entirely on its ability to raise its output per worker" (Krugman, 1994, p. 9).

As the quotation from Krugman implies, we can also link rising productivity to the long-run increase in workers' real wages. Workers in high-productivity industries generally have higher wages than those in low-productivity industries. Wages are also affected by scarcity or the relationship between the demand for the skills and the supply of workers who possess those skills. Productivity and scarcity influence the distribution of income in society and the degree of inequality. We will return to this idea in the last chapter where we will examine how the rising degree of income inequality in the United States might impact community college enrollments.

## Productivity, Costs, and Price

Differences in productivity among sectors in the economy also impact costs and price. If productivity increases faster in one sector (e.g., manufacturing), then the relative price of goods decline in relation to the price of goods and services where productivity growth is slower, like higher education. The relative price of slow-productivity industries will always rise. This is the factor underlying the "cost disease" theory of college cost presented earlier.

There is a critical link between output per worker and the cost of labor that has important implications for higher education. If output per worker increases faster than the cost of labor, the labor cost per unit of output falls. For example, the Department of Labor reported that in the 4th quarter of 2013, output per hour rose by 3.2 percent, while hourly compensation rose by just 1.5 percent, resulting in a decrease in the unit labor costs of 1.6 percent. The cost-output link has important implications for higher education, for in the long run a key factor in controlling costs is to increase productivity. If colleges and universities are able to show that increases in productivity come at the expense of quality, or are unable to develop methods that will raise productivity without reducing quality, then a decision will have to be made as to which is more important—lower prices or higher quality.

When prices are added to the inputs and outputs involved in productivity, a connection can be observed between the price charged for goods and services and the cost of producing them. For instance, if the cost of inputs, such as labor, falls, then the same quantity of output may be produced at a lower total cost. Other things being equal, this will allow prices to fall. Or, if the cost of inputs is rising and productivity, or output per person hour, does not rise proportionately, then costs per unit of output and prices will rise. Alternatively, if the cost of inputs is rising and this is completely offset by a rise in productivity, the costs per unit of output, and thus price, need not rise. All of this assumes that quality is constant, which in turn assumes that there is a suitable measure of quality.

It is important to indicate that if colleges and universities are able to increase productivity in the way we have defined it, there is no guarantee that the surplus produced will result in lower prices. It is possible that the surplus (increase in output and revenue) produced by increasing productivity will be absorbed by the faculty and/or managers in the form of higher wages; or in the case of for-profit colleges, passed on to stockholders. Some, or all, of the surplus might also be used to expand programs or to subsidize more expensive programs and to enhance the image of the college. Thus we find that when additional revenue is generated in colleges or universities through productivity increases or cost saving, "there usually are many claims on . . . [these additional resources] before the possibility of passing the savings on to students comes up: deferred maintenance, filling instructional vacancies, raising salaries (or restoring cuts), etc" (Johnson & Davies, 2014, p. 8).

A major complication to the above discussion is that in higher education the connection between cost and price (tuition) is less direct due to the presence of public and private subsidies. So productivity may rise, holding costs constant, but state subsidies could fall, necessitating some rise in prices (tuition) and/or a reduction in quality. One, if not both, of these things has been happening over the last ten years at both two-year and four-year public colleges in the United States.

## Productivity in Higher Education

Archibald and Feldman (2011) completed an extensive study of productivity in higher education and the cost of going to college. They concluded that "costs in higher education must increase faster than the general inflation rate as long as productivity growth in colleges and universities lags behind productivity growth in the rest of the economy" (p. 114).

What, then, can be done to increase higher education productivity? If productivity is simply the ratio of outputs divided by inputs, then it is easy to see how we can increase it. Either increase the numerator (outputs) or decrease the denominator (inputs). Seen from this point of view, productivity is a throughput measure—more students per instructor, for instance.[1]

The numerator and the denominator can be altered in various ways. Class sizes and faculty workloads can be increased. Admissions can be restricted to students who will succeed. Or more students can be processed though courses with passing grades. These steps would increase the throughput—outputs measured by completion will increase faster than inputs—and the cost per unit of output will fall. But what about the quality of the product and the equal opportunity mission of open-access colleges like the community college?

It is possible, of course, that college quality is going up and that the rising cost of higher education is a fair price for producing a better product. We have little evidence to support this position, although advancing technology and enhanced services have become an important part of the educational process and may have improved the quality of learning.

In an essay on college productivity and costs, William Bowen, the former president of Princeton University and the Mellon Foundation, argued that the information revolution has enhanced output in "ways that do not show up in the usual measures of productivity or cost per student" (Bowen, 2012, p. 6). It is easy to agree with this statement, but, as Bowen indicates, the impact of this revolution has not shown up in measures of improved learning outcomes or lower costs. We will speculate on the potential for technology to lower costs and improve learning in our final chapter on the future.

In the previous chapter, we indicated that community colleges have done a better job of controlling their operating costs, as measured by expenditures, than their four-year public counterparts. They have done so by substituting lower-cost adjunct faculty for higher-cost full-time faculty and by increasing student/faculty ratios. These cost-cutting measures may or may not result in enhanced productivity depending on what happens to output and quality.

Outputs are, at best, difficult to specify and measure in community colleges and quality remains the great unknown. To date, adequate measures of quality have not been developed for any sector of higher education, which means that, from a technical standpoint, we are not able to successfully measure productivity. Nonetheless, there have been attempts to measure productivity in higher education. Among the most notable is the NRC Model, which uses available data to bridge the gap between theory and practice.

## The NRC Model

The most far-reaching examination of the economic conception of productivity and the manner in which it relates to higher education is found in a report (Sullivan et al., 2012) completed for the National Research Council (NRC) of the National Academy of Sciences (Much shorter, less technical versions of the report can be found in Massy, Sullivan, & Mackie, 2012, 2013). The NRC report uses IPEDS and other published data to develop a baseline model for measuring productivity, which is defined "as the ratio of outputs to the inputs required for producing them, where both inputs and outputs are adjusted for quality differences" (Massy et al., 2012, p. 6). Key principles guiding the analysis in the NRC report include the following:

• The focus is on the instructional mission and not on research or public service; community colleges are included.
• The analysis does not include important nonpecuniary outputs such as citizenship and improving the quality of life for students and the community.
• The analysis deals with multifactor productivity including factors like supplies, technology, and capital. This makes the calculation of productivity more difficult, but also more accurate.
• Quality should not be ignored: "Quality should always be a core part of the productivity conversations, even if it cannot be fully captured by the metrics" (Massy et al., 2012, p. 5).

Inputs considered in the baseline multifactor model are:

• expenditures on labor (i.e., salaries, wages, and benefits) and the quantity of labor (i.e., number of full-time-equivalent employees) used in producing outputs;
• expenditures and quantities of other inputs such as supplies, operations and maintenance, including those acquired by outsourcing; and

- capital expenditures (i.e., "depreciation of plant and equipment during use") (Massy et al., 2012, p. 8).

Outputs in the baseline model are:

- credit hours generated over a twelve-month period;
- completions, in terms of "awards or degrees conferred, summed over programs, . . . race or ethnicity, and gender" (Sullivan et al., 2012, p. 65); and
- adjusted credit hours, calculated as "credit hours + (sheepskin effect x completions)" As Massy et al. (2012) note, "the sheepskin effect represents the additional value that credit hours have when they are accumulated and organized into a completed degree. . . ." (p. 8).

The NRC report calculates the actual change in productivity from one year to the next for a particular college and finds that it increased by a little over 2 percent. However, it warns that this figure has not been adequately adjusted for quality measures. It also notes that community colleges must be given special considerations. Among these are the following:

- Community colleges have a different mix of mission and programs than four-year colleges. In assessing outputs, consideration needs to be given not just to degree production but also to transfer success, certificates, remedial, and noncredit workforce efforts.
- Community colleges have a different mix of students than do most four-year colleges. In assessing productivity inputs, outputs and quality, student ability, and preparation must be accounted for.

These factors highlight the difficulties of conducting productivity analyses for community colleges and make a strong case for using the best science available to help the colleges develop better productivity measures.

## Alternative Measures of Productivity

The input-output framework for examining productivity is not the norm for higher education institutions. Instead of focusing on the linkage between cost, productivity, and quality, educators use alternative measures of what they refer to as productivity, such as the number of degrees produced or the number of students who transfer, but without reference to cost or price. These are perfectly legitimate measures of institutional outcomes, but they are not a true measure of productivity.

The current emphasis on measuring outcomes generally ignores inputs in the NRC productivity analysis and concentrates on the efficiency of producing certain outputs, such as graduates. This represents a subtle shift from "productivity" to "efficiency" (e.g. the cost per graduate) in analyses of college performance. A college could increase efficiency not by spending less, but by spending less to produce a given output such as a graduate. This provides a potential opening for increased public support.

A college that increases its credentialing rate, for instance, may be able to argue for greater public funding on the grounds that its cost per credential is falling and that more credentials in turn increases the future personal income and tax revenues and reduces future social welfare expenditures. An excellent paper on the difference between productivity and the efficiency of produc-ing graduates can be found in Jenkins and Rodriguez (2013) who explain in simple terms how current efforts to cut costs may actually reduce productivity and efficiency.

Typical of the alternative definitions of productivity is a conception advanced by Kelly (2009) in a study entitled "The dreaded 'P' word: An examination of productivity in public postsecondary education." Kelly defines productivity as the market value of credentials produced relative to total spending (funding) per FTE student. In other words, he links resources and performance as measured by one outcome: the market value of credentials.

In general, Kelly found that "there is no evident relationship at the state level between resources and performance: higher levels of resources do not result in more credentials awarded per student" (p.17). Kelly's study is lim-ited because it controls for nothing. But it nonetheless compares favorably with simple and unsubstantiated political rhetoric that says that resources don't matter—it's what you do with them that counts.

Such statements are in stark contrast to the research, albeit limited, that shows a positive connection between resources spent per student and gradu-ation rates (Bailey, 2012). The positive link between outputs and resources supports calls for more money to achieve better results and the claim that community colleges are underfunded (Century Foundation Task Force, 2013).

## QUALITY

We have emphasized that an acceptable measure of quality is an important component of productivity analysis. It is difficult to measure, because quality is in the eye of the beholder. Practitioners more often than not conceive of a quality education as one that provides a quality learning experience—one that promotes critical thinking and knowledge through courses that prepare learners for work and further education. Political constituents might think of quality in terms of institutional capacity to promote economic development through spending and outputs created with students.

Students are likely to have a more personal definition of quality. They may refer to a quality experience at XYZ College as an opportunity to explore life and career goals and to build skills they can sell in the labor market. Additional benefits would include making connections and broadening life experiences. These positive aspects of the total college experience are often reflected in alumni surveys taken many years after graduation or in gifts to a college foundation. Research on quality occasionally includes some of these variables, but the majority of academic studies concentrate on two standard measures of quality: peer effects and resources.

## Quality in Four-Year Colleges

In spite of the rhetoric about the importance of outputs (outcomes) over input measures, the latter still hold sway when it comes to measuring quality. The two standard measures of quality in four-year colleges in the research literature are the quality of the students admitted ("peer effects") and the level of resources devoted to the education of students. Peer effects are important because students are one of the inputs that go into the production process: better students, better learning, better outcomes. The quality of students, in turn, is often measured by such factors such as average SAT scores or high school grades, and the selectivity of the college (rejection rate).

The other measure of quality found in the research literature is the level of resources that colleges have to spend on students, which is usually measured by expenditures per FTE student. The assumption is that more resources lead to better outcomes. Well known for using input measures are the *U.S. News & World Report* rankings which use spending per FTE student on instruction, student services, and academic support, as well as faculty compensation, percent of full-time faculty, and low student/faculty ratios as measures of quality.

The message is that higher spending and closer contact with faculty means greater quality. Research has generally shown a high correlation between these inputs and student outcomes in four-year colleges such as degree completion. However, since higher-ability students tend to sort themselves into better colleges, it is difficult to separate the effects of institutional quality and student ability.

## Quality in Community Colleges

No standard measures of quality suitable for community colleges are currently in use. For this reason scholars generally fall back on the input measures cited above. Since community colleges are open-admission institutions, the peer effects on educational outcomes may be negative. Thus, the level of preparation of incoming students must be controlled when conducting outcomes research. When considering peer effects, community colleges should be compared to the population of two-year colleges or less-selective four-year colleges. Research of this genre has yet to be conducted in spite of the fact that about half of all four-year colleges in the United States would fit into this category (Baum & Ma, 2011).

Would expenditures per student suffice as a measure of quality for community colleges? This is the most common proxy measure of quality found in the literature because it is the most readily available and because researchers know that it is correlated with quality in baccalaureate institutions. In spite of the questions raised earlier about underfunding of community colleges versus public master's-level colleges, it is clear that when expenditures per student are considered, efforts to control costs may have come at the expense of quality. Even analysts urging greater control over college costs fear that the community college "imperative to cut costs [may be] sacrificing some aspect of quality" (Wellman, 2006, p. 9).

Practitioners uphold the connection between resources and quality. For example, cognizant of research documenting the positive impact of full-time faculty on student retention and completion, the Maricopa County Community College District (Phoenix) has committed itself to bringing the number of full-time faculty up to 60 percent of the total faculty from its current level of 40 percent within five to eight years (Ashford, 2013). This reflects current thinking that full-time faculty and smaller classes are better for learning and student success—a position reinforced through in-person interviews with top-level administrators at Maricopa, indicating that this line of thinking strongly influenced their decision.

Further supporting this line of reasoning is the behavior of institutions. When budgets improve, colleges hire more full-time faculty and are more likely to retain low-enrollment courses whereas in tight budget years, actions of this type are reversed in an effort to cut costs. College leaders undoubtedly feel that quality suffers in lean years, as Maricopa evidently did, but they rarely have the data to support this belief and even if they did, most would not want to admit it, at least publicly.[2]

## Community College Quality and Outcomes

As we have argued, community colleges have held down costs primarily by substituting part-time for full-time faculty and by increasing the student/faculty ratio. The impact of these actions on quality, however measured, is not certain, given the paucity of studies that have been conducted on this issue. However, the available research, which leans heavily on the standard measures of quality—peer effects and resources—suggests that quality has been compromised.

The most widely cited study of the impact of cost control on outcomes was completed by Jacoby (2006) who examined the impact of increasing use of part-time faculty on graduation rates. Relying on an IPEDS data set, which included 935 public two-year colleges throughout the United States, Jacoby used three different measures of the graduation rate in an attempt to control for part-time and transfer students. For peer effects he used two indirect measures of student quality. He found that as student quality ramped up so did the graduation rate—a predictable result. However, most interesting among his findings was that the increasing use of part-time faculty had a large and negative impact on graduation rates. A similar result was found for four-year colleges by Ehrenberg and Zhang (2004).

An important study contradicting the conclusion that greater use of adjunct faculty has a negative impact on student success was conducted by Bettinger and Long (2010). Using a sophisticated set of controls, Bettinger and Long found that employing adjuncts in occupational fields had a small positive effect on student interest in a subject and on course performance. Although this study was limited to one institution—a public four-year college—it may have implications for community colleges choosing to employ practitioners in occupational fields as adjuncts.

The study confirms the intuitive belief that teachers with practical experience in the field may have a positive impact on students. However, it is not clear whether there is a tipping point at which the addition of adjunct faculty may lead to harmful effects. This is a moot point, however, as most community college programs have moved past this threshold.

Studies of the working conditions of part-time faculty at community colleges show that they work in a marginalized environment, spend less time with students and are less committed to student success than full-time faculty (Umbach, 2007, 2008). Preliminary data from the National Community College Benchmarking Project at Johnson County Community College in Kansas, indicate that part-time faculty spend less than 1 percent of their time tutoring and advising students compared to close to 10 percent for full-time faculty (personal correspondence, March 24, 2014). At this point we do not know what an acceptable mix of faculty, if there is one, in specific programs might be.

Additional evidence that increasing use of part-time faculty has a negative impact on student outcomes in community colleges is provided by Boylan (2010), Egan and Jaeger (2009), and Jaeger and Egan (2009). Egan and Jaeger's work examined the impact of part-time faculty on both graduation and transfer rates. Working with student transcripts and institutional data from the entire California community college system, they followed first-time students who had taken at least eight transfer credits over a five-year period, starting in the year 2000. Controlling for a number of variables, Egan and Jaeger found that greater exposure to part-time faculty reduced the probability of completing an associate degree and of transferring to a four-year college.

In a frequently cited study, Calcagno, Bailey, Jenkins, Kienzl, and Leinbach (2008) used models of student engagement to examine the institutional characteristics that influence student completion rates, measured by certificate or degree completion or by transfer to a four-year college. They considered both peer effects and expenditures per student for a national sample of community colleges.

After controlling for a number of variables, they concluded that expenditures and tuition levels are not related to completion, although traditional-age students seem to be helped by comprehensive student support services. Selected variables did make a difference, however, including college size (small is better), a greater proportion of full-time faculty, and the proportion of minority students (lower is better).

A study by Stange (2009) used national data and expenditures per student, as measures of college quality. Strange found that students do not select a community college based on its quality but generally attend the college closest to their home. More importantly, variations in college quality make no difference in student educational attainment.

This conclusion is contradicted by a Type-3 study of high school graduates in Georgia by Goodman, Hurwitz, and Smith (2015) who found that students attending lower-quality community colleges in that state were much less likely to complete a bachelor's degree than similarly situated students who initially enrolled at a four-year college. Dunlop (2011), however, found that bachelor's degree attainment of community college transfers in the state of Virginia depends on the quality of the college transferred to and not on that of the sending community college.

And finally, recent research has brought new light to the idea that greater reliance on part-time faculty may be compromising quality. Lahr et al. (2014) conducted a series of interviews with mid- and top-level administrators at two- and four-year public colleges in Ohio, Indiana, and Tennessee—states that have well-established performance-based funding (PBF) systems. The interviews were designed to explore the potential impact of PBF on public colleges and universities.

The most frequently cited concern for community colleges was a fear that PBF programs might lead to a "weakening of academic standards" (p. 12). Quality could be sacrificed by lower course requirements, resulting in grade inflation and movement of students through the curriculum at too rapid a pace, especially in remedial programs. Part-time faculty may be particularly susceptible to pressure to demonstrate a strong retention rate in their classes as high standards may be hazardous to job security. Upon further study, it may turn out that performance-based funding and growing reliance on part-time faculty is a lethal combination in community colleges.

## Moving Along

The measurement of productivity and quality has both a theoretical and a practical side. As a matter of public policy, it is important that colleges and researchers move ahead on the technical issues involved in measuring both constructs. Improved data and methodology will accomplish this, albeit, at a slow pace. For now, we cannot wait for the theory and data to arrive at the point where we can make judgments about output measures as proxies for quality in community colleges. The accountability movement demands no less. In the next chapter we provide a detailed description of the outcome measures currently in use or proposed.

## NOTES

1. Throughput should not be confused with facilitating a smoother flow of students through the system. That is clearly desirable and also increases productivity and lowers costs. We can increase throughput by not giving students as many failing grades or by setting academic standards so low that everyone can pass. Most would see this as an undesirable reduction in quality. Smoothing the flow, on the other hand, might come from providing students with better information about pathways, reducing barriers to the transfer of credits among colleges, improving remedial education and reducing financial barriers to completing programs. All these promote desirable outcomes but don't necessarily lower costs.

2. Our discussion of the Maricopa District was written before Arizona policymakers proposed in early 2015 to cut all state funding for that district (See Smith, 2015).

# Chapter 4

# Outcomes

Inputs that drive the process of educating students have long been the primary indicator of quality in colleges and universities. As argued in the last chapter, researchers have used the quality of students admitted and the amount of money spent on them as proxies for quality. Until recently, accreditation agencies concentrated on input measures such as the credentials of faculty, the size of the library, the courses being taught, and the facilities used to house programs. It's not that outputs were totally neglected.

Colleges proudly pointed to successful alumni who became doctors, astronauts, and actors as well as those who came from modest backgrounds and contributed generously to the colleges that helped them achieve their status. Yet, one of the key output variables in the quality equation, the ability of the students admitted, was often left out of this picture. Students were both an input and an output measure.

Admitting high-ability students from privileged backgrounds made it easier to produce favorable outcomes. Colleges further down the higher education hierarchy, especially open-admissions community colleges, insisted that value-added measures would show that they were doing as good a job or better than selective colleges with the students they admitted. Clear indications that this value-added approach can be a good step toward measuring quality have yet to be found. What we can say is that, over the past twenty-five years, researchers have been searching for outputs that will serve as proxy measures of quality for different types of colleges.

The intellectual shift from measuring inputs to measuring outputs has been fueled by a change in attitude toward higher education by the tax-paying public. In the post–World War II period of growing opportunity, rising income, and American hegemony, college graduates with almost any major had a comparatively easy time finding jobs and moving up the income ladder.

But, during periods of recurring recessions from 1980–1982 to the present, the economic returns to college have become more selective, remaining relatively high for graduates in some fields though not for others. As state budgets got tight during each period of economic decline and as the post-war boom gave way to the present era of slow growth, reduced social mobility, and greater income and wealth inequality, the public demanded greater accountability from colleges.

Recessions helped to shift the focus from measuring inputs to measuring outputs. Now, more than ever, the attitude is that "we once trusted you to produce favorable outcomes, but given our limited resources, we need some evidence that you are doing so." Hence we have performance-based funding, college-rating systems, and other forms of public disclosure that do not take positive outcomes for granted.

The shift in emphasis from inputs to outputs is more evident in policy discussions than in the work of researchers who continue to use input measures of college selectivity and college resources (the more the better for both) as proxy measures of quality in their studies. The reason for this is that reliable data on agreed-upon outputs are not yet available.

But the current rush to produce better measures of outputs, framed in the language of outcomes assessment and institutional effectiveness, along with generous funding for research from private foundations, is gradually moving researchers into developing and testing output measures. And although we have not reached consensus on which measures to use and what new data are needed, many states have linked appropriations to outcome measures in performance funding formulas, a topic we will address in the next chapter. This makes it imperative that campus leaders and policy makers understand the strengths and weaknesses of outcomes measures used or proposed in performance-based funding.

We argue in this chapter that outcomes assessment is complicated, especially for community colleges, which have a multimodal mission and a large number of students who have unclear goals and a weak attachment to higher education. We explore the context for assessment by examining four common measures of community college outcomes: credentials produced, transfer rates, learning outcomes, and labor market success. These are the outcomes that are central to most research and around which most evidence has been amassed. Each is accompanied by a "warning" message highlighting important caveats that must be kept in mind as policy makers increasingly turn to outcome measures in funding decisions and in assessments of institutional effectiveness and quality. Output measures beyond the four discussed below, such as momentum points, are less well researched, but are addressed in the next chapter on performance-based funding.

## CREDENTIAL PRODUCTION

Community college credentials are usually awarded in the form of degrees and certificates. Increasing degree production, in particular, is a hot topic as evidence indicates that the United States is falling behind other industrialized nations in the production of postsecondary degrees (for dissenting opinions, see Adelman, 2009; Hauptman, 2012). In addition, evidence indicates that college completion rates are lower today than they were in the early 1970s (Bound, Lovenheim, & Turner, 2010; Goodman, Hurwitz, & Smith, 2015).

The Obama administration, pushed by the agendas of private foundations such as the Bill and Melinda Gates Foundation and the Lumina Foundation, has set ambitious targets to get America back in the lead by 2020 in this category (Obama, 2010). While many experts do not think that these goals can be met, the research and discussion generated by the degree completion movement has resulted in a healthy examination of higher education outcomes in general and of those within community colleges in particular (Kelly & Schneider, 2012). Community colleges are in the limelight because it is generally believed that most of the increase in credential production will come from two-year colleges, where completion rates, as conventionally measured, are low.

Many students come to the community college with the intent of getting a degree, but data indicate that most do not achieve completion. However, we know that the goal of earning a degree is more common among students who initially enroll at four-year colleges than at community colleges. In the latter, students in technical and health programs seem the most focused on completing a degree.

It is hard to imagine students entering a nursing program with the intent of stopping short of the degree or of transferring before getting a degree and license necessary to get a job in the field. Students in computer technology, however, may be less tied to their academic program. If information technology skills are in high demand in the regional labor market, students may terminate enrollment after a year, or less, of study. Labor market conditions have a lot to do with community college outcomes such as degree production and lifetime income.

Students enrolled in liberal arts and business may be even less tied to getting a degree at the community college than those in technical programs. In these programs, transfer after a year of study or dropping-out altogether after testing the waters of higher education is more common. We know that students who require remedial work become more easily discouraged and are much less likely to complete an academic program. Add to this the facts that many community college students come from lower socioeconomic backgrounds, are more likely to be students of color, are more likely to have parents without college experience, and are often educated at marginally-performing high schools, it is not surprising that degree production in community colleges is low. As researchers will point out, these "risk factors" must be accounted for in any assessment of outcomes.

Nonetheless, community colleges are under considerable pressure to increase their degree and certificate production. This could be done by significantly expanding enrollments, but even at the current rate of completion that would require a large increase in capacity and funding that, as we argued earlier, is unlikely to be achieved.

An easier way to increase degree production is to retain more of the students currently enrolled, including those who require remedial work, and to improve pathways toward credentials, including transfer toward a bachelor's degree. Retention becomes more of an incentive if colleges are allowed to keep tuition revenue and if retention is included as a metric in state performance-based funding formulas. However, although community colleges may be described as organizations that have low recruiting costs, they also enroll students who can be expensive to retain.

In the current fiscal environment, rather than increasing the production of associate degrees, colleges have chosen to increase the production of certificates, which have been increasing at a faster rate than degree production (287,642 certificates were awarded in 1994 and 815,334 were awarded in 2009). In fact, only 56 percent of the credentials awarded by community colleges in 2009 were degrees. The remaining 44 percent were either short-term certificates of a year or less (23 percent) or longer-term certificates (21 percent) of at least a year but less than two years in length (Bosworth, 2012; Horn, Li, & Weko, 2009).

Some of the increase in credential production, especially longer-term credentials, has important labor market implications. But in other cases, the benefits are not as apparent. In Pennsylvania, for example, community colleges are awarding certificates to students in general education for passing specific momentum points, such as earning a specified number of credits. Awarding these certificates may increase retention, but they probably have no market value.

## Credentialing Rates Across Institutions

In addition to wide-ranging student characteristics and variations in the types of degrees and certificates awarded, credential production has a lot to do with college mission. Among the most commonly stated mission components in community colleges are remedial education, skill training to prepare students for immediate employment, contract training for local industries, transfer preparation, avocational activities for the local community, and education leading to a bachelor's degree.

The mix of these components differs by state and college depending on public policy and regional economic needs. Ideally, each of these mission components would be assessed individually, but it is clear that not all are designed to produce a credential. Accordingly, an important factor accounting for differences in credential production among colleges is that students use community colleges for different purposes.

College efforts to increase completion rates can also make a difference. The Community College Research Center (CCRC) at Columbia University has been able to document ways in which well-designed programs in remedial education, retention, student learning, and a host of other areas can help move students toward their educational goals. In a new volume that deserves to be widely read, Bailey, Jaggars, and Jenkins (2015) synthesize recent findings from CCRC research and suggest ways that colleges can redesign themselves to increase the institution's impact on student success. They argue that a more structured curriculum with fewer choices and better student support services will be necessary to smooth the pathways toward completion for a greater number of students.

Clearly, colleges can make a difference, but two important studies suggest that a note of caution is also appropriate. The first study comes out of the CCRC and asks whether certain institutional characteristics can make a difference in student success (Calcagno et al., 2008). Using national data from IPEDS and U.S. Department of Education sample surveys, the researchers found that student success rates, as measured by credential completion or transfer to a four-year college, are negatively impacted by college size (small is better) and the proportion of part-time faculty and minority students enrolled.

The second study (Clotfelter et al., 2013) examined the success rate of the North Carolina Community College system in producing credentials. The study linked student data at the college level with data for the same students at their secondary schools. Clotfelter et al. examined the records of over 11,000 students who entered the state's fifty-eight community colleges between 2001 and 2009 and sought to determine if individual colleges differed with respect to the production of vocational credentials (applied success) and the production of transfer credentials and credits (transfer success).

The study found wide differences among colleges, but when results were adjusted for student data, the differences almost entirely disappeared. In other words, it was the differences in student abilities, backgrounds, test scores in high school that were important, not what the individual colleges did. Only colleges at the top and those at the bottom in terms of the two credentialing outcomes examined in the study had either positive or negative impacts on student outcomes.

This suggests that focusing on college outliers might uncover ways that colleges can make a difference, especially among underprepared student populations. Interestingly, the Clotfelter et al. study also compared colleges in terms of measures used by the state for performance funding and found that the state metrics were not effective measures of performance. Again, the highest performing colleges had the highest performing students before college entry (Clotfelter et al., 2013).

These studies highlight how difficult it is to untangle the influence of student background and ability from the influence of institutional programs and services when explaining variations in credential production across colleges. This does not mean that colleges don't make a difference, only that it is difficult to measure the difference. Reflecting on more than fifty years of research, Astin (2013) remarked:

> Decades of longitudinal research have shown that American higher education is so stratified in terms of student inputs that institutional differences in such outcomes [as credential production, graduation rates or earnings] are primarily attributable to the kinds of students who enroll—their abilities, social class, etc. —rather than to anything about the colleges' educational programs. Indeed, when one takes into account the types of students who enroll, some of the colleges with modest outcomes turn out to be doing an excellent job, while others with much better outcomes sometimes turn out to be doing a mediocre job. (para. 1)

While colleges must not fall victim to a mind-set of educational determinism that reinforces existing inequalities, this line of research underscores the difficulty of developing measures of institutional effectiveness that capture student success within the multidimensional mission of the community college and with the variety of goals and ability levels of its students.

One matter is certain: Credentialing rates are strongly correlated with income levels. Students from lower-income groups but with similar ability have a much lower completion rate than students from higher-income groups, no matter what type of college they attend. This inequitable outcome is something that community colleges can address. Noting the strong correlation between degree completion and socioeconomic status (SES), Bailey, Jenkins, and Leinbach (2005) point out that

> If this correlation represents systematic difficulties faced by lower income and minority students, then colleges should try to ameliorate them. Alternatively, if systematic differences in expectations result from SES, community colleges need to strive to raise the expectations of poorer students, even when they

themselves do not seek degrees, by helping them recognize the opportunities for advancement in education and subsequently in employment. (p. 3)

## Measuring Credential Production

As reported by Snyder and Dillow (2015), about one in five first-time, full-time community college students graduate with a degree or certificate within three years of the normal time it takes to earn these credentials (three years for the associate degree, less for a certificate). This "official" graduation rate comes from the U.S. Department of Education's federally mandated IPEDS survey to which virtually all colleges contribute data and which is a major source of information about postsecondary education. It was developed in 1992 to satisfy the requirements of the Student Right-to-Know and the Higher Education Opportunity Acts.

This figure includes only students who enter in the fall semester and graduate from the initial college of entry (this significantly undercounts both enrollments and graduates for the community college). It excludes part-time and transfer students and only captures about one-third of the students attending community colleges.

IPEDS data have been widely criticized as painting an incomplete and even an inaccurate picture of what is happening in higher education, especially for community colleges (Dellow & Romano, 2002). When looking at student outcomes, such as graduation and transfer rates, IPEDS does not stand up well when compared to other national databases like those maintained by the National Student Clearinghouse (NSC) and those derived from Department of Education sample surveys, such as the National Education Longitudinal Study (NELS), the National Longitudinal Survey of Youth (NLSY), and the High School and Beyond (HS&B) Survey. This is primarily because IPEDS data track student progress only within institutions and do not factor in student progress across institutions within the larger system of higher education.

For instance, NSC data, which follow all students for six years at public and private colleges and across state lines show that for the Fall 2007 cohort, about 40 percent of community college entrants completed a degree or certificate at either the college of initial enrollment or at a transfer college (NSC, 2013, p. 6). This is almost double the rate calculated from IPEDS data. If we look at only full-time students, the NSC graduation rate increases to 58 percent, but for students attending part-time exclusively it falls to 20 percent.

Responding to the criticisms of IPEDS data, Secretary of Education Arne Duncan appointed a Committee on Measures of Student Success in 2009 to recommend changes in the outcomes measures and the way they are calculated for community colleges. The Committee, headed by Thomas Bailey from Columbia University, urged the Department of Education to "refine and update current methods for calculating federal graduation rates by measuring progress more broadly and adding student subgroups to reflect the student populations served by two-year institutions," including part-time degree-seeking students, students needing remedial instruction, and those receiving Pell grants and other forms of federal financial aid (Committee on Measures of Student Success, 2011, p. 27).

The Committee also urged further work on clarifying which students should be considered degree-seeking students. The Committee's recommendations represented a balance of what is needed and what is possible, given existing legal constraints and the desire not to burden colleges with excessive data collection costs.

New outcomes measures proposed for the 2015–2016 IPEDS data collection cycle attempt to broaden the scope of completion indicators, tracking the progress of the 2007 entering cohort of students. The Institute for Higher Education Policy (IHEP) reports that the new information will capture outcomes information on more students, including part-timers and students who are non-first-time entrants. But the IHEPS analysts caution that these measures, although an improvement, will likely be a disappointment to both individual colleges and researchers for what they do not contain. For instance, the new data will not be able to answer such basic questions as, "How many students transfer from a particular community college to a four-year institution?" (Voight et al., 2014, p. 7). Readers interested in a detailed analysis of what the new IPEDS information will and will not contain are directed to the IHEP Report.

It is clear that modifying a large national database such as IPEDS takes a long time and will always lag behind what researchers feel are important data elements to capture. As the head of the Committee on Measures of Student Success notes:

A fundamental problem is that IPEDS can't track accurately the longitudinal path of students who transfer among institutions. This is a particularly serious deficiency for judging the effectiveness of community colleges since preparing students to transfer is a fundamental part of their mission. The Commission recommended the development of a longitudinal unit record system that would solve this problem, but current federal law prohibits the development of such a system. As long as we cannot track students among institutions, outcome measures reported through IPEDS will be frustrating and incomplete. (comments from Thomas Bailey, personal communication, June 14, 2014)

Since community college success rates depend not only on credential completion but also on what transfer students do, let's look at transfer rates in more detail.

WARNING: *Different components of college mission and student goals create variable credential production rates. Knowing how completion rates are calculated and what goals students are pursuing can be useful when explaining low credential completion rates to constituents.*

## TRANSFER

Transfer to a four-year college is a goal for many students entering community colleges and ought to be considered as much a part of student success as completing a degree or certificate—and it is. The most widely cited national transfer rate calculated from IPEDS data is in the low 20 percent range (Mullin, 2012); but, as we have stated, IPEDS data vastly undercounts the number of transfer students. Community college graduates, for instance, who transfer are not counted because graduation trumps transfer. A student can only be counted once.

The new IPEDS measures will correct for some of these problems and soon colleges will be able to calculate a new measure of institutional success defined as the percentage of entrants who, after a specified period of time, are still enrolled, have transferred, or have earned a credential (Voight et al., 2014). But, as Bailey has indicated, users are likely to be unhappy with other elements of the new data, especially the calculation of transfer rates.

### Numerator and Denominator

The transfer rate is the percentage of students from a target population that transfer; but, the rate will differ depending on the numerator and denominator selected. Considering the *numerator*, for instance, should students who transfer to another two-year college (called lateral transfer) be counted? Many researchers feel that only transfer to a four-year college (called upward or vertical transfer) should be counted as a positive outcome. What about the time of transfer? If a student transfers ten years after attending a community college, should he or she be included in the transfer rate? The answer is probably "no," but nothing is definitive.

Cohen has suggested that to be counted as a transfer, the student should take one or more classes at a four-year college within four years of leaving the community college (Cohen, 1991). Others have advocated a minimum of a semester's worth of credit at the transfer college in the definition of a transfer student (Adelman, 2005).

The new IPEDS data system will not provide a resolution to most of these issues. For instance, colleges will report all transfers together in the same category. Grouping in this fashion will obscure the type of institution to which students transfer. Data from the National Student Clearinghouse (NSC) indicate that 40 percent of all transfers are lateral—transferring from a community college to another community college or from a four-year college to another four-year college. If these transfers are included in the numerator, the result is a significantly higher transfer rate. In fact, when lateral transfers are included in the transfer rate, community colleges actually receive more transfer students than they send to four-year colleges (NSC, 2012). This confusing swirl of students creates difficulty in calculating the transfer rate.

In addition to decisions that must be made about whom to include in the numerator, there must also be a means of tracking individual students to determine if they transfer. IPEDS requires that the transfer number be reported but does not provide a means for doing so. Most public colleges would use statewide system data to report transfer numbers, but the most accurate tracker available is the NSC.

The NSC is an improvement over most statewide databases because it can track students who transfer to public or private colleges within states and across state lines. It can also track degrees earned, as well as the enrollment status of students (full-time, half-time, three-quarter time, less than half-time, and withdrawn). This is potentially valuable information for tracking transfer students, but the NSC data are not publically available for research and a fee is charged for colleges choosing to track their own students. State systems of higher education would do well to negotiate a system-wide fee for NSC data use, as some states have done. The State University of New York has integrated NSC data into its own statewide data system so that students can be tracked without sending a separate query to the Clearinghouse.

What about the *denominator*, which Hom (2009) feels is the more difficult problem to solve? How long do community colleges have to retain students before counting them in the target population? Should they count any student who takes a single credit course? Should they only count students who take courses designed for transfer? Or, perhaps they should only count graduates who receive a credential.

Most feel that the right answer is somewhere in between the extremes, perhaps requiring that students take ten to fifteen, or roughly one semester's worth, of credit, before inclusion in the target population. Eliminating incidental students who accumulate less than a semester's worth of credits, as Adelman (2005) suggests, is appropriate and helps produce a more accurate graduation and transfer rate. Eliminating students who already have a bachelor's degree or who are taking noncredit courses from the denominator would also be appropriate. Certainly including all students in the denominator is inappropriate and produces an inaccurate picture of both transfer and graduation rates.

Although successful transfer is in itself an important outcome, community colleges should track transfer students to determine how many complete a bachelor's degree. Recent studies have shown that community college transfer students are just as likely to complete a bachelor's degree as students who start at a four-year level (Melguizo, Kienzl, & Alfonso, 2011). Other studies (e.g., NSC, 2012) have suggested that while obtaining an associate degree before transfer is not necessary for many students, those who do are more likely to complete a bachelor's degree than those who do not.

Certainly, the more limited the time spent by students at a community college prior to transferring, the more difficult it becomes to estimate the percentage of bachelor's degree attainment that can be attributed to the community college experience and the less useful the transfer rate is as a proxy measure for quality.

Finally, using statewide data sets as well as NSC databases to track student success after transfer can be useful in advising students who enroll with the intent of transferring. Some four-year colleges prove to be more transfer friendly than others. Community colleges could direct more students to these colleges and, armed with transfer information, could publish degree outcomes on their websites. Although this information might be politically sensitive, it can be used as leverage in improving support services at receiving institutions.

## Self-Reported Student Goals

The question of student intent is an important factor in discussions of how transfer rates can be calculated. It would seem appropriate that only those students who really intend to transfer be counted in the target population. If an accurate measure of student intent can be established, community colleges would be able to calculate a more accurate transfer rate.

Palmer (2000), for example, cited a study in Illinois yielding a 22 percent transfer rate when all enrolled students were included in the denominator; but this rose to 34 percent when the denominator included only those students who enrolled in transfer programs and declared upon entry that they intended to transfer. In another study, using a national sample of community college entrants indicating an intention to complete a bachelor's degree or higher, 36 percent had transferred to a four-year college within five years (Bradburn, Hurst, & Peng 2001).

Accurately measuring student intent is a challenge. Although research indicates that upward of 80 percent of students entering community colleges state a long-term educational goal of a bachelor's degree or higher (Horn & Skomsvold, 2012), the real figure is probably lower for a number of reasons. First, aspiration to the bachelor's degree is a socially acceptable answer when students are asked about educational intention. Second, students change expectations as they move through the educational pipeline. And, third, many students who enter the community college are less committed to higher education and have uncertain educational expectations compared to those who enter four-year colleges (Pascarella, 1999; Romano, 2004; Schneider & Stevenson, 1999). As Kane and Rouse (1999) state, these are students who are "at the margin between college and work" (p. 68).

If the 80 percent figure is inflated, how do community colleges obtain a more accurate figure? In 2004, Romano used a comprehensive set of questions to determine intent to transfer at an upstate New York community college. In a survey of entering students, which achieved a 75 percent return rate, respondents were asked a single question about how far they would like to go in school. In line with national averages, 73 percent (n = 1,110) replied that they would like to obtain at least a bachelor's degree at some college.

However, the percentage expecting to achieve at least a bachelor's degree fell to 51 percent when students were asked a series of questions about how far they actually expected to go, given their ability, their finances, the time available to them, and, when, in addition, they were asked to estimate the strength of their belief about the probability of attaining a bachelor's degree. The 51 percent figure is probably a more realistic estimate of those aspiring to a bachelor's degree. Following up on this group, it was estimated that 75 percent actually did transfer. These results were replicated in a series of entering student questionnaires at the same college over a period of six years.

Interestingly, a study previously conducted to assess the aspirations of the same students while they were in high school identified a clear trajectory for students headed to the community college (Rehberg & Rosenthal, 1978). On balance, they exhibited less decisiveness and greater uncertainty with respect to educational goals than students out of the same group who entered four-year colleges.

It would be hard to argue with the statement that improved knowledge of student goals would help colleges better direct their resources to improve student success. Hom (2009) seems to be on the right track in concluding that a single question on a student survey about educational intent "is not an adequate signal to admit that student into the target population" of transfer students (p.137). In a review of the reasons that impel students to inflate intent to transfer, Hom suggested that a complex set of questions may not be cost-effective in measuring student intentions about educational goals.

## Behavior as a Signal of Intent to Transfer

A better and less costly method of inferring intent to transfer involves examining student course-taking behavior, as suggested by the Committee on

Measures of Student Success (2011). It stands to reason that students taking transferable courses are more likely to intend to transfer than students taking courses that are not transferable. This line of thinking has attracted considerable attention and is notably reflected in the work of Clifford Adelman, Peter Riley Bahr, and MPR Associates.

**Adelman's research.** The most frequently cited study tracking community college course enrollment patterns was conducted by Adelman in 2005 under the auspices of the U.S. Department of Education. Drawing from longitudinal studies of the National Center for Education Statistics, Adelman focused on a national sample of traditional-age (18–24) students enrolled in community colleges. Looking at the course-taking behavior of the students, as well as data on goals and transfer collected from the students and their transcripts in the years following high school graduation, Adelman classified students into three categories.

The "homeowner" was the vocationally oriented student and constituted 37 percent of the total. The "tenant" was the transfer-oriented student who started at the community college, completed more than ten credits, and transferred to a four-year college and subsequently completed more than ten credits toward the baccalaureate degree. This group had a strong academic background and constituted 18 percent of the total. The "visitor" was the largest group at 45 percent of the total. This group typically completed less than 30 credits and left college, usually without a credential. Adelman found that 37 percent of those who completed more than ten credits at the community college eventually transferred and 60 percent of that group eventually earned a bachelor's degree when followed for 8½ years after their high school graduation in 1992.

In addition, Adelman's data on the educational aspirations of community college entrants suggest that the community college raised the aspirations of 19 percent of its students toward a bachelor's degree and lowered the aspirations (i.e., cooled out) the aspirations of only 7 percent of the students. This reinforces the results of Romano's (2004) study, which showed that community colleges "heat up" more students than they cool out (34 percent vs. 3 percent). Other studies have yielded similar results: The percentage of students who are heated up exceeds the percentage who are cooled out at both the two- and the four-year college (Alexander, Bozick, & Entwisle, 2008; Leigh & Gill, 2003).

After reviewing the limited number of studies on heating up, Rosenbaum, Deil-Amen, and Person (2006) concluded that "overall warming up is more frequent than cooling out" (p. 46). The "heating up" phenomenon is an outcome that deserves greater attention and could prove to be an important metric to consider when measuring community college effectiveness.

**Bahr's research**. A series of recent studies by Bahr, focusing on students enrolled in California community colleges, confirms Adelman's finding that the manner in which students intend to use community colleges can be detected from their course-taking behavior (Bahr, 2010, 2013). In one study, Bahr (2010) used cluster analysis to analyze the enrollment and course-taking behavior of 165,921 first-time students who entered California community colleges from 2001 to 2008. The California data set used by Bahr included transcript and demographic data for all students and was linked to the NSC data used to track transfers to public, private, and out-of-state colleges. Bahr identified six clusters of behavior classified as *transfer, vocational, drop-in, no-credit, experimental,* and *exploratory.*

Students in the transfer cluster (13 percent of the sample) took the highest number of transferable courses, such as English and math, and exhibited the highest persistence rates. Students in the vocational cluster (3 percent of the sample) also exhibited a high level of persistence and course completion, but took mostly non-transferable vocational courses. The drop-in cluster of students (32 percent) attended for a semester or less, but were generally successful in course work. Students in the noncredit cluster enrolled in some credit courses, but were more interested in noncredit offerings. This group comprised 3 percent of the sample and included mostly female adult learners returning to college after an extended period of time away from education.

The experimental (30 percent of the sample) and exploratory (19 percent of the sample) clusters were students who were testing the waters or exploring areas of interest by taking a variety of courses. They exhibited a low success rate in terms of persistence and course completion. The course-taking behavior of students in the last two clusters revealed that approximately 50 percent of the total first-time student population in California had come to the community college for a short duration and either decided that they did not want to continue, could not do the work, or had satisfied their goals.

The upshot of Bahr's work is that a limited number of students enrolling in California community colleges had well-defined academic goals. The drop-in, experimental, and exploratory clusters comprised more than three quarters (84 percent) of the total population of students. Among the credit students, only the vocational and transfer clusters seemed to have had clear goals with which they were able to pursue with some degree of success. It is also worth noting that in these two clusters and in the drop-in cluster, the students' self-reported academic goals (intent) upon entering matched the outcomes they achieved.

Following up on the students after they left the community college, Bahr found that 55 percent of the transfer cluster actually transferred to a four-year college, with or without a credential, and 29 percent of the students in the vocational cluster completed a degree or certificate. As one might expect, the vast majority, over 90 percent, of the students in the other four clusters did not transfer or complete a credential. Did these students fail to achieve their goals? Removing the noncredit students, all would be counted as failing to complete.

Bahr draws several possible policy implications from this typology of first-time community college entrants: (1) efforts to retain students who have short-term objectives may waste effort and money, whereas efforts to heat up those students who are exploring or experimenting might be a better use of resources; (2) defining transfer-intended students too broadly (e.g., including all those with twelve credits in the denominator of the transfer-rate calculation) may be unwarranted—the more credits the better; and (3) self-reported academic goals for students who end up in academic or vocational clusters may be more accurate indicators of intent than research suggests. Some of the students who left the community college early undoubtedly did so for financial reasons. Turning uncertain goals into sound educational objectives takes money—perhaps more money than the taxpayers of California were willing to give.

**The MRP study.** California enrolls over 20 percent of community college students in the nation and ranks low in completion and transfer rates. The community college system in California funded MPR Associates, an independent research organization, to study transfer and completion rates in the state, thereby adding to the work undertaken by Bahr and others. MRP found that upon initial enrollment, one-third of the first-time students in California community colleges indicated they expected to transfer and an additional 10 percent expected to complete a credential. This is well below the national average on both of these measures. In addition, MRP found that first-time students were "fairly uncertain about their initial education goals" (Horn & Lew, 2008, p. 2).

Not relying solely on self-reported intent data, MRP calculated transfer rates based on student course-taking behavior. Six different denominators were used, three based on any credit accumulation and three based on transfer-oriented course completions. Over 500,000 students were tracked over a six-year period in three entering cohorts between 1993–1994 and 2000–2001. Transfer rates ranged from 24 percent using the most inclusive denominator, to 67 percent for the most restrictive denominator.

## Implications for Funding

The Adelman, Bahr, and MPR studies, among others, imply that community college outcomes are difficult to document because students enroll with a variety of goals, many of them uncertain and changing. Ideally, individual student goals should be taken into account before counting successes and failures, but this might be impractical and expensive. If funding is to be tied to outcomes, colleges will need to be careful. Student goals might simply amount to testing the waters. Even students enrolled in transfer or vocational programs can be exploring options in contrast to pursuing a degree.

We noted earlier that students who enroll in community colleges are often less certain of that decision than students entering four-year colleges. They are uncertain about their ability to finance their education, but they are also uncertain about their interests, their academic ability, and the benefits they will receive from a college credential. According to Stange (2012), students reduce these uncertainties during the educational process. Entering the community college may be seen as a low-cost way for students to acquire information about interests and ability without committing to continuing on to a four-year college.

"In addition to directly making college less expensive, community colleges increase the option value of enrollment because dropout is less costly [than at four-year colleges], so more people experiment with school" (Stange, 2012, p. 80). This position applies, for the most part, to young students recently out of high school and does not address other components of the comprehensive community college mission, such as retraining of displaced workers.

If enrolling in a community college is a low-cost screening mechanism for some students, then elected officials must decide whether they are willing to pay for this function or propose an alternate mechanism for doing so. The social cost of the alternatives may be higher. In our view, community colleges are probably a reasonable place for young, undecided students to sort out their interests and willingness to pursue postsecondary education. Enrolling in a community college would be less burdensome on students, with minimal cost to taxpayers, if students left less financial aid on the table and student debt were tied to an income-contingent repayment scheme.

## Additional Transfer Issues

Beyond students' goals, and forces outside of academic life that impinge on their success, it is important to look at both the sending and the receiving colleges for characteristics and procedures that constrain student success. One line of research indicates that the diversion of capable students from four-year colleges to community colleges reduces the likelihood that students will transfer and complete a bachelor's degree.

In other words, for students interested in a bachelor's degree, enrollment in a community college comes with a penalty. In a balanced review of the literature on this topic, Pascarella (1999) concluded that students "planning on a bachelor's degree who begin postsecondary education at community colleges are about 15% less likely to complete a bachelor's degree . . . [than]

students of similar background who start at four-year colleges and universities" (p. 10).

Two recent Type-3 studies support the now widely accepted, penalty rate of 15 percent. Long & Kurlaender (2009), estimated the penalty at 14.5 percent after following students for nine years using a database in Ohio. A second study by Monaghan and Attewell (2014) estimated the penalty at 17 percent using a national sample of 13,000 students. This study examined student transcripts and determined that despite the penalty rate, students who managed to transfer were just as likely, perhaps more likely, to complete a bachelor's degree than students who started at the four-year college. After using sophisticated statistical techniques to examine a number of possible reasons underlying the penalty, Monaghan and Attewell concluded that loss of credit during the transfer process was a primary factor.

A Type-3 study by Brand, Pfeffer, and Goldrick-Rab (2014), however, questioned the assumption of a penalty rate for students seeking a bachelor's degree who begin study at a community college. Working with data from Chicago public high schools, they argued that advantaged students are hurt when they are diverted from a four-year college to a community college. But they found that disadvantaged students who did not go to college within one year of high school graduation were actually helped by starting at a community college rather than a four-year college.

For these students, the community college may be the only option available for postsecondary study, reinforcing Cohen's observation that discussions of the community college penalty rate must be tempered by the realization that for many students, the choice is not between the community college and a four-year college; "it is between the community college and nothing" (Cohen, Brawer, & Kisker, 2014, p. 63). Thus, when looking at outcomes it is important to realize that policies can have a variable impact on different student populations (Brand, Pfeffer, & Goldrick-Rab, 2014).

Practitioners should not restrict their focus to community colleges when looking for reasons that might explain low transfer rates. Receiving four-year colleges are also part of the problem. In a study of the transfer pipeline in California, Neault (2012) found that public four-year colleges in the state used variable transfer admissions as an enrollment management tool. When economic conditions slow enrollment growth at universities, they relax transfer admission requirements; but when demand is high they reduce the number of transfers they admit. Thus, the transfer rate ebbs and flows with changes in the economy and state budgets that limit capacity at the four-year level. This is an area that deserves attention from policy makers, particularly in states that suffer capacity constraints.

Overall, a considerable body of literature on transfer offers important lessons. First, community colleges need to make sure that students who aspire to the bachelor's degree are encouraged to transfer and that campus cultures, pathways and support systems are set up to assist them in the process. Second, states need to monitor transfer admissions policies of four-year public colleges to eliminate unnecessary bottlenecks in the transfer process. This might include providing financial incentives for enrolling more transfer students from in-state community colleges. Third, states need to focus on transfer pathways and ensure that the loss of credits transferred from community colleges to public four-year colleges is minimized.

This also means that community colleges need to limit the number of credits required for an associate degree to sixty credits for most programs. Faculty preferences for adding additional courses to program requirements only increase the cost to students and add to the likelihood that more credits will be rejected by the receiving institution. All of these efforts are underway around the country and early research findings indicate they will be successful.

WARNING: *Student differences and the business cycle impact transfer rates as well as credential production. Funding can be linked to both of these outcomes, however, be prepared to defend low-output numbers with data on student goals. The quest for new outcome measures must continue. Beyond degree and transfer rates, successful completion should also be measured by the number of students who discover new interests or who develop and pursue educational goals short of traditional outcome measures.*

## LEARNING OUTCOMES

Two outcome measures that have attracted considerable attention of late are student success in the labor market and whether and what students learn in colleges. Less is known about these measures than either credential production or transfer success. Student learning is a particularly difficult nut to crack, but from the perspective of faculty it is clearly the most important outcome.

Ask almost any instructor what the most important goal of higher education is and they will repeat a litany of desirable learning outcomes such as critical thinking, communication, quantitative literacy, global awareness, civic education, etc., as well as an array of career and knowledge area skills. Faculty will contend that knowledge and skills are developed through the courses they teach and that their work with classroom assessment of student learning is endless. This is part of the faculty role. Isn't this enough?

It's not enough because knowledge and skills are cumulative and build with use. General intellectual skills like critical thinking are taught in literature as well as mathematics courses. They are shaped by activities outside the classroom and by peers both inside and outside of classes. If we are looking for an overarching measure of the general intellectual skills that students acquire, institutional assessment on a level beyond what instructors assess in courses will be necessary. This is a broadly accepted principle, although faculty do not readily buy into it because institutional-level assessment often involves using standardized tests as an assessment tool.

Standardized tests are acceptable when it comes to measuring the knowledge and skills that pertain to vocational and technical job fields. Passing rates of graduates on licensing exams for nurses, dental hygienists, engineers, and accountants are examples. Test scores validate student learning in certain areas and are a standard part of the learning outcomes measured by community colleges. They are also a useful measure of college quality.

However, using standardized tests to measure cumulative learning in general skills, such as critical thinking, across courses at the program or college level can be a daunting task. In addition, providing measures that are comparable between colleges may not be possible given increasing diversity among institutions in terms of the students they serve and the programs they offer.

A promising approach to the development of standard learning proficiencies for college degrees, including the associate degree, is the Degree Qualifications Profile (DQP), developed and promoted by the Lumina Foundation. The DQP is an American adaptation of a movement underway in Europe (the Bologna Process) to standardize degree expectations in order to promote greater student mobility among and between countries (Adelman, 2008). The DQP has been pilot-tested in the United States by 106 colleges at the associate degree level, 195 at the bachelor's level, and fifty-six at the master's level. The National Institute for Learning Outcomes Assessment (NILOA) has been tracking the use of the DQP and reporting on the results (Jankowski et al., 2013).

The DQP is an attempt to shift the focus from what colleges should teach to student outcomes. It outlines a flexible framework for assessing learning in five different areas: specialized knowledge, broad integrative knowledge, intellectual skills, applied learning, and civic learning. Specific performance objectives are identified which focus on what students should know and be able to do at various degree levels. The American Association for Community Colleges—in a newly developed Assessment tool, The Voluntary Framework for Accountability (VFA)—has suggested that the DQP might be an appropriate way for colleges to assess learning outcomes. The AACC has committed itself to studying the DQP and has asked member colleges, who sign on to use the VFA, to report what they are doing in assessment of learning within the NILOA framework.

The VFA looks like a promising approach to assessing learning outcomes in community colleges, but only for the associate degree. At this time, the DQP has not been widely embraced by colleges, in part because it may be seen as a step in the direction of establishing national standards for measuring quality. Even if widely accepted, however, colleges will need to resolve problems involving the movement of students who "swirl" in and out of two-year and four-year colleges. It will be difficult to find a cohort of students who receive the full effect of a well-designed set of learning objectives.

Thus, even though the DQP articulates proficiency standards for outcomes at different degree levels, when students attend multiple institutions on the path to a credential, determining what individual colleges contribute to that proficiency is problematic. As Adelman (2011) has said, "you can't do learning outcomes for people in motion" (para. 1). As an assessment tool for individual colleges, the DQP provides limited information about the vast majority of students who attend and graduate and/or transfer from the community college.

The challenge of measuring learning outcomes or the value added by a particular college is exacerbated by the fact that individual differences among entering students remains the strongest predictor of college learning outcomes. Responding to a recommendation in the Spellings Report (Secretary of Education's Commission, 2006) to develop standardized tests of learning, Banta (2007) argued that "while standardized tests can be helpful in initiating faculty conversations about assessment," there are serious doubts about the validity of "aggregating . . . [student] scores for the purpose of comparing institutions" (para. 7). She noted that "differences in test scores reflect individual differences among students taking the test more accurately than they illustrate differences in the quality of education offered at different institutions" (para. 8). In the end, she argued, enthusiasm for testing as an approach to documenting institutional impacts on learning is not supported by research:

> For nearly 50 years measurement scholars have warned against pursuing the blind alley of value added assessment. Our research has demonstrated yet again that the reliability of gain scores and residual scores—the two chief methods of calculating value added—is negligible. (para. 9)

Although Banta is not a fan of standardized testing for general intellectual skills, she supports campus-level assessment processes such as electronic portfolios "that illustrate growth over time" and with assessment measures developed by faculty in academic disciplines (Banta, 2007, para. 11). These types of assessment tools are already in use by colleges throughout the country. The electronic portfolio used to assess learning in general education at Salt Lake Community College (2014) is an example.

And, finally, the obvious: learning outcomes would improve if entering students were better prepared for college-level work. It is hard to assign blame solely to public K-12 schools, but perhaps reforms like the common core will eventually work. It would be desirable if the need for remediation was greatly reduced. Not only would outcomes improve, but resources would be freed up for services bringing students to a higher level of success.

WARNING: *Student differences matter and funding should not be tied to outcomes that are difficult to measure. Using courses completed as an outcomes measure is a reasonable first step to measuring student learning, but, at this time, standardized tests of general intellectual ability are not suitable for measuring differences in learning exhibited by most students.*

## LABOR MARKET SUCCESS

Success in the labor market may be the single most important metric associated with performance funding in the future because it is becoming easier to measure and is uniquely relevant to technical and vocational programs. Among elected officials, labor market outcomes may be the only outcome they are interested in for all of higher education.

In chapter 1 we suggested that the benefits of higher education may be divided between those that flow directly to the student (private benefits) and those that spill over to the rest of society (public benefits). A key private benefit is a good job and a higher level of lifetime income. Higher levels of education generate, on average, both higher lifetime income and more stable employment. A recent estimate is that the average worker with a bachelor's degree can expect to earn over $1 million more, and those with an associates degree about $325,000 more, than a worker with only a high school degree (Abel, Deitz, & Su 2014).

### Education\Earnings Profiles

One way to look at income gains is to plot lifetime earnings against the level of education attained. Results indicate that the income path of community college graduates is somewhere between that of a high school graduate and students with a bachelor's degree. This speaks to the benefits accrued to both students and taxpayers through the production of community college graduates. But these numbers are averages for the entire population and considerable variation from the average exists.

Research conducted by Carnevale, Strohl, and Smith (2009) shows considerable overlap between the earnings of those with an associate degree and those with a bachelor's degree. "For instance, 22 percent of those with an occupational or vocational . . . [associate degree] earn more than the median earnings of those with a . . . [bachelor's degree] and 14 percent earn more than the median earnings of those with graduate degrees" ( p. 22).

Educators are increasingly aware of the fact that earnings depend, not just on degrees, but on what is studied and where one works. This is a key factor underlying the national push to promote STEM and other programs with high-wage potential. A recent study by the Brookings Institution estimated that "half of all STEM jobs are available to workers without a four-year college degree" (Rothwell, 2013, p. 1). As we will note in the next chapter on performance-based funding, colleges that increase their output in STEM fields are often rewarded.

Lifetime earnings are also dependent on the economic conditions at the time students enter the labor market. A study by Oreopoulos, Wachter, and Heisz (2012) lends support to research and observations that recessionary economies not only reduce the quantity of jobs available, but also the quality of jobs (i.e., lower wages). During expansionary periods following a recession, the supply of high-wage jobs expands and the wages of individual workers increase. By studying the wage patterns of workers over time, research shows that students experiencing the misfortune of graduating during a recession may suffer "persistent earnings declines" and some may never recover (p. 1). The adverse impact on earnings is especially pronounced for workers who are less skilled and have lower levels of training.

This is important because a fall in the wage gain to a particular college's graduates may result from conditions in national and regional labor markets, not from what colleges do to promote student success. This is not to say that the economic returns of college programs are unimportant outcome measures. They are indeed very important. But linking institutional funding to these fluctuating outcome measures over which colleges have only partial or no control can be problematic.

## Rates of Return

Aside from the income/education trajectory, another way to look at labor market effects of community college education is to calculate the rate of return. This approach is derived from the model of human capital, which views education as an investment involving a return over cost expressed as an annual percentage. Private rates of return are reflected primarily in the present value of lifetime income. Social rates of return include spillover benefits to the community, including some that are nonpecuniary in nature. All rates of return, but especially social returns, are notoriously difficult to measure (Rosenbaum & Rosenbaum, 2013, provide estimates for community colleges).

Based on research findings, community colleges perform favorably on rates-of-return measures. In a review of the literature on earnings gains, Belfield and Bailey (2011) concluded that "almost all studies have found" that the "average earnings gain from an associate's degree . . . is 13% for males and 22% for females," while "the average earnings gain for those attending the community college without obtaining a credential is estimated at 9% for males and 10% for females" (pp. 49–51).

A recent study of rates of return for the associate degree by Abel, Deitz, and Su (2014) showed that some of the gains, especially for women, may be due to employment in the health care field. Positive rates of return for certificate programs were also found by Rosenbaum and Rosenbaum (2013), and in an oft-cited study, Kane and Rouse (1995) found that the economic value of a community college credit was equivalent to a credit earned at a four-year college.

When examining income gains attributed to community college education, it is important to adjust wage gains to the business cycle or at least be prepared to explain why variations in the income of graduates may be outside of the college's control. In addition, securing accurate income information can be difficult. A recent report by the American Institutes for Research (Alva & Schneider, 2013) purported to provide reliable information on the income of community college graduates.

The earnings data were collected by a private organization called PayScale, which has a website posting data on jobs held by graduates, as well as salaries and benefits earned. Data of this type is potentially valuable, but the validity of PayScales' data has been severely criticized by higher education policy analyst Donald Heller. Writing in the *Chronicle of Higher Education*, Heller explains that the earnings data is self-reported and is often based on a small sample of graduates. After citing several examples, Heller concludes that the data "is careless at best and grossly misleading at worst" (Heller, 2013, para. 17).

## UI Wage Data

The most reliable method for tracking the incomes of students leaving the community college is to link college student records to state unemployment insurance records (often called UI wage data). As of 2014, the U.S. Department of Labor has given grants to thirty-three states to help them extend their student database to include employment and wage information. The U.S. Department of Education has made a major investment in supporting research that will connect employment and income data, with postsecondary education enrollment.

In 2011 it funded the Center for Analysis of Postsecondary Education and Employment (CAPSEE) to produce a number of studies measuring labor market outcomes. Although UI wage data has a number of shortcomings, it is likely to become the standard measure of student success for community college vocational and technical programs.

States collect quarterly wage information for most workers so that unemployment benefits can be calculated should they lose their jobs. One problem with the data is that it is hard to determine if the wages reported are for part-time or full-time employment. In addition, each state's database only covers workers who are employed in that particular state, which means that the state data systems must be connected to acquire a more complete picture. At this time, twenty-two states have signed data-sharing agreements. Self-employed and federal workers, including those in the military, are also left out of state UI wage data.

Ideally community colleges could use UI data to compare the wages earned by students who were working before they entered college with the wages earned by the same students after leaving college. These comparisons would help colleges determine if the skills gained during attendance led to any gains in income. The cause-and-effect assumption underlying these comparisons seems reasonable, but it would be more meaningful if wages after training could be compared with the trajectory of expected income without training.

It is worth noting that before-and-after comparisons of income work better for younger workers. Abstracting from an example used by Mullin (2013), consider the case of a 45-year-old worker who loses her $60,000-a-year job in a Ford manufacturing facility. She enrolls in a community college, completes a degree in a health field, and begins a new job at a yearly salary of $40,000. Calculating the value added by the college through the analysis of pre- and post-earnings would result in a negative number. This example underscores the fact that calculating value added for older displaced workers can be problematic.

The increasing use of UI wage data and the growth of statewide data sets focusing on the employability of graduates have led some to voice concern over the coming "witch hunt for college programs that don't pay off" (Kelly & Whitfield, 2014, p. 60). But despite its shortcomings, UI wage data is the best information available on earnings. Community college leaders should urge states to make UI wage data available so that it can be used to measure the outcomes of vocational and technical programs.

Privacy issues are a major obstacle to widespread use of this system, but recent changes in Family Educational Rights and Privacy Act (FERPA) regulations will allow more states to share UI data with colleges. Over the next few years we can expect to see an expansion of research using UI wage data. Most recently the Department of Labor in New York has signed an agreement with the State University of New York (SUNY) that links UI wage data to system-wide student records. SUNY is using UI data to provide outcomes-based bonus payments to community colleges.

WARNING: *Wage gains are a reasonable outcome measure for vocational and technical programs, but not for transfer programs. Be aware that*

*student-reported incomes are not accurate and that few states presently have
the data to calculate income gains accurately. For states that do have the
data, income gains are more accurate for younger workers. Colleges should
be prepared to show how business cycles have impacted economic returns
to their graduates. Colleges desiring to see how labor market data can be
used to measure student success can consult a guide prepared for this purpose by the Aspen Institute at:* http://www.aspeninstitute.org/publications/
aspen-guide-using-labor-market-data-improve-student-success.

## UNMEASURED BENEFITS

In the introductory chapter, we argued that public benefits (spillovers) of
higher education are difficult to measure, especially for community colleges.
Even private benefits are not fully reflected in additional lifetime income.
Besides its "investment value," some students enjoy learning and receive
"consumption value" from college attendance. Many discussions with college
faculty will reveal a belief that education is not just about workforce training.
But, communicating the idea that education also has a loftier purpose is a
difficult message to get across in the community college where the attachment to the values of liberal and civic education, for instance, is often weak
(Higginbottom & Romano, 2006).

Campus voices that view the mission of community colleges as something
more than economic in nature need to be listened to when curriculum decisions are made. As Mike Rose (2012) put it in his wonderful little book on
the educational lives of community college students, people *do* go to college
for economic reasons, but they

> also go to college to feel their minds working and learn new things, to help their
> kids, to feel competent, to remedy a poor education, to redefine who they are, to
> start over. You won't hear any of this in the national talk about postsecondary
> access and success. (pp. 141–42)

Not all student-centered benefits can be measured in terms of private or
public rates of return, yet those who teach in community colleges know they
exist.

Closely connected to the idea that important benefits of college have gone
unmeasured is the idea that we have not fully appreciated or measured the
impact that expanded educational opportunity has had on the social mobility of the extended families of disadvantaged students. We may be able to
estimate the impact of college attendance on income and jobs for any given
cohort of students, but we have yet to produce data on the benefits extended

to the children of those given an opportunity to attend the community college because of its open-admissions policy.

Attewell and Lavin (2007) provide an excellent examination of these extended benefits in their study of the City University of New York's open-admissions experiment in the 1970s. Looking at mounds of data over a thirty-year period, they were able to show that graduates, especially women, of the open-admission program, including those who attended community colleges, not only improved their own lives, but also those of their children who were more likely to attend college and achieve upward mobility.

The idea that educated parents have a positive impact on their children has also been highlighted in a recent study by Reeves and Howard (2013) demonstrating that parenting behavior has a large impact on children's future income and social mobility. It is interesting to note that the impact of education on the extended family is not included in any of the analyses undertaken to assess the economic rate of return to college attendance.

And finally it is important to mention the largely unmeasured benefits of the community colleges as an integral part of the social safety net. All colleges perform this function to some extent, but it is especially important for the community college, one of which, on average, is within driving distance of 95 percent of the U.S. population. Things happen in the lives of young adults that bring them home, often on a temporary basis. A parent gets sick and needs caring for, a death in the family occurs, a breadwinner loses a job, a student gets into trouble at the state university and needs to get his life back on track, etc. It is difficult to estimate the percentage of these students attending community colleges, but many are no doubt part of the group that Adelman called visitors and Barr grouped into clusters of drop-in and exploratory students.

Oft overlooked by elected officials and policy makers is the fact that community colleges are there, accepting all who need them, whether they intend to stay or not. Betts and McFarland (1995) referred to community colleges as a "safe port in a storm" and documented their sheltering role during recessions. Sociologists Kalogrides and Grodsky (2011) wrote about community colleges as "something to fall back on" for students who are forced to leave four-year colleges for academic or financial reasons and are caught by community colleges on the "way down."

Their research shows that these students "have more favorable academic and labor market outcomes than similar students who drop out of postsecondary school altogether" (p. 853). Clearly some of the safety-net functions performed by community colleges can be measured, especially if students graduate or return to the four-year college, but most of the outcomes of this type must be considered as unmeasured successes.

## CHALLENGES TO COLLEGE LEADERS

Higher education institutions in the United States are increasingly stratified along economic, ethnic, and racial lines. Some see the expansion of community colleges as creating or adding to this problem. Properly funded, community colleges can be part of the solution to restoring some degree of social mobility in the nation. Without a doubt, public two-year colleges have been a major force in expanding access to higher education. This is a mission that four-year colleges did not want to assume following the surge in enrollments after World War II and the introduction of Pell grants in 1972.

Circumstances will continue to dictate that increasing numbers of students will enroll in community colleges because they are comparatively inexpensive and geographically convenient. A major challenge is to provide a method of funding for community colleges that will allow them to continue their primary mission, which is access.

This is not to deny that the outcomes of these open-access institutions are also an important part of the process of institutional evaluation and have a role to play in funding community colleges. Student success should matter more than it currently does in most state funding formulas. Nevertheless, the arguments presented in this chapter are intended to promote "a healthy dose of humility in our efforts to come up with [standard measures] of institution-wide outcomes" (Clotfelter et al., 2013, p. 820).

Community colleges are faced with potentially conflicting outcome agendas. Should they accept an open-ended agenda in which there may be as many desirable outcomes as there are student goals? Or, should they define a more limited number of outcomes and direct policies and resources toward those ends? In a tight fiscal environment, taxpayers seem likely to favor the latter. Their attitude is, increasingly, that students can pursue all of the interests they want, up to a point, but beyond that they should pay for exploration themselves.

Public policies limiting the number of credits that a student can experiment with and restricting the number of times a course can be repeated are indications of this preference. These policies may seem reasonable given limited resources, but they also limit the ability of disadvantaged students to explore interests and repair past failures. Colleges should not shy away from indicating that this is a cost of the choices that limited resources are forcing them to make.

Clearly, leaders and staff should not be deterred by the difficulties involved in measuring and improving student success. Colleges can make a difference in the lives of students and must constantly search for better ways to measure their impact. They should not settle for an educational determinism that reinforces the increasing social stratification in society. The linkage of funding to outcomes measures promises to create a new incentive structure for achieving goals that are important to community colleges. The next chapter discusses the evolution and use of these incentive structures for funding community colleges.


# NOTE


A modest proposal—Although many students who enter community colleges may be ambitious, they are also directionless. If colleges could reduce the uncertainty of career choice, perhaps they could cut down on the costly movement of students between programs and the mismatch between what the labor market needs and what students want and expect. Devoting time in a student's first semester, or perhaps in the last year of high school, to testing aptitude and identifying their educational and career interests would be a good first step. Armed with this information, students could research jobs that fit them, the education required for those jobs, and what the labor market will look like for those jobs. The U.S. Department of Labor has the resources necessary to carry out these tasks. Hopefully this process would improve the fit of student interests and abilities with realities of the world of work. Extended programs might integrate internships with coursework or at least the shadowing of employees in areas of interest. If community colleges did not have the expertise to accomplish this, career search programs could be outsourced to a vendor who would develop the program and train faculty or counselors to coordinate it. Career search programs might benefit both students and taxpayers over the long run.

## Chapter 5

# Performance-Based Funding

*Performance-based funding* (PBF) in higher education is an attempt to tie multiple forms of state funding to institutional performance. It is a direct extension of public accountability measures used in what Burke (2005) called *performance reporting*, which attempts to document institutional outcomes without an explicit connection to funding. According to the National Conference of State Legislators ([NCSL], 2015), 24 states tied at least some portion of funding for community colleges in 2015 to specified performance measures, usually related to student outcomes such as course completion, transfer, or credential attainment.

But estimates of the number of states with PBF systems vary, "because state officials not infrequently disagree in their understanding of what performance funding is and whether their state has it" (Dougherty & Reddy, 2013, p. 17). In addition, the number of states employing PBF systems has varied over time as initial PBF approaches are abandoned or modified in an ongoing process of experimentation that continues today.

As Jones (2013) aptly points out, "tying funding to achievement is not a new idea" (p. 2).[1] Historians have traced the concept of PBF in higher education to a long line of attempts by managers to measure the performance of individuals, institutions, or public agencies in order to improve the efficiency and quality of the goods and services being produced. Understanding the origins of PBF helps place the concept within a broader context and provides clues as to whether it might work in its current form and how it may evolve.

After a brief discussion of historical roots, which draws largely on a recent Rand Corporation analysis (Stecher et al., 2010), we examine the thrust of early state PBF initiatives in higher education from the 1970s to the early 2000s, describe the more ambitious PBF systems that have emerged, and conclude with a discussion of lessons learned through experience with PBF programming—specifically the impact of PBF on public expectations of community colleges, the factors that impede or facilitate the implementation of PBF programs, and the difficulty of isolating the impact of these programs on the work of community colleges and the educational experience of students.

## HISTORICAL ORIGINS OF PERFORMANCE-BASED FUNDING

All of us in the working world get paid directly or indirectly for performance. Some workers, like certain salespersons, get paid directly through commissions that tie their income to productivity. Others get paid indirectly through negotiated wages and salaries. Nevertheless, annual salaries are connected to productivity or at least to the joint productivity of industries with which workers are affiliated. Generally workers in high-productivity industries get higher wages than those in low-productivity industries.

Managers and owners of enterprises have tried to increase productivity by offering monetary and other incentives to encourage harder or smarter work. This has worked in a wide range of industries. However, research by economists and psychologists has shown that performance-related pay for individuals may backfire and actually diminish performance. This happens most frequently in industries where cognitive, rather than physical, skills are required (Stecher et al., 2010). When the focus shifts from motivating individuals to motivating complex organizations such as colleges, a whole new set of issues arises. This is borne out by the history of pay-for-performance schemes within private- and public-sector organizations.

### Pay-for-Performance Systems

A long line of pay-for-performance schemes has preceded and contributed to the present era of performance-based funding. During the gilded age, for example, individuals contracted with farmers or craftsmen to produce a given good or service, often at home, and if it was not satisfactory, payment was not made. In simple enterprises owners were close to workers and could keep track of performance and the quality of work.

But as enterprises grew more complex, owners became detached from workers and managers, forcing them to look for ways to assess performance. This led to the growth of piece work, often associated with sweatshops. It also led to the application of principles of scientific management. Both were used as vehicles to track performance and link pay to worker output. There is a direct link between these early forms of pay for performance and the modern versions that appear under titles such as *total quality management* and *performance-based accountability systems* (Stecher et al., 2010).

Dating back to the early nineteenth century, pay for performance was also applied in government enterprises as a method to improve efficiency and performance (Stecher et al., 2010). In 1863, Florence Nightingale published a report card comparing the mortality rates of English hospitals. This led to improvements in the condition of hospitals and is an antecedent of accountability measures that are routine in hospitals today. By the 1980s, the idea of performance-based incentives to change behavior was well established in England and aggressively implemented in Australia and New Zealand. In Japan and the United States, the idea had taken hold for business enterprises but not so much within the public sector (Stecher et al., 2010).

By the turn of the century, pressing demands for an accounting of agency performance in the public sector led the U.S. government to widespread use of performance-based assessment. In 2002, the Federal Office of Management and Budget developed a Program Assessment Rating Tool "to help . . . evaluate the effectiveness of government programs" (Stecher et al., p. 28). In education, the No Child Left Behind Act of 2001 brought performance-based accountability systems to public schools. And in higher education, President Obama sought to link college funding to college performance by suggesting that federal financial aid be used as a motivating lever (Jaschik, 2013).

This initiative has been reinforced by the president's plan to eliminate tuition at community colleges through federal subsidies that would be contingent on actions taken by colleges to "adopt promising and evidence-based institutional reforms to improve student outcomes" (Hudson, 2015, The Requirements section, para. 2).

## Elements of Success

The history of pay-for-performance systems has left us with a reasonable understanding of what works in this approach to funding and what does not. For example, the Rand Corporation study cited above examined performance-based accountability systems in five different industries: transportation, childcare, education, emergency response, and health care. In general, the study found limited evidence of the effectiveness of performance-based payments across all five industries.

But, when PBF funding *was* successful, six elements were present: (a) a goal that was widely shared among all stakeholders; (b) unambiguous and easy-to-observe measures; (c) incentives that apply to individuals or organizations with control over relevant inputs and processes; (d) incentives that are meaningful to those being incentivized; (e) minimal competing interests or requirements; and (f) adequate resources to design, implement, modify, and operate performance-based reward systems (Stecher et al., 2010).

A good example of a successful system can be found in the construction and road building industry. Here it is common practice to provide bonuses for early completion of projects and penalties for late deliveries (Stecher et al., 2010). Within this industry, all six of the elements of success were found to be present.

But when applying these elements of success to higher education, it might be argued that control over relevant inputs and the ease of measuring agreed-upon goals is problematic. In community colleges, for example, not all of the success elements are present. Colleges do not control one of the most important inputs into the educational process—entering students—since they are open-access institutions that, for the most part, do not screen students based on ability. Nor do community colleges have measures of student success that are unambiguous and easy to observe. Community college advocates would also claim that they do not have the last of the six elements—adequate resources to design and operate the system.

Without these six elements, PBF systems reward organizations for something, but it is unlikely to be what was intended. In addition, the limited ability of pay-for-performance schemes throughout history to capture the quality of output presents important problems for higher education. As economists Ehrenberg and Smith (1997) have pointed out, "in an environment [such as education] in which not all aspects of output can be measured," attention to quality may suffer (p. 390). This does not, however, negate the obligation of colleges to be accountable in some way for the resources given to them by the public.

## Business Interests and the Erosion of Trust-Based Funding

Despite the challenges of implementing pay-for-performance systems in higher education, the establishment of PBF systems remains a compelling goal for many policymakers, largely because the idea that "material incentives" can motivate the behavior of both individuals and institutions is deeply rooted in the business world where incentives are seen as essential to profitability (Dougherty & Reddy, 2013, p. 10).

Indeed, business interest in promoting performance-based funding for colleges has been strong. In an extensive study of the political origins of state performance-based funding systems, Kevin Dougherty and his colleagues found that "business demand for greater higher education efficiency and lower costs, and a rising Republican presence in state legislatures" were forces that played an important role in the adoption of PBF for higher education (Dougherty et al., 2011, pp. 103–104).

A similar business influence can be found in many European countries. With some exceptions (notably the United Kingdom where student fees are a primary source of operating resources), national governments continue to provide 60–80 percent of university budgets with few strings attached. Still, historical "trust-based" funding through block grants gave way to at least some performance-based funding in the 1980s under the influence of tight budgets, growing enrollments, and what Europeans saw was happening in U.S. higher education funding systems (Sörlin, 2007).

In contrast to the United States, where most of the discussion and action on performance-based funding has been at the undergraduate level, university funding in Europe has become more of a policy instrument to promote research and increase the global competitiveness of European businesses. With respect to undergraduate education, however, European nations (as we noted in the last chapter) have come much further than the United States in defining learning outcomes, even at the associate degree level (Adelman, 2008). The purpose of standardizing learning outcomes in Europe is to allow greater student mobility among universities, rather than serving as a form of leverage employed to influence student and institutional behavior, as it is in the United States.

Viewed through the European lens, one could certainly describe college funding models in the United States (until perhaps 1980) as based on trust— that is, the trust of tax payers in colleges and universities to do the right thing with the public money they were given. That trust, however, is increasingly subject to question. The explosion in college enrollments, tight state budgets, and the rising cost of college attendance have brought forth demands for increased accountability and for efforts to tie even decreased levels of funding to performance.

## EARLY PBF EFFORTS IN U.S. HIGHER EDUCATION

The first state PBF systems affecting community colleges emerged in the 1970s and 1980s as add-ons to enrollment-based state funding formulas developed in the post–World War II growth years. As Dougherty et al. (2014) point out, early PBF programs provided colleges with relatively small bonuses on top of regular (i.e., base) enrollment-based appropriations and were championed by state higher education agencies and by institutions themselves as a way of securing "new state funds for higher education in a time of increased resistance to taxation and criticism of higher education's effectiveness and efficiency" (p. 166). These early systems, commonly dubbed "performance funding 1.0" (Dougherty & Reddy, 2013, p. 6), attempted to sustain predictable enrollment-based funding streams while at the same time acknowledging demands that funding be tied to results.

A "pioneering example" of performance funding 1.0 was the PBF program initiated by Tennessee in 1979–1980 (Dougherty & Reddy, 2013, p. 30). The Tennessee program initially awarded bonuses equaling 2 percent of a college's budget on the basis of performance indicators related to program accreditation, graduate performance on exams related to their majors, student performance on general education assessments, and assessments of instructional and academic programs based on input from "current students, recent alumni, and community members or employers," as well as "peer review teams of scholars from institutions outside the state and/or practicing professionals in a field" (Dougherty & Reddy, 2013, p. 31).

The system remains in operation today, though the bonus a college can earn now stands at 5.45 percent of its budget, and indicators have been dropped and added. For example, job placement has been added to the list of indicators, as have measures of institutional success in increasing enrollment, retention, and graduation of specific student subpopulations selected from a list that includes minority group members, adult students, males, and students majoring in health and other high-demand fields (Tennessee Higher Education Commission, 2010).

The approach of tying a small proportion of total appropriations to indicators of performance is based on "the theory that small rudders can move large ships" (Bogue & Johnson, 2010, p. 14). This principle has been applied— according to an estimate by Dougherty and Reddy (2013)—in the higher education systems of twenty-seven states. Approaches used among the states vary. Some have set aside a proportion of base funds to be tied to performance on specific indicators. Illinois's short-lived performance incentive program (1998–2002), for example, aimed at allocating 2 percent of the state's total fiscal support for community colleges to performance on indicators of student satisfaction, student success (e.g., remedial course completion, transfer, retention, credential attainment, subsequent employment), and service to the district (Dougherty et al., 2010).

Another approach, employed in North Carolina community colleges from 1999 to 2007–2008, "allowed institutions to carry over unexpended funds if they performed effectively [on student success indicators] and to share the state pool of unexpended funds if they performed exceptionally well" (Dougherty & Reddy, 2013, p. 24). A third approach abandoned add-on funding altogether, holding back a small proportion of state appropriations until institutions demonstrated adequate performance on specified indicators. This approach was used by the state of Washington in a performance funding program initiated in 1997 based on indicators related to transfer, the earnings of vocational program graduates, and "time-to-degree efficiency" (Dougherty & Reddy, 2013, p. 33).

In a notable move, Washington abandoned this "hold-back" approach in 1999, and in 2007 initiated a Student Achievement Initiative that now offers community colleges additional monies for performance on indicators related to student progression through the curriculum. These indicators gauge basic skills achievement (including gains on tests of basic skills as well as completion of developmental writing and math courses); first-year retention (earning the first fifteen and thirty credit hours); second-year retention (earning the first forty-five credit hours); the completion of college-level math courses; and the completion of degrees, certificates, or apprenticeship programs (Dougherty & Reddy, 2013; National Conference of State Legislatures, 2015, Washington section).

The intent was to focus "students and institutions on shorter term, intermediate outcomes that provide meaningful momentum towards degree and certificate completion for all students no matter where they start" (Washington State Board for Community and Technical Colleges, 2014, para. 6). This development is important because it moved performance-based funding away from a predominant focus on acquisition of credentials to rewarding institutions for success in guiding students to those credentials, step by step.

Although states continue to experiment with add-on funding, as evidenced by Washington's Student Achievement Initiative and (as discussed below) New York's Job Linkage Program, Dougherty and Reddy (2013) note that of the 27 states that have initiated add-on programs, "two thirds . . . abandoned performance funding at some point and 8 of those states have not reinstated any type of performance funding" (p. 32). The meager amount of funding was one factor contributing to the instability of these programs.

In the wake of the recession of the early 2000s, institutions focused on protecting base funding (Dougherty et al., 2014), and bonus funding lost its meaning. For many institutions it simply served as partial compensation for reductions in state funding (Dougherty & Reddy, 2013). In addition, PBF programs lost political "champions" as governors and legislators who had promoted PBF left. Opposition from institutions also came into play, stemming from concerns that college-level personnel had not been sufficiently consulted in the development of PBF programs, that performance indicators used to allocate bonus subsidies were inappropriate, and that the requirement to earn back withheld appropriations (where this approach was used) "left institutions uncertain about how much of the holdback they would eventually recover" (Dougherty et al., 2014, p. 170).

From the limited evidence available, it is reasonable to conclude that the first phase of PBF systems for community colleges did not succeed in terms of motivating colleges to produce better outputs. Beyond the relatively small amounts of money involved, the limited success of early PBF experiments reflects the challenges states faced in meeting the six elements of success outlined by the Rand study discussed above (Stecher et al., 2010).

Given the wide-ranging backgrounds and goals of students admitted through open-door policies, it is difficult to gain consensus on outcome indicators that adequately capture the community college mission and reflect performance on factors that colleges have control over. It is no wonder that institutional opposition played a role in the checkered history of early PBF efforts.

## THE SECOND PHASE: PBF 2.0

Despite the failed history of most initial efforts, a renewed emphasis on PBF emerged in the late 2000s, driven by the recession (2007–2009) coupled with a concern that higher education institutions remained unresponsive to state economic development needs at a time when a more highly educated citizenry was needed to initiate and sustain economic recovery.

Citing these developments, along with burgeoning higher education enrollments and the diminished capacity of states to increase higher education funding, McKeown-Moak (2013) noted that the "economic crisis of the states led to demands for graduation of more students, with higher quality educations, more efficiently, and more quickly" (p. 4). This, in turn, led to a renewed focus on PBF but with "a twist" (p. 4). Unlike PBF 1.0, which aimed primarily at sustaining institutional funding, new PBF initiatives focused on aligning college efforts with state economic development goals. As McKeown-Moak put it, the "new funding models reflect the needs of the state and its citizens, not merely the needs of the institution" (p. 4).

The second wave of PBF programs, dubbed "performance funding 2.0" by Dougherty and Reddy (2013, p. 6), also differed from earlier PBF initiatives by tying performance to base funds, rather than simply adding bonuses to base funds. This was an attempt not only to reward colleges for documented performance aligned with state priorities, but also to move away from, and perhaps eventually replace, state funding formulas based primarily on enrollment (rather than outcomes) that are a legacy of the post–World War II growth years of higher education when "a primary policy question was how to allocate state appropriations equitably among a growing and diverse number of public colleges and universities . . . ," taking into account "enrolments and costs by programme (from English to engineering) and by level (from undergraduate to graduate)" (Bogue & Johnson, 2010, p. 13). This was an ambitious goal that, if realized, would constitute a sea change in higher education funding.

The second phase of PBF programs also reflected, to a greater extent than the first, the research that had been conducted on community college outcomes. This is evidenced in Tennessee, which, as in the first stage of PBF, has taken a leading role in this new phase of performance funding. The Complete College Tennessee Act of 2010 mandated, among other provisions, the development of an outcomes-based funding model for higher education that "shall consider factors unique to community colleges" and that will incorporate outcomes related to "end of term enrollment for each term, student retention, timely progress toward degree completion and degree production" (p. 2).

The bill also specified that other outcomes might include "student transfer activity, research, and student success, as well as compliance with transfer and articulation principles" (p. 2). The funding formula developed in response to this mandate allocates monies to community colleges on the basis of productivity including the number of students who accumulate their first 12, 24, and 36 credit hours; the number of students in dual-enrollment programs; the number of certificates and associate degrees awarded; the number of students who successfully complete college-level courses within three years of passing a developmental course; the number of graduates employed in fields for which they were trained; the number of students transferring to other institutions after earning at least twelve credit hours, the number of contact hours generated in workforce training programs, and the total number of certificates and associate degrees awarded per 100 full-time-equivalent students (Tennessee Higher Education Commission, n.d.).

It is important to note that weights assigned to these measures within Tennessee's outcomes-based funding formula vary across institutions according to mission emphasis (Tennessee Higher Education Commission, n.d.). Accordingly, 20 percent of funding for an institution with a strong emphasis on transfer might be tied to the number of students transferring, compared to only 5 percent at an institution with a strong emphasis on vocational education.

In addition, the formula provides a premium for outcomes generated with adult and low-income students, reflecting the state's concern for retraining and workforce development. Tennessee's long-standing performance funding program (discussed earlier) continues in place today, allowing colleges to earn bonuses beyond allocations accrued through the new outcomes-based formula and complementing the productivity emphasis of the formula with attention to program quality. With its PBF system firmly in place, Tennessee is headed toward basing 100 percent of its appropriations on performance "after a base amount is set for operational support" (NCSL, 2015, Tennessee section).

Ohio is another state with a notable PBF 2.0 program, tying (in fiscal year 2014) 25 percent of base funding for community colleges to "success points" related to students who earn the first fifteen and thirty college-level semester hours, students completing developmental courses and then moving on to college-level courses, students earning "at least one associate's degree," and students transferring to a university after earning at least fifteen college-level credit hours at a community college (Ohio Board of Regents, 2013, pp. 5–6). An additional 25 percent of base funding is tied to course completion, and the remainder is calculated on the basis of enrollment (NCSL, 2015; Ohio Board of Regents, 2013). Overall, 50 percent of state funding in Ohio for fiscal year (FY) 2014 was based on outcomes. Lahr et al. (2014) report that this figure will rise to 100 percent in FY2015.

Perhaps the most extreme, and unusual, example of a state linking performance to funding is found in the eleven campuses that make up the Texas State Technical College System (TSTCS). Here, 100 percent of the state contribution to the operating budget for instruction and administration is tied to one outcome—the increase in wages earned by college completers. TSTCS colleges receive, in effect, a commission on the increased income and state tax revenue generated within the state by their job-training activities.

In this model, state funding for the system is based, in part, on direct and indirect additions to state tax revenues that can be attributed to the education experienced by TSTCS students. Drawing on state unemployment insurance (UI) wage records over a five-year period, the model calculates direct additions to state tax revenues in terms of "the incremental state tax revenue attributable to former TSTCS students' jobs, based on the difference between former TSTCS students' annual wages and a base wage representing a full-time employee earning minimum wage" (Texas Higher Education Coordinating Board, 2013, p. 2).

Indirect additions were defined "as the direct value-added multiplied by 1.5, an economic multiplier derived from a U.S. Bureau of Economic Analysis study" (Texas Higher Education Coordinating Board, 2013, p. 2). Here we see an attempt to base institutional funding not on student advancement through the curriculum, but on estimates of the state's return on investment in the TSTCS system. While Texas seems to regard its technical college system as serving a single labor market purpose, it does not see the community colleges in the same way, allocating 10 percent of appropriations on the basis of performance measures that reflect student academic achievement (NCSL, 2015).

Other states allocating, or planning to allocate, substantive proportions of funding to community colleges through PBF mechanisms include Arkansas, where performance-based monies are expected to reach 25 percent of funding by 2017–2018; Louisiana, where PBF monies account for 15 percent of base funding; Massachusetts, which bases 50 percent of state funding for community colleges (after operational support) on performance metrics; and

Wisconsin, where 10 percent of funding for technical colleges is based on performance, with plans to increase to 30 percent in 2016–2017 (NCSL, 2015).

In contrast to the examples above, most PBF systems allocate smaller proportions of funding to public colleges based on performance. In Indiana, for example, approximately 6 percent of higher education funding for fiscal years 2014 and 2015 was tied to performance on (among other metrics) indicators focusing on credential completion as measured by certificates or associate degrees awarded to students overall and to at-risk students specifically; student progression as measured by students completing the first 15, 30, and 45 credit hours, as well as by student success in developmental courses and subsequent college-level courses; and by productivity as measured by on-time graduation (Indiana Commission for Higher Education, n.d, 2013; NCSL, 2015).

Additional examples of small-scale programs include the PBF program in Illinois, which accounts for less than 1 percent of state funding (NCSL, 2015); Minnesota's appropriations bill for the 2014–2015 biennium, which stipulated that an allocation of 5 percent of the total appropriation for the Minnesota State Colleges and Universities system would "be available" upon evidence that the system had met three of five goals related to degree attainment, retention, and job placement (Omnibus Higher Education Appropriations Bill, 2013); and the legal stipulation that the Kansas Board of Regents will determine the level of new state funding (i.e., funding beyond monies appropriated in the previous year) that institutions will receive, "taking into account the . . . institution's level of compliance with . . . [a] performance agreement" based on indicators related to the state's goals of increasing degree attainment and developing the economy (Kansas Board of Regents, 2014, p. 5).

New York's Job Linkage Program is yet another small-scale program that uses the bonus approach for its community colleges. The state's 2013–2014 and 2014–2015 budgets included $3 million dollars that were to be divided among the thirty community colleges within the State University of New York (SUNY) system and another $2 million for the community colleges in the City University of New York (CUNY). Within the SUNY system, the largest bonus in the first year was $260,479 and the smallest was $20,531.

These bonuses only apply to technical and vocational degree and certificate programs and reward colleges that have a program mix favoring these areas. Bonus awards for the first year were based on employment and wage gains in the second quarter after college completion/graduation. Extra points were given if students were veterans, Pell recipients, had a disability, were females or minorities in a STEM field, or were initially enrolled in remedial courses.

Progress toward completion (twenty credits) was also included. The heaviest weights were given to job placements and wage gains based on unemployment insurance wage data (discussed in the last chapter). Because calculations for the bonuses were made by SUNY's central administration using existing system data, no additional collection costs were imposed upon individual colleges. And, because the calculations were made at the close of the year, colleges had no incentive to change internal policies to maximize awards. In effect, this was a small bonus payment meant to reward colleges for meeting state workforce needs and not a performance-based measure meant to change behavior. It is too early to tell if the SUNY program is a trial run for a more ambitious performance-based funding model in the future.

Overall, with the exception of a few bold moves, notably those undertaken by Tennessee, Ohio, and the Texas State Technical College System, most states employing performance-based funding adhere to the paradigm of attaching only a small proportion of funding to indicators of student outcomes. This cautious approach seems appropriate in light of the fact that community college outcomes are broad-scale, difficult to measure, and not adequately captured by standard measures of course completion or credential attainment. It remains to be seen if the goal of abandoning enrollment-based funding will be achieved or even found to be desirable.

It is worth noting that all of the outcomes-based funding models under discussion are centered only on funding streams that come from the state. There are no examples of a college's total revenue stream based on performance outcomes. The proportion of revenue coming from tuition is still enrollment based. For instance, if a state based 50 percent of its appropriation on outcomes but only provided 25 percent of a college's total operating revenue, then only 12.5 percent of its total revenue would be based on outcomes. Whether this is sufficient to alter institutional behavior is an open question.

## WHAT HAVE WE LEARNED?

The future of PBF is uncertain. But past experiments with PBF systems have left us with important insights, including an understanding of what state policymakers value in community colleges and practices that facilitate PBF programs. Past experience has also underscored the need for further research that will enhance our understanding of how PBF programs affect institutional behavior.

### Policymaker Priorities

Community college leaders have long held an open-ended view of student outcomes, arguing (as we have in chapter 4) that students often pursue idiosyncratic goals that may have nothing to do with degree attainment.

Fundamental to this view is a belief that student perceptions of whether or not they have achieved their goals should be the primary measure of institutional success. But public policymakers hold a different view, as evidenced in Table 5.1, which details outcome indicators employed by states that, according to the National Conference of State Legislatures (2015), utilized PBF systems at least partially for community college funding as of January 2015.

Credential completion, transfer to baccalaureate-granting institutions, and the achievement of intermediate goals leading to credential attainment or transfer (such as success in remedial courses and the completion of the first 15, 30, or 45 credit hours) constitute the primary focus of states with PBF systems. This emphasis is an important signal to community colleges, urging greater attention to policies and services that will lead students to timely degree or credential completion. Efforts to create "guided pathways for the acceleration of transfer or credential attainment," as advocated by Columbia University's Community College Research Center (Bailey, Jaggers, & Jenkins, 2015; Jenkins & Cho, 2014), will become critical to sustaining state fiscal support.

Table 5.1 also notes the extent to which policymakers tie concerns for completion to workforce and economic development, as evidenced by indicators related to job placement and income, pass rates on licensure or certification exams, and credentials awarded in science, technology, engineering, and mathematics (STEM) fields. This emphasis may lead to further efforts in future PBF programs to base funding not only on labor market outcome measures, but also on more direct indices of college impacts on the economy.

An example is the value-added model of the Texas State Technical College System explained above. However, as we noted in the previous chapter, outcomes, especially those related to jobs and income, are subject to the state of the economy. Only a robust economy produces favorable results. Students who graduate in a strong labor market have strong outcomes, those who enter the market during a recession, may not. In addition, outcomes related to credential completion and employment, though critically important, do not reflect the totality of the community college's educational impact.

A key challenge in the future will be to match the emphasis on economic efficiency (in terms of credential completion and employment outcomes) with an emphasis on equity. As evidenced in Table 5.1, some states have attended to equity in their PBF systems through metrics that factor in the progress of low-income and minority students. These metrics include the calculation of outcome measures for these populations specifically, or they may simply take the form of weighting systems that provide disproportionately large subsidies for demonstrated success in helping low-income and minority students succeed.

**Table 5.1   Student Outcomes Indicators Used in Performance-Based Funding Formulas for Community Colleges in 2015, by State**

| Indicator | AR | HI | IL | IN[a] | KS[b] | LA[c] | MA | MI | MN | MO | MT[d] | NV[e] | NM | NC | OH | OK | TN | TX | UT | VA | WA | WV[g] | WY |
|---|---|---|---|---|---|---|---|---|---|---|---|---|---|---|---|---|---|---|---|---|---|---|---|
| **Student progress and retention** | | | | | | | | | | | | | | | | | | | | | | | |
| Course completions or completion rates | ✓ | | | | | | | | | | | | | | | | | | | | | | ✓ |
| Completions or completion rates in math, writing-intensive, or reading-intensive (gateway courses) courses | | | | | | ✓ | | | | | | | | | | | | | ✓ | | ✓ | | |
| Achievement of specified milestones (e.g., first fifteen credits completed, first thirty credits completed, etc.) | ✓ | ✓ | ✓ | ✓ | | | ✓ | | | ✓ | | | | | | | | ✓ | | | | | |
| Credential completions or completion rates (e.g., certificate, associate's degree) | ✓ | ✓ | ✓ | ✓ | ✓ | ✓ | ✓ | ✓ | ✓ | ✓ | | | ✓ | | ✓ | ✓ | ✓ | ✓ | ✓ | ✓ | ✓ | | |
| Retention | | | ✓ | ✓ | | ✓ | ✓ | | | ✓ | | | | | | | | ✓ | ✓ | ✓ | | | |
| On-time or timely graduation | | | | ✓ | ✓ | ✓ | | | | | | | | | | | | ✓ | ✓ | ✓ | | | |
| Graduated or still enrolled in higher education within a specified time period (student success index) | | | ✓ | | | ✓ | | | | | | | | ✓ | | | | ✓ | | | | | |
| **Developmental education** | | | | | | | | | | | | | | | | | | | | | | | |
| Remedial course completions or course completion rates | ✓ | | | | | | | | | | | ✓ | | | ✓ | ✓ | | | | | | | |
| Student transition from developmental to college-level courses | | | ✓ | | | | | | | | | ✓ | | ✓ | | | | | | | | | |
| Educational-level gains of adult education students | | | ✓ | | | | | | | | | | | ✓ | | | | | | | | | |
| Student transition from adult education to college-level work | | | ✓ | | | | | | | | | | | | | | ✓ | | | | | | |
| Credentials awarded to students who had taken developmental courses | | | ✓ | | | | | | | | | | | | | | | | | | ✓ | | |
| Math, reading, or writing test score gains | | | | | | | | | | | | | | | | | | | | | ✓ | | |
| GED/high school credential attainment | | | | | | | | | | | | | | | | ✓ | | | | | | | |
| **Specific populations** | | | | | | | | | | | | | | | | | | | | | | | |
| Persistence or credential completions by adult students | ✓ | | | | | | | | | | | ✓ | ✓ | | ✓ | ✓ | | | | | | | |
| Persistence or credential completions by minorities | ✓ | ✓ | | | | | | | | | | ✓ | ✓ | | ✓ | ✓ | | | | | | | |
| Persistence or credential completion of Pell grant recipients or low-income students | | | | | | | | | | | | ✓ | | | ✓ | | | | | | | | |
| Persistence or credential completion of veterans | | | | | | | | | | | | ✓ | | | | | | | | | | | |

Persistence or credential completions of state residents with partial credit toward a degree

Transfer
- Students transferring to a four-year college
- Performance of students at four-year colleges after transfer
- Students transferring laterally to another community college

Labor market outcomes
- STEM credentials awarded
- High-demand credentials awarded
- Job obtainment
- Wages of students hired
- Pass rates on licensure and certification exams
- Student performance on Workkeys or industry-sponsored certificates
- Apprenticeship completion

Other measures
- Student performance on benchmarking surveys

*Note:* States represented in this table are those that, according to the National Conference of State Legislatures ([NCSL] 2015), employed PBF mechanisms to allocate at least some portion of state monies on the basis of student outcomes to community colleges. North Dakota, though listed by the NCSL as having a PBF system, is not included, because its PBF system is based on credit hour completion (NCSL, 2015). The table details only student outcomes indicators employed in PBF programs, not curricular or other measures that might be employed (e.g., monies tied to increases in the use of distance learning technology, in the development of articulation agreements, etc.).

*Sources:* Arkansas Department of Higher Education (2014), Illinois Community College Board (n.d.), Indiana Commission for Higher Education (n.d., 2013), Kansas Board of Regents (2014), Louisiana Board of Regents (2014), Missouri Department of Higher Education (2014), Montana University System (n.d.), NCSL (2015), Nelson and Keller (2014), Nevada System of Higher Education (n.d.), New Mexico Department of Higher Education (2013, 2014), North Carolina State Board of Community Colleges (2013), Ohio Board of Regents (2014), Oklahoma State Regents for Higher Education (n.d.), Omnibus Higher Education Appropriations Bill (2013), Performance Indicators Task Force (n.d.), Tennessee Higher Education Commission (n.d.), Texas Legislature (2013), University of Hawai'i System (2014), Utah State Legislature (2013), Virginia Higher Education Opportunity Act of 2011, Washington State Board for Community and Technical Colleges (2012), Wisconsin Technical College System (2015).

[a]Proposed metrics for 2013–15. In addition to a measure of on-time graduation, each institution will employ one additional "productivity metric linked to their strategic plan" (Indiana Commission for Higher Education, n.d., p. 13). [b]Kansas colleges and universities enter into performance agreements with the Kansas Board of Regents (KBR). New monies are "contingent upon achieving compliance" with those agreements (KBR, 2014, p. 3). Measures listed here include those that institutions can select from in meeting two goals in the KBR strategic plan: "increasing higher education attainment" and "meeting the needs of the Kansas economy" (KBR, 2014, p. 6). Community and technical colleges must also include three additional institution-specific indicators related to the KBR's strategic plan, "one of which measures a non-college ready student population" (KBR, 2014, p. 6). [c]Institutions enter into six-year performance agreements committing them to meet "specific performance objectives in exchange for increased tuition authority and eligibility to participate in certain autonomies" (Louisiana Board of Regents, n.d., para. 1). Performance objectives include curricular and efficiency measures (e.g., elimination of programs not aligned with state needs or that have low completion rates) in addition to the outcomes indicators listed here. [d]Proposed performance metrics for fiscal years 2016 and 2017. [e]Proposed metrics. [f]In addition to mission-specific measures. [g]Technical College System only.

Notably absent from the list in Table 5.1 is any reference to specific learning outcomes. Nor as Jones (2013) has indicated, has any "state explicitly included a quality metric in its funding model" (p. 6). This seems appropriate, given the inability of colleges and universities to this point to come up with an acceptable way of measuring these two interrelated outcomes.

## Factors That Impede or Facilitate PBF

In addition to improving our understanding of what the public values and is willing to pay for, prior experience with PBF systems has enhanced our understanding of what facilitates their development and use. These factors are summarized in Table 5.2, which details selected recommendations in key writing on the implementation of PBF systems.

Some of the recommendations address fiscal impediments in the design and use of PBF, including the danger of tying PBF programs to a small proportion of funds, thereby making it unprofitable for institutions to devote time and effort required for data reporting, and the temptation to designate funds as add-ons to base funding, which increases the probability that PBF programs will be cut from state budgets during economic downturns (Dougherty & Reddy, 2013). Stop-loss provisions have also been recommended as an assurance that institutions will sustain at least minimal financial support.

Other impediments to developing and implementing PBF systems are administrative or structural in nature, such as launching a PBF program too quickly and without adequate input from institutional stakeholders, especially faculty and staff who work with students; making the PBF formula so complex—and the process of complying with the PBF mandate so difficult—that the PBF effort simply collapses or succumbs to those who would "game the system"; and failing to recognize the substantial investment in institutional research that compliance with a PBF program will require.

The latter may be especially problematic at community colleges, which often have small and overworked institutional research offices. Dougherty and Reddy (2013) argue that at a minimum, colleges will need "funds to acquire new data management systems, expand the number of institutional researchers, and train faculty members and institutional research staff to analyze performance data" (p. 85).

They will also need assistance in "becoming learning organizations . . . capable of continuously monitoring their performance, identifying problems, developing strategies to solve them, and evaluating how well those strategies work" (p. 86). The reader will note that all of these recommendations align with the elements of success developed by the Rand Corporation's historical analysis of pay-for-performance systems (Stecher et al., 2010) discussed earlier in this chapter.

**Table 5.2  Selected Recommendations in the Literature for Implementing PBF Systems**

| Recommendations | (Dougherty et al. 2014; Dougherty & Reddy, 2013) | Jones (2013) | Miao (2012) | National Conference of State Legislatures (2015) |
|---|:---:|:---:|:---:|:---:|
| **Avoiding fiscal impediments** | | | | |
| Assure that PBF systems are tied to meaningfully high proportions of institutional funding. | ✓ | ✓ | ✓ | ✓ |
| Be careful that the proportion of state funds tied to performance are not, on the other hand, so high that they promote unintended consequences, such as lowered academic standards. | ✓ | | | |
| Incorporate performance funding into the state formula for base funding rather than using PBF to provide colleges with add-ons to base funding. | ✓ | | ✓ | |
| Employ stop-loss provisions assuring that institutions will not lose more than a certain proportion of funding in a given year. | ✓ | | ✓ | |
| Do not wait for increased state monies before starting a new PBF program. | | | | |
| **Avoiding administrative or structural impediments** | | | | |
| Provide financial and other support needed by colleges to develop and sustain the institutional research effort that will be required to calculate and report data embedded in the PBF formula. | ✓ | ✓ | | |
| Assure that indicators used in the PBF formulas are simple and readily understandable. | | ✓ | | ✓ |
| Construct the PBF formula around a small number of variables that reflect key state priorities. | | ✓ | | ✓ |
| Design the PBF system with meaningful input from institutional-level personnel, including faculty members and student affairs staff. | ✓ | | ✓ | ✓ |
| Implement PBF systems gradually, phasing them in over time. | | ✓ | ✓ | ✓ |
| Seek consensus on the goals of the PBF program. | | ✓ | ✓ | ✓ |
| Assess the PBF system on a continual basis. | | | ✓ | |
| **Avoiding damage to the educational mission, equity, and quality** | | | | |
| Assure that indicators applied in the PBF formulas are appropriate in light of the institution's mission. | ✓ | ✓ | ✓ | ✓ |
| Tie the funding formula to economic and workforce development needs, including preparation for high-demand occupations. | | | | ✓ |
| Take steps to assure that the PBF program does not ultimately lead to lower academic standards so that the goal of learning is not displaced by the goal of completion | ✓ | ✓ | | ✓ |
| Factor in weighting schemes that provide institutions with additional funding for low-income, minority, and other high-risk or underrepresented students. | ✓ | ✓ | | ✓ |
| Employ indicators that reflect student progress on the way to the degree, not just indicators of ultimate outcomes (e.g., graduation) | | ✓ | ✓ | ✓ |
| Reward institutions for "continuous improvement, not attainment of a fixed goal" (Jones, 2013, p. 6). | | ✓ | | |

*Note:* This is not an exhaustive list of all recommendations made by the four publications cited.

Finally, other recommendations in Table 5.2 focus on educational mission, equity, and indirect measures of quality. These recommendations reflect concerns that PBF formulas might impose inappropriate measures on institutions, fail to reward institutions for hard-won student progress on "intermediate student outcomes" (Dougherty & Reddy, 2013, p. 7) such as continuing enrollment from one year to the next, pressure instructors to diminish academic standards, or lead colleges away from open access by pushing them to seek out qualified students who are more likely to perform well on PBF metrics.

In response to concerns that outcome measures may not always be appropriate to community colleges, Dougherty and Reddy (2013) recommend that measures employed in PBF formulas factor in student intent (e.g., calculating transfer or graduation rates on the basis of those who intend to transfer or graduate in the first place).

Along with other authors, Dougherty and Reddy also recommend metrics that factor in low-income and underrepresented students. And, in response to concerns about academic standards, Dougherty and Reddy recommend state efforts to "monitor degree requirements and course grade distributions," facilitate "anonymous surveys of faculty to see whether they report substantial pressure to weaken academic requirements," and intensify efforts to assess student learning (p. 88).

Thus, the need for a robust data management and analysis infrastructure is matched by a need for a robust effort aimed at sustaining academic standards and documenting student learning. Tennessee's efforts to complement its new outcome-based funding formula with quality measures from its long-established performance-based funding system, which includes indicators of learning in general education, may provide a workable model for this. But the warnings of Trudy Banta (2007), discussed in chapter 4, underscore the difficulty of using value-added measures to assess institutional contributions to learning. Widely accepted measures of student learning have yet to be developed, and none are included in current PBF systems with the exception of standard licensure and certification exit exams.

## The Uncertain Impact of PBF

Do PBF programs have the effect that policymakers intend? Despite a growing body of research on these programs, this remains an open question. The first phase of PBF did not seem to improve measures of student success, due in part to the fact that many PBF schemes initiated early on were short-lived and never had a chance to take root in state funding mechanisms. However, prospects for the second phase seem more promising, as evidenced by the wider range of metrics now employed in PBF formulas (see Table 5.1), a development propelled by advances in data collection and management since early phase-1 experiments (Jones, 2013); by a growing body of research on community college outcomes; by the commitment of funding (in some states, at least) to incentivize colleges to produce better outcomes; and by today's strong policy emphasis on enhancing student success, which lends a greater urgency to monitoring and fostering student persistence and achievement.

Nonetheless, the results of PBF systems are unknown at this point. Bridging the gap between early and subsequent phases of PBF, Donna Desrochers of the Delta Cost Project at the American Institutes for Research conducted an analysis for this volume, offering tentative insights into the potential impact of state PBF programs (personal communication, September 1, 2014). Using IPEDS data, she compared states in terms of average annual percent changes between 2002 and 2012 in (a) total degree or certificate completions per 100 full-time-equivalent (FTE) students, (b) graduation rates, (c) retention rates for full-time students, and (d) average undergraduate credit hours per completion.

Testing the hypothesis that performance-based funding would have an impact on these outcomes, she compared average percent changes in outcomes for four groups of states: those with well-established PBF programs, those with smaller or less-well-established PBF programs, those with recently implemented PBF programs, and those with no PBF programming. Results (Table 5.3) were mixed.

Table 5.3  Percent Change in Selected Performance Outcomes at Public Two-Year Colleges, 2002–2012

| | Completions per 100 FTE students (%)[a] | Graduation rate (%)[a] | Retention rate for full-time students (%)[a] | Credit hours per completion (%) |
|---|---|---|---|---|
| States with wide-scale and well-established PBF programs | 31.1 | 16.0 | 63.0 | −30.6 |
| Florida[b] | 35.6 | 34.0 | 62.0 | −19.8 |
| Ohio | 22.0 | 12.0 | 48% | −27.4 |
| Tennessee | 28.7 | 12.0 | 52% | −100.3 |
| States with smaller or less-well-established PBF programs[c] | 29.3 | 18.0 | 59% | −40.4 |
| States with recently-implemented PBF programs[d] | 24.5 | 18.0 | 60% | −32.0 |
| States without PBF Programs | 23.6 | 22.0 | 57% | −35.7 |

*Note*: Compiled by Donna Desrochers, personal communication, September 1, 2014. Data are from the Delta Cost Project IPEDS database, 1987-2010 and the Delta Cost Project analysis of IPEDS 2010–2011 and 2011–2012 data: 11-year matched set.
[a]Completion and performance rates are enrollment weighted (using full-time equivalent enrollments); weighted graduation rates and credit hours per completion were calculated from summed data. [b]Funding for Florida's program, begun in the mid-1990s, lapsed in 2008. Consequently, Florida is not included in table 5A. [c]Includes Indiana, Louisiana, North Carolina, Utah, and Washington. [d]Includes Arkansas, Hawaii, Illinois, Kansas, Massachusetts, Michigan, Minnesota, Missouri, Nevada, New Mexico, North Dakota, Oklahoma, and Texas.

For example, states with well-established PBF programs outperformed states without a PBF program in terms of completions per 100 FTE students and retention rates for full-time students. But this was not the case for graduation rates or for credit hours per completion. It is important to note that this analysis did not contain any controls and that although the results are suggestive, they do not prove causation. In general, however, these results are similar to those found in more robust studies of this type.

Extensive interviews with educational leaders in states with PBF programs, as well as a thorough review of empirical studies, also led Kevin Dougherty and his colleagues to mixed findings (Dougherty et al., 2014; Dougherty & Reddy, 2013). On the one hand, interviews conducted by Dougherty et. al. (2014) suggested that the implementation of PBF programming induced colleges to take actions that help retain students and guide them to transfer or credential completion. These actions include curricular or policy modifications that eliminate unnecessary barriers to graduation; "improvements in developmental education, tutoring, and other supplemental instruction" (Dougherty & Reddy, p. 48); and beneficial "modifications to registration and graduation procedures," counseling and advising practices, and job placement assistance (Dougherty & Reddy, 2013, pp. 49–51).

On the other hand, their review of statistical analyses attempting to isolate the impact of performance-based funding on student outcomes failed "to find evidence that performance funding improves graduation and retention," leading them to conclude that it is difficult to isolate the impact of performance-based funding on changes in desired student outcomes from the impact that other factors might have on these outcomes, including "changes in-state tuition and financial aid policies, other efforts to improve student outcomes . . . , or institutional decisions to avoid admitting less-qualified students" (Dougherty et al., 2014, p. 173).

Hillman, Tandberg, and Fryar (2015) echoed this conclusion in their analysis of Washington's Student Achievement Initiative, pointing out that PBF programs are part of a "larger performance accountability package" and that "it can be difficult to disentangle which specific feature of the . . . package is responsible for any observed effect." They noted that "a college may improve its performance, but it is unclear whether this was due to . . . financial incentives, . . . compliance reporting, the establishment of . . . goals, or any combination of these factors" (p. 2).

In the end, it is difficult to determine when improved student outcomes are the product of incentives in a PBF system or the product of actions undertaken by colleges to improve student success regardless of the state funding mechanism. After all, the PBF systems that have emerged in the wake of the Great Recession are themselves a product of a larger movement endorsed by the media and influential foundations to focus on efficient student credential completion. While these systems may ultimately have a positive impact, they are only one of many contemporary influences on institutional behavior.

## POLICY RECOMMENDATIONS

Performance-based funding seems to be here to stay and is a welcome addition to the community college's emphasis on access. However, access should be the primary goal, and if PBF is appropriately viewed as a means to an end, and not an end in itself (Jones, 2013), it is better to start with this end in mind when designing a PBF system. Here we see a potential conflict in that Phase-2 PBF systems may be better aligned with state goals than with the goals envisioned by the colleges or their students.

While this seems appropriate at first glance—we are talking about state money after all—students come to community colleges for a variety of reasons, and, as we argued in chapter 4, not all of them fit the outcome models currently in use. A PBF system that focuses on credential completion alone without recognizing the goal of sustaining access—even if that access serves only to help students test the waters—offers only partial recognition of personal and societal returns on investment in community colleges.

In addition, as a growing proportion of state funding becomes tied to performance measures, the goal of performing well on formula metrics may displace the goal of assuring a quality educational experience, regardless of a student's educational goal. This concern was raised by community college administrators and instructors in Indiana, Ohio, and Tennessee who, during interviews conducted by Lahr et al. (2014), noted instances in which state performance funding schemes actually did, or potentially could, lead colleges to screen out less-prepared students through restricted admissions or by subtly influencing faculty members, particularly (as we noted in chapter 4) part-time instructors, to lower academic standards as a way of increasing completion rates. Both factors could significantly threaten the access and outcomes goals of community colleges.

The recommendations in Table 5.2 offer sound advice for avoiding these problems, among others. But we distill from these recommendations four overall principles that are critical to aligning PBF systems with the community college mission. First, it will be critically important to focus rewards (and thus metrics) on recruiting and supporting low-income and other at-risk students. As Table 5.1 suggests, these metrics do not appear to be as commonly used as those devoted to retention, persistence, or completion of students generally, or to employment outcomes. Additional weighting for the disproportionately large number of at-risk students enrolled at community colleges has the potential to further state equity goals for higher education, which are largely achieved through the open-access function of community colleges.

Second, PBF formulas should, as we have previously noted in this chapter, factor in quality indicators that will protect the academic integrity of the curriculum. In light of the growing evidence (discussed in chapter 4) that increased reliance on adjunct faculty may reduce retention and completion rates, and that part-timers might be particularly vulnerable to pressure to lower standards as a way of increasing rates of course completion, it may be prudent to include threshold levels for the proportion of instructors who are employed on a full-time basis. Evidence of student learning may over the long run also be a useful addition, though as we have previously noted, current testing mechanisms are not yet up to the task.

Third, in the rush to develop PBF programs, the costs associated with these funding schemes should not be underestimated. As Dougherty and Reddy (2013) have noted, the reporting requirements of PBF may strain the institutional research capacity of many colleges. To the extent possible, PBF metrics should be confined to data that are already collected by colleges and states.

The inclusion of data not currently collected should be considered only after careful analysis of the additional cost involved and weighed against the anticipated benefit. One has only to think of higher education's past experience with cumbersome and eventually abandoned budgeting schemes, including zero-based budgeting and program planning budgeting systems (PPBS), to realize that complicated and labor-intensive analytic frameworks for the allocation of funds—however enticing in theory—are ultimately unworkable in practice (Birnbaum, 2000).

Finally, policymakers should be cautious in terms of the proportion of funding tied to performance. An ideal PBF system for community colleges would probably account for no more than 10 percent of total institutional revenues, a figure large enough to "command attention" (Jones, 2013, p. 8) yet perhaps not so large that it inadvertently leads to the untoward consequences noted by Lahr et al. (2014) or diverts institutional attention from the important educational outcomes fostered by open access that aren't easily captured in PBF metrics. But this approach has its challenges. Because institutions vary in terms of the proportion of total revenue coming from state funding, states would need to vary PBF allotments across institutions, which from a practical and political standpoint will be difficult. And because state appropriations vary over time with the business cycle, adjustments would need to be made from year to year as well.

As a more workable compromise, we recommend that a flat 25 percent of state appropriations, phased in incrementally over time, be tied to performance, and that this level of funding be reconsidered over time after we gain greater insight into the validity and impacts of the metrics used in PBF formulas. A flat rate of 25 percent would admittedly lead to considerable variation across institutions. If the state contribution to a college's total revenue is 10 percent, as it is in some colleges in Illinois (Fain, 2014d), the proportion of total revenue tied to performance-based monies would be 2.5 percent. Where state funds account for 50 percent of revenues, the figure would be 12.5 percent.

Most colleges would certainly fall within this range of 2.5–12.5 percent, and though the strength of PBF incentives would vary across colleges, the overall impact of PBF funding would certainly be felt. A single flat rate is easier to explain to college constituents than a complicated rate that changes every year, and tying the flat rate to previous (let's say) three years of outcomes makes budget planning at the campus level less burdensome.

Jones (2013) has noted that the 25 percent figure is "reasonable" (p. 8) and a "normative ultimate target" (p. 11) that several states seem to be working toward. He also argues that PBF funding should be phased in over time. But we differ from him in at least one respect. While we concede that our recommendation for a flat rate of 25 percent would mean that the percentage of total institutional funding tied to performance—and hence the relative influence of the fiscal incentives built into the PBF program—would decline as the share of total funding derived from the state declines, Jones argues that "as a general principal, the smaller the share of institutional resources derived from the state the greater the percentage of state funds that should be directed toward outcomes" (p. 8).

Our stance is that the flat rate puts the onus on the state to ante up funds that are commensurate with the influence that states want to exert. The flat rate carries with it an implicit message to state policymakers: "If you are not giving us much, how can you hold us accountable for increased performance on statewide persistence and completion goals beyond the goal of access that community colleges provide?"

Our position is admittedly more aligned with an institutional than with a state perspective, and we recognize that states, hard pressed to increase funding might simply respond by ratcheting up the proportion of appropriations that are tied to performance. But in that case the state is simply demanding that colleges do more with the same or less, a self-defeating strategy that may, without vigilance, diminish quality and neglect the real personal and social benefits that accrue through student pursuit of goals that do not lead to the most easily measured outcomes such as transfer or credential attainment.

## DO NO HARM

PBF systems have the potential to focus institutional attention on helping students advance through the curriculum to further study and/or career advancement. But as Dougherty and his colleagues have stressed (e.g., Dougherty & Reddy, 2013; Lahr et al., 2014), care must be taken to assure that PBF systems do no inadvertent harm. In addition, it is important to remember Jones's (2013) admonition that despite the attention now being paid to PBF systems, outcome-based funding is simply one component of a larger system of fiscal support.

Desrochers and Wellman (2012) put it well in their observation that continued work on PBF programs should not divert "attention from deeper issues affecting state funding for higher education that must be addressed," including (e.g.,) the substantial limitations imposed on institutions by the growing cost associated with employee benefits and "the decline in state funding for all public institutions" (p. 6). As noted in chapter 2, employee benefits do not appear to be as much of a cost pusher for community colleges as they are for public four-year colleges. However, cost-cutting efforts undertaken by community colleges in response to personnel obligations, notably through increased reliance on part-time instructors, may reduce the quality of education, especially for the least advantaged students. The likely consequences of this will be discussed in the final chapter.

## NOTE

1. Dennis P. Jones (2013), writing for Complete College America, has done an excellent job of outlining the principles that states should follow in designing and implementing a performance-based funding system.

*Chapter 6*

# Issues on the Horizon

This chapter examines lesser-known or emerging ideas on the revenue and expenditure (cost) side of the budget that may become important in the near future. Included are proposals that can affect revenue streams directly or indirectly through alterations in financial aid, including changes in the federal loan and Pell programs as well as experiments with performance-based student aid; reconfigured tuition strategies, including differential program pricing or perhaps the elimination of tuition charges altogether in the wake of the "free tuition" movement; increased emphasis on enrollment management; and experiments with educational vouchers.[1]

On the cost side, we examine initiatives that focus on calculating the cost of degrees and implementing activity-based costing. Both have the potential to help managers reallocate funds within a college, which might improve efficiency and student success.

## FINANCIAL AID

In preparation for reauthorization of the Higher Education Act (HEA) expected in 2015, lobbies, think tanks, and advocates from all parts of the political spectrum have weighed in with a spate of reports and recommendations concerning financial aid. With new reports coming almost weekly, it is virtually impossible to stay current on what is happening. However, since the HEA sets the rules for Pell grants and federal loans, many of these reports focus on recommendations for change in programs that could have a major impact on community college budgets and student success.

In this chapter we review a few of the proposals that we feel are well supported by research and that fit our policy agenda of benefiting the least

115

advantaged students. By the time this book is published some of these proposals may have already influenced the new HEA.

## Tinkering with Federal Loans

As we argued in chapter 1, the availability of federal loans (credit) helps to
correct for market failures. Even with well-functioning credit markets, student borrowing is limited by an individual's aversion for risk (uncertainty
about outcomes) and/or their aversion for debt (psychic costs of holding
debt). These will be briefly considered in the next chapter. For now we
can say that without the availability of this credit, higher education will be
under-produced.

It is worth pointing out, however, that federal backing of student loans does
not necessarily require that they be subsidized. Subsidies do not remedy market failure, but the availability of loans does. Our argument in support of the
federal student loan program should not be interpreted to mean that private
loans cannot be used to finance higher education, although, once again, the
government need not guarantee these loans.

Figures were provided earlier (chapter 2) that showed federal loans to be
a more important source of student support than Pell grants for undergraduates at four-year colleges. But these loans are not widely used by community
college students. In fact, the Institute for College Access and Success (2014)
argues that community college students are too often denied access to federal
loans, noting that "more than one million students in 31 states" are enrolled
in colleges that do not even participate in the loan program (p. 1). Greater use
of federal loans can help students persist and succeed, but the terms under
which loans are repaid must be changed or many students will encumber
unreasonable debt that will have a negative impact on their future and that of
the economy.

Dynarski and Kreisman (2013), in an analysis of the student debt problem
conducted for the Brookings Institution, provide some straight-forward thinking about the undergraduate student debt problem and present a different picture of student debt from that projected by the media. They show that student
loans are an important part of the financing of higher education and that debt
levels are moderate compared to the potential return on a college education.

The authors suggest that we do not have a debt crisis, but rather a repayment crisis given that in 2013, seven million loans were in default. Most of
the students in default are young. "We have a repayment crisis because student loans are due when borrowers have the least capacity to pay—when they
are young and have not yet settled into the higher paying jobs that reflect the
value of their education" (Dyranski & Kreisman, 2013, p. 6).

The answer proposed by Dyranski and Kreisman is to replace the existing federal loan programs, with their confusing array of applications, interest rates, and repayment schemes, with a single—and much simpler—federal program employing an income-based repayment schedule. It would allow loans to be paid back over a 25-year period, if necessary, through payroll deductions in much the same way that income and social security taxes are now collected. Additional payments would be optional to pay the loan down faster, and outstanding balances after twenty-five years would be forgiven.

Under such a plan, payments would be low when income is low and increase progressively as income rises until the loan, plus interest and collection costs, is paid in full. Dynarski and Kreisman also propose sensible adjustments in the program to account for students who do not enter the workforce or who are tempted to borrow more than they need with the hope that the loan will eventually be forgiven.

The approach suggested by Dynarski and Kreisman seems all the more reasonable in light of research by Carnevale, Hanson, and Gulish (2013) showing that loan repayment under current policies is forced upon young graduates too early. Working with labor market data from their Georgetown Public Policy Institute, they document that "young adults [today] do not reach employment and earnings levels similar to those of young adults in 1980 until later ages" (p. 3).

In fact, the point at which young adults reach the median wage of all employed individuals has increased from age twenty-six in 1980 to age thirty in 2012. And while some may argue that an extended loan repayment system based on income and some degree of loan forgiveness may be too expensive, Dynarski and Kreisman note that the plan they propose will not cost the tax-payers any more than the current system and may, in fact, cost less. To offset the cost of this program they suggest that the federal government stop paying the private sector to collect loans thus saving $360 million a year (it will not be needed anymore); eliminate the tax deduction for loan interest, thereby saving $1 billion annually; and eliminate "the in-school interest subsidy," converting "the billions saved . . . into grant aid" (Dynarski & Kreisman, 2013, p. 13).

A long line of research has promoted the idea of an income-based repayment plan. The United States has such a system in place but it is small and too restrictive to reach the students who need it the most. More simplified and successful programs are at work in Australia, New Zealand, and the United Kingdom, (Johnstone & Marcucci, 2010), but to this point the United States has lacked the political will to follow their lead. Community college leaders can do the nation and enrolled students a great service by pushing for a program of this type.

## Tinkering with Pell Grants

Research has left little doubt that Pell grants have expanded access for low- and moderate-income students. As data from the College Board (2014) reveal, the number of students receiving Pell grants has expanded greatly over the past twenty years (from 3.8 million in 1993–1994 to 9.2 million in 2013–2014), propelled by growing income inequality and by enrollment surges during the recessions of 2001–2002 and 2007–2009, when many students could not have attended college without Pell subsidies. This track record, along with research substantiating the impact of Pell grants on access, provides a strong case for increased funding for the program and for efforts to restore cuts made in 2012 that eliminated funding for students in summer programs and for students without a high school degree.

However, as with any large government expenditure, the Pell program has its critics. Space does not allow for an extensive review of these criticisms, but some of the more interesting research-based proposals for change have been driven by concerns that the application process for Pell monies (or for any federal financial aid) is onerous, that Pell guidelines offer insufficient incentives for timely degree or credential completion, and that Pell subsidies may, of themselves, be insufficient to encourage enrollment and completion by low-income students.

In addition, there are some who have argued that the Pell program, as we know it, should be scrapped in favor of other approaches to subsidize low-income students. Federal financial aid policy aside, there are also growing concerns that the goals of the Pell program may be thwarted by institutional practices that divert resources to wealthier students and by the phenomenon of under matching, where uncertainty about net prices leads high-achieving, low-income students away from selective institutions. All of these factors have a bearing on policy discussions surrounding the future direction of America's signature needs-based aid program.


**Simplifying the application process.** A common criticism of the Pell program is that it would be more successful if the application was simpler. As it is, the Free Application for Federal Student Aid (FASFA) form is unnecessarily complicated and discourages students from applying. Efforts have been made to simplify the form in recent years, but its complexity continues to undermine its potential.

In fact, research has demonstrated that a short form can produce the same results as the current FAFSA application, which has over one hundred questions. With the Republican victory in the Senate in 2014, Lamar Alexander took over as chair of the Education Committee and one of his favorite themes has always been to "simplify, simplify, simplify" (Field, 2014). At one time

Alexander touted a "Pell on a Postcard" proposal with just two questions on it (Alexander & Bennet, 2014).

In any case, political support for simplifying this form is strong and it seems likely that some action on this will be part of the new Higher Education Act. This will not only have a positive impact on student access and success, but could cut the cost of administering college financial aid offices, and allow the savings to be used to boost other support services for low-income students.

Another promising idea for streamlining the process, although one that seems less likely to be enacted, is tying the Pell application to parents' and students' federal tax forms, thereby making it easier to determine a student's eligibility for Pell grants. In an interesting experiment, Bettinger, Long, Oreopoulos, and Sanbonmatsu (2009) did just that, using H&R Block software to help low-income students in the Boston area complete the FASFA form. This resulted in a significant increase in student enrollment.

**Disincentive for completion.** Another common critique of the Pell grant is that it is structured in a way that discourages the timely completion of degrees because it only requires a student to take twelve credits per semester to be considered full time. Some argue that if fifteen credits were required, it would encourage students to take more courses and finish sooner.

Others point out, however, that at many community colleges, tuition for full-time students is not a fixed amount, but based on the number of credits taken. Therefore, if the definition of full-time enrollment were moved up to fifteen credits, and if Congress does not approve additional dollars for more than twelve credits, then more of the grant would go toward tuition payments and less would be available for other student expenses. Under such a system, the lowest-income students would be penalized (Baum, Conklin, & Johnson, 2013).

**Attending to access barriers**. Other proposals to redesign the Pell program call for new money to reduce access barriers identified in research. Among the best of these is the proposal by Baum and Scott-Clayton (2013) in a discussion paper prepared for the Hamilton Project of the Brookings Institution. Along with supporting recommendations for simplifying the FAFSA and using IRS data to determine eligibility, the Baum and Scott-Clayton proposal would provide new money to support coaching and guidance services for students as early as high school. Their proposal also recommends paying Pell recipients a bonus for completing degrees on time.

A similar call for additional funding for disadvantaged students was made in a report by the New America Foundation (Burd, 2013). Subsequently, the New America Foundation, along with the Education Trust, Young

Invincibles, and the American Association of State Colleges and Universities, called for an even bolder federal and state effort to guarantee that for students eligible for a full Pell grant, no more than 10 percent of family income, each year, would be necessary to finance their college education (Consortium for Higher Education Grants and Work-Study Reform, 2014).

This proposal also attempted to address the problem that although net price may be low, it is the sticker price that discourages entry. The veil of uncertainty over the real price is especially relevant for low-income students in community colleges. Indeed, research indicates that student applications to community colleges are discouraged by high sticker prices even though the net price might be less than zero. The "free tuition" movement explained below is one approach to dealing with this. Another is to find a better way of displaying the net price, up front, so that low-income students can see, at first look, what their price will be.

**Eliminate Pell.** Perhaps the most extreme critique of the Pell grant comes from Sara Goldrick-Rab. In a paper written for the American Enterprise Institute (Goldrick-Rab, Schudde, & Stampen, 2015), Goldrick-Rab calls for elimination of voucher-like programs such as Pell, recommending instead a financial aid policy that makes college more affordable for all students. She recommends a change in the focus of federal and state subsidies from the student to the institutions they attend. Major strings would be attached. Subsidies to institutions would depend on how well they kept costs under control, the extent to which they shifted resources to the most disadvantaged students, and their ability to narrow the outcomes gap between low- and middle-income students.

Goldrick-Rab's proposal goes beyond tinkering with Pell and other grants; it represents a major redirection of funds to lower college costs for all students, especially the least advantaged. The philosophy underlying her approach is that education is more of a public good than is currently recognized by the dominant human capital model of economists. In a statement prepared in advance of the reauthorization of Higher Education Act, Goldrick-Rab has called for the redirection of federal aid to colleges for the purpose of making the first two years "free" at any public college (Goldrick-Rab & Kendall, 2014; Goldrick-Rab et al., 2015). This expensive program would represent a new role for the federal government in financing colleges and is discussed later in this chapter.

**Counterproductive institutional practices.** Other studies are less critical of the Pell program, focusing more on how colleges subvert the purpose of the program by directing funds away from the neediest students. Burd (2013), for instance, argues that institutional financial aid funds, though originally viewed as monies that would fill in the gaps that federal and state did not cover for low-income students, have been used by both private and public colleges to compete for students who are not needy.

Driven by an enrollment management industry and the goal of maximizing revenue, colleges have found that rather than offering a $20,000 scholarship to one needy student it is advantageous to offer four $5,000 scholarships to wealthier, but not necessarily brighter, students who can pay the balance of the full price and who are more likely to become donors. Burd suggests that this is one reason that "even after historic increases in Pell grant funding, the college-going gap between low-income students and their wealthier counterparts remains as wide as ever" (p. 2). Even more troublesome, are reports noted by Burd that some colleges reject students even before they apply based on their application for a Pell grant.

**Under-matching**. If the practices, noted above, of reduced preference for low-income students were to become more widespread, calls to restructure the Pell program in ways that would reestablish its original purposes would emerge. If retained in its present form, the program would push more students down the selectivity ladder, and some would end up in community colleges. This, however, would also result in under-matching of students and probably reduce the bachelor's degree completion rate.

The under-matching phenomenon, where students fail to apply to the most selective colleges that will accept them, has gained recognition as a problem in its own right. In a widely cited study, Hoxby and Avery (2013) hypothesized that the undermining of Pell described above is not widespread and that highly selective colleges are continually in search of low-income, high-achieving students.

But in a complex analysis that involved the top 10 percent of students in the high school class of 2008 who took either the SAT or ACT test, Hoxby and Avery found that the majority of the low-income, high-achieving students did not apply to selective colleges and ended up in less-selective four-year or community colleges, even though the more selective colleges could offer them a better financial aid package and a lower net price. It was not that these students preferred the community college, since virtually none of them "reported that a two-year degree was their educational goal" (Hoxby & Avery, 2013, p. 34). In a follow up with these under-matched students, Hoxby and Avery found that the students were much less likely to persist and graduate than the comparable group of low-income students who had attended a more selective college.

Efforts can be undertaken to help students avoid under-matching. In a widely cited study of 40,000 students across the country, Hoxby and Turner (2013) demonstrated that when low-income, high achievers were provided with information about more selective colleges (at an estimated cost of $6 per student) and an application fee waiver, applications and admission to these colleges increased dramatically.

This and other studies have shown that a lack of information about net pricing and the complexity of applying for financial aid are keeping disadvantaged and academically capable students from applying to colleges that match their ability levels (Hoxby & Turner, 2013). Information provided on net price on college websites is not enough. Fortunately, as Hoxby and Turner and others have demonstrated, there are low-cost interventions that are scalable to help high-achieving, low-income students reach their potential.

Recently the governor of Delaware acted on the research of Hoxby and Turner to encourage low-income students to attend top-level universities. According to media reports, the program was a great success and increased the attendance rate of under-matched students to 98 percent (Leonhardt, 2014).

Interestingly, the under-matching problem does not seem to apply to high-achieving students alone. Goodman, Hurwitz and Smith (2015) conducted a study on degree completion rates at public colleges in the state of Georgia. Looking at students who graduated from high school from 2004 to 2007, they found that even lower-ability students (as measured by SAT test scores) were much less likely to complete a bachelor's degree if they first enrolled at a public two-year college. The positive effect of initially enrolling in a four-year college was particularly strong for low-income students who benefited from strong peer effects. Community colleges did benefit those who might not have gone to college at all, but it hurt those who could have enrolled in a four-year college. This unintended negative consequence would seem to apply to any policy that diverts students from four- to two-year colleges.

Proposals to correct the under-matching problem for high achievers are bound to gain support in the near future. No matter what one's political persuasion, it would be difficult to argue that low-income, high achievers should not be encouraged to attend more selective colleges. Few of these students now attend community colleges, so the impact on enrollment should be minimal in most areas. But the ethics of offering special scholarships to recruit these students or hold on to them in community colleges are subject to question.

Perhaps it is too much to expect that a community college finding these students in its entering pool will assist them in moving along as quickly as possible, or for highly selective institutions to actively pursue community college transfer students. Yet the occasional linkages forged between two-year and elite four-year institutions such as programs developed by Amherst College (n.d.) and Cornell University ("Cornell Transfer Program," 2008), suggest that initiatives facilitating transfer are possible. Beyond this, it appears that lower-ability students respond proactively to high academic standards—a factor that should encourage community college instructors to challenge students as much as possible in their classrooms.

## Performance-Based Student Aid

Pell grants and federally supported student loans target access, not student success. But political support for performance-based funding (PBF) for colleges has spilled over into the student financial aid arena and is bound to influence federal and state public policy in the coming years. Although not a new idea and not widely in place as yet, the strategy of using scholarships as an incentive for improving academic performance is gaining attention.

As the last chapter suggested, paying colleges for performance can produce mixed results. When it comes to paying individuals rather than organizations for positive outcomes, experience within the private sector also shows mixed results. The same undoubtedly holds for college students. In both cases, PBF systems can provide individuals with incentives that produce favorable outcomes, but only under the right conditions.

An example of a PBF scheme aimed at individuals within higher education can be seen in the high compensation packages received by Division 1 coaches, whose jobs and salaries are linked to winning performance. Beyond that, some university presidents are subject to PBF standards. Weisbrod, Ballou, and Asch (2008) discuss the performance bonuses and incentives provided for one of every six presidents at large public universities. They conclude that some performance bonuses based on easily measurable outcomes, such as graduation or retention rates, might be "counterproductive for presidents, encouraging them to disregard hard-to-measure elements of a school's overall mission" (p. 261).

What about students? We want them to perform well in college, lead happy and productive lives, and become good citizens. We know that positive outcomes are less likely to occur among lower-income students, many of whom have a loose attachment to higher education because of their life experience. Offering these students a monetary reward for keeping their grade point average (GPA) up or enrolling full time should provide an incentive to study more, to persist, and to move toward their degree and other goals. Over the long run, we would expect that this would, on average, produce better job prospects and higher lifetime incomes along with the other positive outcomes.

But when we start anticipating the unintended effects of performance-based student aid, it becomes clear that several factors need to be recognized and monitored. For instance, students might be encouraged to take easier courses

in order to comply with benchmark goals such as minimum GPA requirements associated with grants. They might withdraw from certain courses
or change majors to improve their academic record, actions that would not
always be in the student's best interest. If performance-based scholarships are
employed, care must be taken—as in the case of PBF funding schemes for
colleges—to assure that no harm is done.

## Linking Financial Aid to Institutional Performance

In August 2013, President Obama put forth ideas on how the federal government could make college affordable and accountable (Jaschik, 2013). Under
the plan, parts of which will require Congressional approval, colleges would
be rated according to access (number of students with Pell grants), cost,
graduation rates, transfer rates, and the earnings of the graduates. Enhanced
data on these metrics would be added to the existing U.S. Department of Education's College Scorecard—an online database that provides basic information on individual college prices, graduation rates, loan default rates, median
earnings and employment.

An early version of the Administration's plan also contained proposals for
tying financial aid to academic progress and enabling students to cap their
federal loan repayments to 10 percent of their income. Under one of the more
controversial aspects of the plan, students who attend highly ranked colleges
would receive higher Pell grants and more favorable loan rates, and colleges
that enroll more lower-income students would be given bonuses.

But community college advocates, who are generally leery of any attempts
to rank colleges because their missions are so diverse, also fear that if existing
Pell funds are diverted to goals other than access, it will negatively impact
opportunities for lower-income students. Clearly, Pell grants should be
reserved for the goal of access for low-income students and attempts to divert
Pell funds for other purposes should be resisted.

All of these plans are political initiatives and subject to significant change
over time. Some, such as tying the rating system to mandatory accountability
measures, will require political action and Congressional support. It is clear
that at least some of the change proposals directed at the political system are
influenced by research that shows what works, including the proposal that
loan repayment rates be capped at 10 percent of income.

## What the Research Shows

A vast amount of research has been conducted on how effectively financial
aid policies work. The overwhelming evidence from the research is that
grants, such as Pell and other need-based aid, expand access to college and

increase persistence, especially among two-year college students (Rouse, 1994). This finding is supported by recent Type-3 analyses of financial aid policies.

A study by Castleman and Long (2013) showed that need-based grants, beyond Pell, not only increased access to college but also had a positive impact on persistence, credits completed, and degree completion for students seeking a bachelor's degree at four-year public colleges in Florida. Additional research, including Type-3 studies of community college students, provide further evidence.

**Louisiana study**. In 2004–2005 a study completed by MDRC at three community colleges in Louisiana involving approximately 1,000 students found a strong relationship between the availability of performance-based financial aid and student outcomes. Roughly half of the participating students were assigned to a treatment group (they were given performance-based scholarships in addition to whatever other aid they may have received), while the other half acted as a control group (they were also on aid but received no additional help).

Assignments were random but the population had eligibility requirements. The targeted groups of students were low-income first-time students, eighteen to thirty-four years old, who were also parents and willing to attend school at least half time. These eligibility requirements meant that students in the study were mostly female and poor, and were "generally more likely to possess characteristics that are associated with an increased risk of failing to complete a degree than the typical community college student in Louisiana or the nation" (Barrow et al., 2014, p. 574).

None of the students in the study had their Pell or other need-based aid reduced because of participation in this experiment. The students in the treatment group were given an additional $1,000 scholarship for two semesters if they maintained at least a C average. They were also given additional counseling services by the college. Partial payments were made as certain benchmarks were reached during each semester over a two-year period. Students reported using the additional money, which was paid directly to them rather than the college, to pay for books and supplies, and to pay for household expenses including child care.

Controlling for a number of characteristics, the results were promising. College transcript data and data from the National Student Clearinghouse showed that students in the treatment group completed nearly 40 percent more credits than the control group over a two-year period and showed evidence of increased effort toward improving academic performance. Little evidence was found that students changed courses or majors to game the system. This preliminary evidence indicates that "the benefits of performance-based financial aid programs in terms of academic performance and increased future income . . . seem to outweigh the cost of providing the scholarship" (p. 592).

**Six-state study.** Following up on the Louisiana study, MDRC designed an experimental study in six states—Ohio, New Mexico, New York, California, Arizona, and Florida—to investigate the effect of performance-based scholarships. In this study, the scholarship amounts and duration, as well as the academic benchmarks and additional counseling help given to students in the target population, were varied to capture differences that were not studied in Louisiana analysis. The results suggest that, at least in the short term, "performance-based scholarships can move the dial on some important markers of academic success" for low-income students (Patel & Richburg-Hayes, 2012, p. 8).

The results of the six-state study are modest, but they do provide some evidence that performance-based scholarships supplementing traditional need-based aid can have a positive effect on student outcomes. The longer-term impacts on outcomes such as graduation rates and income will have to await further study. The results of these studies have lent a good deal of credibility to the argument that financial aid with strings attached can produce positive outcomes.

**Lessons learned.** Dynarski and Scott-Clayton (2013) have provided a non-technical survey of the type of research mentioned above and summarized the lessons learned as follows:

1. Money, especially in the form of grants, increases college access and possibly persistence and completion.
2. Program complexity, such as the complex FAFSA form required of Pell applicants, undermines aid effectiveness and limits low-income student enrollments.
3. Performance-based incentives and aid "with strings attached" (p. 86), appear to augment effectiveness and improve short-term outcomes.
4. "Evidence on the effect of student loans [on access and outcomes]" (p. 83) is limited but appears to be mixed.

In many ways the success of the Pell program has set the stage for vouchers and grants given directly to students that can be carried to the colleges in which they enroll. Governments like the idea of vouchers because they allow greater student choice. And vouchers have a history of generating successful outcomes. One only needs to consider the impact of the GI Bill after World War II to understand what vouchers can do. Other voucher systems such as those that support charter schools are more controversial and will require more time for evaluation. The idea of using different types of vouchers for higher education will be discussed later in this chapter.

## TUITION PROPOSALS

Emerging policy debates will of necessity need to factor in tuition, which has become the fastest growing source of revenue for community colleges. Some policy makers have recently promoted initiatives to reduce net tuition to zero for the purpose of attracting greater numbers of students. These proposals are often couched in the rhetoric of "free tuition," invoking a low- or no-tuition policy that community college advocates of the post–World War II era cherished, but that Lombardi (1976) declared a "lost cause" by the 1970s (p. 1). Other proposals involve the creation of differential tuition in which colleges charge different rates per credit hour across academic and vocational fields depending on program cost.

### The "Free" Tuition Movement

The "free" tuition movement at community colleges has captured media attention, after being referenced in President Obama's State of the Union message in 2015 (Fain, 2015a). The president's proposal was not fully developed at the time of this writing, but it follows the lead of the program at Tulsa Community College, and more widely known programs in Tennessee and Chicago. As described by Fain (2014a) and Kelchen (2014), the Tennessee Promise Program and Chicago's Star Scholarship program are really "last-dollar" scholarship programs for high school graduates designed to cover tuition and fees after federal and state aid have been applied.

The Tennessee plan offers all high school graduates a tuition and fee waiver at a state community college if they enroll full time, apply for financial aid through FAFSA, maintain a 2.0 GPA, and complete eight hours of community service. Students are also provided with volunteer mentors and an on-campus orientation program. The program has widespread support with 35,000 applicants in the first two months of implementation, exceeding the 20,000 applicants that were expected to sign up. Because all students are eligible, some critics claim that it will benefit primarily middle- and upper-income students. To the extent that it diverts students from four-year colleges, it could reduce completion rates.

The Chicago program is directed at lower-income students. To become eligible, students must enroll full time and apply for Pell and other need-based grants. This program also has merit-based provisions as it eliminates students who require remedial work. It requires students to maintain a 3.0 high school

GPA. These provisions effectively restrict the number of students who will qualify for scholarships because 94 percent of Chicago public school graduates require remediation. Of course, the hope is that the prospect of a scholarship will encourage high school students to work harder in order to meet the remediation and GPA requirements.

In both the Tennessee and the Chicago plans, most low-income students who would qualify for last-dollar scholarships are already eligible for "free" tuition based on Pell and state need-based aid. In Chicago, for instance, 85 percent of low-income students have their full costs covered by Pell grants (Kelchen, 2014).

A few new students will benefit, but the cost of administering the programs is unknown. While community colleges have welcomed free tuition programs, they need to be vigilant about fine-print details. One positive effect of the "free tuition" movement however, is that media attention will encourage more students to apply to community colleges and increase awareness of the availability of financial aid to pay for college. Promising a zero sticker price at least puts the word "free" upfront.

The "messaging power of free" (Baum & Scott-Clayton, 2015, para. 1) is dramatically illustrated in the Obama proposal, which is a welcome addition to public policy, but has little chance of getting through Congress. Unlike the existing Tennessee and Chicago programs, it is not a last-dollar payment, but covers tuition and fees for most students enrolling in community colleges, leaving Pell and other grants to pick up additional costs.

The generosity of the program also leads to its high estimated operating cost of $60 billion over a ten-year period (Fain, 2015c). It would require the states to pick up 25 percent of the cost and would increasingly federalize the funding of community colleges. Students would need to maintain a 2.5 GPA, have an adjusted gross income below $200,000 and be able to show progress toward a degree (Fain, 2015a).

Research support for the "free" tuition movement has been provided by Goldrick-Rab and her colleagues who propose that high school graduates be provided a "free" education for the first two years at public two- and four-year colleges (Goldrick-Rab & Kendall, 2014; Goldrick-Rab, Schudde & Stampen, 2015). This would be accomplished largely through government subsidies to institutions, which would be held accountable for justifying costs and provided with incentives to enroll low-income students.

The Goldrick-Rab proposal eliminates student tuition payments and allows low-income students to bypass the onerous application process for need-based financial aid. It also covers living expenses through stipends, "guaranteed employment at a living wage," and "unsubsidized, dischargeable loans of a small amount . . . available for those who need them" (Goldrick-Rab & Kendall, 2014, p. 19).

Goldrick-Rab and her colleagues provide a strong argument for making the first two years of college "free," arguing that current financial aid policies do not reach all who are eligible; do not cover the total costs borne by many of the students; and do not hold institutions accountable for containing costs, increasing completion rates, and improving quality. They also point to the simplicity of their proposal, arguing that "the messaging involved in means-tested programs is inherently divisive and more difficult to communicate when compared to the wide-spread and consistent messages that can be conveyed with universal programs" (Goldrick-Rab & Kendall, 2014, p. 18).

Our basic objection to most of the "free tuition" proposals, especially the one put forth by President Obama, is that students who don't need the money are the most likely to benefit, and the promise of "free tuition" is likely to distort student choice and divert some from their preferred four-year degree programs. In addition, it is not clear that the Obama proposal will increase college revenues, though it will certainly make more demands on individual colleges for accountability. Free tuition will not increase completion rates. We repeat our argument that targeting funds to lower-income students and expanding underfunded support programs that promote student success are more important uses of any new federal funds.

## Oregon "Pay-it-Forward" Proposal

Among other proposals that have attracted media attention is the Oregon "Pay-It-Forward" plan, which calls for the elimination of up-front tuition and fees for students, using state loans to cover these costs for undergraduates regardless of income. The loans would be repaid by requiring students to pay up to 3 percent of their future income to the state (with a cap of 24 years). Unlike the "free tuition" plans described above, this is essentially an income-contingent repayment plan extended to in-state students and is similar to initiatives in Washington and California that were never enacted and to a plan at Yale University that was used but abandoned in the 1970s (Kiley, 2013).

The Oregon plan has been widely criticized as unworkable and as a possible way for the state to shift more of the cost of higher education to students and parents. Critics caution that students who earn high incomes after graduation will not like the idea of paying back more than their share of the loans (they could borrow for less under existing plans) and that the state would have to come up with a substantial sum of cash to start the program.

In addition, the difficulty of collecting the loans would require the participation of the Internal Revenue Service, which seems unlikely. This is not to say that income-contingent loans are a bad idea; on the contrary, they are a good idea. But they would need to be implemented at the federal level and they should not be a mandatory form of aid for all students.

## Differential Tuition

It costs colleges more to educate a nursing student than it does a history major. Undergraduates also cost less than graduate students, and lower-division undergraduates help finance the education of more expensive students. While cross-subsidies within college programs are an accepted part of financing higher education, high-cost programs are increasingly scrutinized in an environment where resources are tight. When high-cost programs produce students who are in high demand, colleges might move to bring the cost of those programs down or, alternatively, charge tuition that is closer to cost. While "one price fits all" is a long-standing tradition in setting tuition levels, many universities and some community colleges have sought to increase revenue by charging differential tuition.

For example, it is now common practice for four-year colleges to charge more for upper-division courses and for high-cost programs such as engineering, business, and nursing. A 2011 survey conducted by Cornell University found that 41 percent of public doctoral-level universities used differential undergraduate tuition rates to increase revenue (Ehrenberg, 2012). But students are somewhat sensitive to price.

Stange (2013) examined the impact of differential tuition on student choice of undergraduate majors at 142 public research universities and found that higher pricing had a negative impact on the number of students graduating in engineering and, to a smaller extent, in business, but not in nursing. Women and minorities were among the most impacted student groups. These negative impacts on enrollment were not remedied by the additional aid given to these students.

While a detailed study of this nature has not been conducted at the community college level, we know that the lower-income and minority students that community colleges attract are more price sensitive than the students in Stange's study. That does not mean that a differential tuition policy would not increase college revenue. Demand is still inelastic even at the community college level, so revenue would go up as long as enrollment did not decline proportionally. But it is likely that those students who are more price sensitive or less committed to a particular curriculum will be discouraged by higher pricing. Differential tuition can increase college revenue, but it will come at a price.

In community colleges, the four most frequently cited examples of colleges that use differential tuition are Aims Community College in Colorado, Pima

Community College in Arizona, Lone Star College System near Houston, Texas, and Bristol Community College in Massachusetts.

**Aims Community College.** In 2009, Aims set different tuition rates for high-cost programs in three tiers. For the Fall 2013 and Spring 2014 semesters, the standard tuition per credit hour was $67.36 for in-district residents, but separate tuition rates were set for programs in higher-cost fields. The first-level differential was for programs like communications media and fire science at $118.45; the second level was for programs like surgical technology at $123.60; and the third and highest was for programs like aviation, radiologic technology, and nursing at $128.75 (Aims Community College, n.d.).

Tuition rates for the highest differential programs were almost twice the standard tuition rate at the college and did not include additional lab fees associated with some of the programs. According to the budget director at Aims (quoted in Moltz, 2010, para. 19), "we do an analysis of program costs each year" and base the differential tuition rates on that analysis. Student demand for programs and employment prospects for graduates in higher-wage jobs were major considerations in setting differential tuition rates.

It is notable that Aims is one of two community colleges in Colorado that is not a part of the statewide community college system. It has its own local governing board, which probably provides the college with greater discretion in fiscal management. Not all community colleges have that discretion. A study completed by the University of Alabama's Education Policy Center showed that local boards determine tuition rates in only twenty-one states. As the Center's director, Steve Katsinas, has pointed out, colleges in these states are more likely to have the freedom to charge differential tuition rates (Moltz, 2010).

**Pima Community College.** Arizona, where Pima Community College is located, is one of the states in which local boards set tuition rates. The idea of differential tuition was introduced to the Pima governing board in 2010. High-cost programs were designated to carry a 10–30 percent additional charge. The idea was not immediately accepted, but for the Spring 2012 semester the board agreed to a plan in which courses costing at least twice as much as the median course cost for at least two consecutive years qualified for differential tuition.

Tuition differential A is for those courses that cost between two and four times the average. For those courses, a 30 percent fee was added. For the differential B category, where courses cost more than four times the median, a 40 percent premium was added. Officials at the college consider the program a success, generating an additional $200,000 in revenue in 2012–2013 ("Differential Tuition," 2013).

Pima's website explains why differential rates are needed, noting that "some courses . . . are more costly for the College to offer" because of "class size requirements of accrediting agencies, or expensive equipment that must be regularly updated to meet industry standards" (Pima Community College, n.d., para. 1). The College website currently lists fourteen programs in the tuition differential A category and seven in the tuition B category. Course costs and tuition rates are evaluated each year.

**Lone Star System**. The Lone Star College system near Houston has instituted an extensive differential tuition system (Fain, 2012a). Regular in-state tuition for a three-credit course in 2013–2014 was $200. Additional tuition for 23 high-cost programs ranged from a low of $3 per credit hour for agriculture to a high of $12 per credit hour for dental hygiene and two other high-cost programs. These are modest increases for relatively expensive programs.

**Bristol Community College**. Efforts to institute differential tuition at Bristol Community College in Massachusetts ran into a political backlash (Fain, 2012b). Initially college trustees implemented a higher tuition charge for popular eHealth programs, which featured online and hybrid degrees and certificates. Tuition for the program was increased to $246 per credit hour, compared to $166 per credit hour for other programs. Revenue increased, but constituents lobbied against it based on a belief that students should not pay different prices for the same degree they could get through regular classroom instruction.

Differential tuition was eliminated as of the Fall 2012 semester. In its place, trustees approved a $50 extra fee for high-cost nursing and dental hygiene programs. At Bristol, the political cost of implementing differential tuition was judged to be too high in comparison to the revenues such a policy would yield.

**Other proposals**. A host of other proposals for differential tuition have made the news in recent years. Most pertain to problems in particular states that are unlikely to be repeated elsewhere. An example is the two-tiered tuition proposal for the California community colleges, which emerged in 2012 when Santa Monica College tried to charge a higher tuition for over-enrolled general education courses like English and math as a way of circumventing state regulations favoring low tuition.

Advocates argued that thousands of students were being driven into for-profit colleges for over-enrolled courses and that the principle of low tuition had diminished access. Critics felt that the policy would favor higher-income students and violate the philosophy of open access and fairness (Fain, 2012b,

2013b, 2013c). In stark contrast to the use of differential tuition for high-cost programs, Santa Monica College wanted to use it for low-cost but high-demand courses, arguing that California's revenue problems would be solved by allowing colleges to raise tuition and keep the revenue.

Differential tuition is a policy that is likely to receive considerable attention in community colleges. In some instances it will be used as leverage to increase state appropriations, and in other instances it will be used as leverage to cut high-cost programs. For differential tuition policies to work, governing boards must have the ability to set tuition rates and colleges must be able to retain tuition revenue. Colleges will have little incentive to charge differential tuition if tuition revenue moves directly into state coffers.

## ENROLLMENT MANAGEMENT

Enrollment management is the "process that brings together often disparate functions having to do with recruiting, funding, tracking, retaining, and replacing students as they move toward, within, and away from institutions" (Kurz & Scannell, 2006; Roots and Purpose section, para 5). As community colleges become more tuition dependent, and assuming that they get to keep tuition revenue, failure to meet enrollment targets can result in budget cuts. This prospect fits best for many colleges in the midwest and east that face population declines and reductions in the number of students graduating from local high schools.

The literature on enrollment management is vast, and since most colleges are familiar with enrollment management models we will not repeat them here. One promising idea that is just beginning to receive attention, however, involves a city in upstate New York that has two public colleges, one a highly selective research university, the other a community college (Foderaro, 2011).

The community college needs students and the four-year college, which rejects over 60 percent of its applicants, would like to replace students that leave the college after the first year in an effortless, low-cost manner. In the first year of the program the university took a group of 600 applicants who had been rejected for the fall semester and sent them a letter promising guaranteed admission if they first attended the community college for a year or two and maintained a 3.0 GPA. This extends the transfer agreements that are typically in place at most community colleges. It is a profitable arrangement for both institutions and has the added advantage of protecting the university's standing in the ratings game by admitting students with lower entry scores in this way.

Students in the deferred admissions program are guaranteed housing at the university while they attend the community college. Paperwork and payments are administered jointly. The students pay the lower tuition rate at the community college, but are assessed a $2,500 fee by the university for the "privilege" of participating in the program. Meals and transportation are arranged, and students are made to feel a part of the university environment while enrolled at the community college.

The first class of forty students enrolled in the program in the Fall 2011 semester. The number has increased to over 200 students for the Fall 2014 semester. Using the National Student Clearinghouse to track the first cohort of students, researchers found that thirty-nine of the forty students enrolled in Fall 2011 returned to the community college the following Spring semester, and thirty-one had been "picked up" by the university after one year of study at the community college.

Most of the remaining students had transferred to other four-year colleges (personal communication with authors, June 2014). The program appears to be a win-win for both colleges, but whether it benefits students is an open question. Clearly students have other options. It is too early to tell if enrollment in the program delays degree attainment, raises the cost of a bachelor's degree, or diverts students to less or more desirable occupations.

## VOUCHERS

The use of school vouchers in the United States in primary and secondary education is a politically charged issue that has received considerable attention. Research studies and political opinions written on student choice and charter schools at the K-12 level are in stark contrast to the limited literature on the applicability of voucher systems to higher education. Nevertheless, some of the ideas from the theory and practice of applying vouchers to compulsory education have carried over to the postsecondary sector where efficiency is a greater concern than student choice. These ideas have made their way into the political arena and could affect the way community colleges are funded in the future.

### History and Politics

Vouchers have a long history. West (1997) traced the idea back to Tom Paine's *Rights of Man,* but in modern times the idea is associated with free market economist Milton Friedman (1962). Although vouchers usually find their greatest support from the political right as a means of increasing choice and therefore freedom, this is not always the case. The system has also found support from the political left for the purpose of expanding equality of opportunity (Jencks, 1970). For Jencks, vouchers would have strings attached so that the scale is tilted in favor of the less advantaged. More recently, Harbour and Jaquette (2007) have argued that a voucher system, as they define it, can help advance the equity agenda of community colleges.

It is clear that student vouchers and the form that they take are strongly influenced by politics. This is well illustrated by the current debate in the United States over the vouchers in K-12 education. Proponents of vouchers are motivated by what they see as the failure of public schools, which they attributed, in large part, to teachers' unions, politicized local school boards, and the lack of parental role models for children.

In postsecondary education, the focus is different—vouchers are seen as a way of reining in costs by promoting competition among colleges. Vouchers could be used to replace state appropriations as a method of privatizing higher education. Some free market advocates view subsidies going directly to students as a means of increasing student choice. This would be true if a voucher could be carried to either a public or a private college and carried out of state. The Pell grant can be seen as fulfilling important elements of the voucher system, but it is a targeted form of aid directed at low-income students. Likewise vouchers are targeted to veterans and other groups that governments identify as deserving of a subsidy. Which groups and interests will be favored in the future is a matter that is sorted out through the political process.

## Advantages and Disadvantages

Among the advantages of vouchers in higher education touted by proponents are increased competition among suppliers, increased efficiency (lower costs), and improved quality. Vouchers, it is argued, would give students greater freedom of choice, and colleges would become more responsive to consumer demand. Colleges that provide more value for the money would be rewarded; those that do not would be motivated to change or go out of business.

Disadvantages, according to critics, center around the possible adverse impact of vouchers on lower-income groups, increased segregation of students by income and race, and limited information consumers have to make rational choices. Realistically, competition is difficult to achieve since many community college students are place-bound and would have few choices even with a pure voucher system. This would change if students were free to take widespread advantage of distance education. But, as noted in chapter 4, there are lingering concerns that many students may not do as well in online courses as they would do in face-to-face courses.

## Types of Voucher Systems

Governments provide subsidies to public two-year and four-year college students by allocating money directly to institutions through budget appropriations. Another approach is to channel money to colleges through students by way of a voucher. This could be accomplished though appropriations to a college for each full-time-equivalent student who enrolls in the college. This is a producer-side or supply-side voucher that goes directly to the college. Students are not aware that they are receiving this subsidy, as the sticker price (tuition) does not reflect the total value of the voucher. In fact, voucher funding linked to enrollment is not usually referred to as a voucher, but is more often referred to as a state subsidy or stipend paid to the college.

Another type of voucher is labeled a demand-side or consumer voucher. Here the student is aware of the state subsidy, as the college's sticker price (tuition) will capture the value of the voucher. In this case, states may provide in-state students with a voucher that they will come to see as an entitlement. Because, at least theoretically, this type of voucher puts money directly into the hands, or at least under the control, of the student, it is referred to as a consumer subsidy and becomes analogous to consumer spending on a good or service.

The value of either the supply- or demand-side voucher is determined by the government, but in either case money follows the student. Whatever form vouchers take, there is general agreement that an approved list of colleges or eligible institutions would be an important part of the quality control of any voucher system.

## Pure Voucher Systems

As we have stated, a voucher may be defined broadly to include a subsidy based on enrollment, or it may be defined narrowly to exclude supply-side subsidies allocated directly to colleges even if they are based on enrollment. Were we to define state vouchers broadly as payments from the public sector that follow student enrollment, then many states, such as New York, could be said to employ a voucher approach in financing their community colleges. For our purposes, however, we will follow Jongblod and Koelman (2000) and define a pure voucher system as a payment that is demand-side in approach excluding state payments or appropriations that go directly to institutions irrespective of enrollment.

What would a pure voucher system look like? For purposes of illustration we will define a pure voucher system as one where all state appropriations to higher education are eliminated. This would likely be restricted to undergraduate education since graduate education and research need not be funded in the same way. All operating budgets would be funded through demand- (consumer-) centered vouchers given to all students regardless of income. Vouchers would be completely portable between public and private providers as long as they were on the approved list of providers.

Furthermore, at the extreme, vouchers would be portable between states, which means that they would need to be federal in nature. Such a system would effectively privatize all of public higher education. A national voucher system would be easier to implement and administer in countries that, unlike the United States, have a centralized college system.

Under a pure voucher system, providers may or may not have freedom to set tuition and fees, but the government would be under no obligation to increase the size of the voucher to correspond to provider fees. A publicly-funded, non-means-tested grant would be a windfall for middle- and upper-income students. Although such systems have been discussed, no state or country has implemented a pure voucher system. However, some of the elements of such a system, along with the intended advantages, are woven into current and proposed financing systems.

After reviewing the case for and against voucher systems in higher education, Jongblod and Koelman (2000) concluded that it was "difficult to formulate a conclusion on the relevance of vouchers in general . . . [and that their effects] will depend on the characteristics of the scheme" (p.13). While this is certainly true, it is clear that voucher systems in higher education will continue to attract the attention of policy makers at the state level, especially during periods of economic stagnation and tight budgets. All of the proposals made to date would fit under the heading of supply-side vouchers.

One example comes from Pennsylvania, where the governor has announced support for the idea of funding higher education with vouchers. However, the program that has attracted the most national attention is the voucher system enacted in Colorado in 2005.

## Vouchers in Colorado

The passage of the 2004 legislation that created the Colorado voucher system (College Opportunity Fund, or COF) was widely touted as revolutionizing higher education funding and hailed by the governor as "a new day for higher education in America" (quoted in Strayer, 2004, p. 29). Advocates advanced market-based arguments favoring vouchers as a means for increasing student choice and squeezing inefficiencies out of the system. It was, in fact, nothing close to the pure voucher system described above, but did contain some of the elements of a demand-side voucher system.

The COF was designed to replace direct state appropriations to two- and four-year public colleges that were based on the prior year's allocation, with an adjustment for inflation and enrollment growth. While the ideology of greater choice and improved efficiency was part of the debate surrounding enactment of the system, its main purpose was to circumvent a voter-mandated change in the state's constitution called the Taxpayer's Bill of Rights (TABOR). Passed in 1992, TABOR limited growth in state revenues and spending and tuition revenue, counted as state revenue, was subject to the same limitation.

Under COF, a separate state agency (trust) was set up to transfer money from the state to a student's college of choice. Students never actually touched the money, but the process was designed to inform the students, up front, that the value of their voucher was subsidizing at least part of their education. The value of the voucher was proposed to be $4,400 per year for a full-time, in-state undergraduate student, but was reduced to $2,400 by the time of implementation in the Fall of 2005.

Students receiving Pell grants at three private in-state colleges were eligible for one half of that amount. The expectation was that colleges would raise tuition by the amount of the state voucher, thus allowing them to capture the full value of the voucher. In fact, most colleges—starved for revenue for a number of years by TABOR—raised tuition by an amount greater than the value of the voucher, thereby increasing the out-of-pocket cost to students in the face of the political promise that college costs would fall or remain stable.

In 2008, Colorado commissioned the Western Interstate Commission for Higher Education (WICHE, 2008) to evaluate the voucher system. The WICHE report showed that the voucher system was successful in enabling public colleges to bypass the revenue restrictions of TABOR, but in most other respects was a failure. It decreased rather than increased the participation of low-income and minority students. It reduced overall college enrollments, with community colleges taking the greatest hit (enrollments fell by 5 percent in the first year under the voucher system and by 9 percent the next year).

Students, especially in community colleges, were confused by the system and found that costs were rising instead of falling. Colleges were faced with increased administrative costs, and systems set up to change college behavior, in terms of student recruitment and cost efficiencies, did not work. In the final analysis, the WICHE report described the voucher plan as one "that undermined the principles of good government by creating a Rube Goldberg-like state higher education financing structure" that created bureaucratic inefficiencies and left the colleges with the same amount of money they would have received if the voucher system had not been implemented (Prescott, 2010, p. 9).

In spite of problems highlighted in its report, WICHE argued that the Colorado experiment did not provide a fair test for student vouchers as an alternative way of financing higher education. Preparation and implementation were flawed, and the system was not designed effectively to encourage positive educational outcomes. Writing about the WICHE report, Prescott (2010) noted that "a truer test of vouchers . . . awaits a state to implement them in a way that preserves the market-oriented incentives that champions of vouchers generally attribute to them" (p. 25).

In short, the idea of vouchers is on the table, driven in part by ideology and waiting to be picked up by others who resonate with the idea of greater student choice at lower cost. For the time being, ideological arguments might be expected to carry greater weight in subsequent battles over voucher systems, because the Colorado program has yet to be rigorously evaluated by scholars; Harbour, Davies, and Lewis (2006) lay out relevant research questions that might be pursued.

While we do not see, or support, the implementation of anything approaching a pure voucher system in the United States that would, in the words of the 2008 WICHE report, "provide a truer test of vouchers," we do see the use of supply-side vouchers as a growing trend. Fewer and fewer community colleges will be funded directly through state appropriations. Vouchers are likely to take the form of state stipends that follow the student. Supply-side vouchers as a way of funding community colleges are not undesirable, but in order for them to work, colleges will need to gain greater control over operating revenue and how it is spent.

Demand-side vouchers, on the other hand, are more likely to be used in workforce development. State and federal money could be allocated directly to the student to use at an institution of his or her choice. A set of rules designed to increase student choice at reduced public cost might be established to encourage industries to provide skill training (while capturing voucher revenue) and increase the number of workers with skills in short supply. This would increase competition for community colleges in noncredit workforce development and potentially reduce the role that they play in this market. Colleges might be contracted to assist in workforce training but at a reduced rate of compensation over what they now enjoy.

## Voucher Systems Worldwide

No other country has tried to implement a pure voucher system as defined above. Versions of a modified program can be found in Denmark, Sweden, Hong Kong, and the United Kingdom, and most European systems of higher education have directed more and more money to students and away from institutions themselves.

Jaquette (2009) describes a voucher-like program in England and Wales that applies to Colleges of Further Education (the rough equivalent of U.S. community colleges). However, the most comprehensive proposal for a nationwide voucher system for higher education was put forth in Australia. The Australian plan is widely cited and mined for ideas worldwide.

In 1997, the conservative government in Australia commissioned a study of the country's financing of higher education. The resulting report, commonly known as the West Report (West, 1998), recommended that student-centered, market-based forces replace government control and financing of postsecondary education. In the face of widespread criticism, the report's recommendations were never implemented, but its underlying ideas provided a political base for future reform.

Among the recommendations in the West Report was: (a) a national student voucher, designed to act as a lifetime individual entitlement of public funding for postsecondary education which could be used at any college; (b) freedom for colleges to charge whatever additional fees they liked; and (c) access to deferred payment loans which would cover the cost of attendance (Johnstone & Marcucci, 2010, provide a comprehensive discussion of higher education funding systems worldwide).

In the United States, both federal and state governments have been moving in the direction of channeling a greater proportion of higher education subsidies through students. This trend will likely continue. Voucher systems are one of the paths that state allocations to community colleges could take; certainly not in the pure form as we have defined them, but in a modified form that allows money to follow students and puts pressure on colleges to satisfy student consumers of their services.

## WHAT DOES A DEGREE COST?

Although this chapter has focused on initiatives that could affect revenues, new developments in the management of expenditures (costs) are equally important. Indeed, it is often said that one of the most important sources of revenue for colleges can be found within their own budgets. This means that colleges will seek to improve efficiency and continuously reevaluate existing programs from both sides of the budget. A careful analysis of program revenues and costs will assist managers in reallocating resources to better achieve institutional goals and increase efficiency.

Harris and Goldrick-Rab (2010) have completed an interesting study of the cost-effectiveness of various strategies used by community colleges to improve student success. They have shown that some strategies are more cost-effective than others and that failure to use cost-effective methods has constrained colleges from achieving their productivity potential.

Knowing what a degree costs is an important starting point in efforts to correct this shortcoming. Producers of any good or service need to know the cost of what they are producing. Colleges are producers of important services that have both private and social benefits. Yet, few colleges calculate the cost of what they produce. Most have a crude estimate of what degrees cost; when they want precise figures they hire an outside agency to do it. However, these agencies are expensive and often provide a one-shot look at degree costs.

It would be better and more cost-effective over the long run, for colleges to develop an internal system for calculating the cost of degrees, which can be updated periodically. Even though community colleges might argue that degrees and other credentials are not their most important product, they are a product on which constituents measure college performance.

An early attempt to measure the cost of degrees at the community college level was completed by Romano, Losinger, and Millard (2011).[2] This is a case illustration of an actual institution called, for the purposes of this study, Upstate Community College, and follows a method suggested by Johnson (2009) in a white paper produced for the Delta Cost Project. Johnson's degree cost study was directed at state systems and used state-level data from Florida and Illinois. He did not include community colleges in the study, but did provide the necessary methodology and insights for doing so. What follows is a brief overview of the process and results of this case study.

### Direct Instructional Costs Per Credit Hour

Calculating the cost of a degree begins by determining the direct instructional cost per credit hour for all campus departments. In this analysis, "departments" are defined loosely to include discipline or program areas required for degrees. Thus the "math department" is designated as that area that teaches MAT courses, whether or not it constitutes a separate department or offers a degree itself.

To calculate direct instructional costs, all courses taught at the college are allocated to departmental cost centers according to their catalog designator. Courses taught by the English department, for example, include all English, literature, and other courses taught by the department.

If an instructor is shared with another department, only the proportion of personnel expenditures used by English are allocated to that department. If secretaries are shared, proportional costs are allocated to the appropriate cost center. If faculty members have released time for a campus-wide project, that cost is not charged to the department, but is allocated to an institutional support budget line and counted as an indirect cost. All costs are proportioned to the proper cost center, thus departmental costs reflect actual expenditures associated with offering courses taught by a specific department each semester.

Costs per credit hour include all direct instructional costs, which are primarily personnel expenditures—the main driver of degree costs. For 2008–2009, the highest direct instructional departmental cost per credit hour at Upstate was mechanical engineering technology at $475, and the lowest was foreign languages and English as a second language at $72.

Table 6.1 shows the direct costs per credit hour of the five most expensive and the five least expensive departmental cost centers in the case study. These data highlight the relatively high cost of health care and vocational-technical fields. (For a complete list of the departmental costs used in the original study, see Romano et al., 2011).

## Full Costs per Credit Hour

To determine the full (total) degree cost by program, indirect costs (e.g., student support, administration, etc.) are added until all college operating costs are accounted for. Actual expenditures in the case study showed 51.6 percent going for direct instructional costs and 48.4 percent for indirect costs in the 2008–2009 academic year. For all departmental cost centers at Upstate, the average direct instructional cost per credit hour for 2008–2009 was $144. To arrive at full cost, indirect costs were added to the calculation: $29 for academic support, $60 for institutional support, $30 for plant operation and maintenance, and $17 for student services. These costs totaled to an average cost per credit hour of $279 for all direct and indirect costs at the college.

It is important to note that in calculating cost per credit hour, indirect costs are spread proportionally over all departments. This is a short-cut method of allocating indirect costs that is easier to explain and does not materially affect the results. The calculation of cost per credit hour by department takes time and effort. But once a method for doing so is established, it can be modified

Table 6.1    Direct Instructional Cost per Credit Hour for the Five Highest-Cost and Five Lowest-Cost Departments in the Upstate Community College Case Study

| Departments | Cost per credit hour ($) |
|---|---|
| Highest-cost departments | |
| Mechanical Engineering Technology | 475 |
| Dental Hygiene | 454 |
| Radiologic Technology | 440 |
| Electrical Engineering Technology | 371 |
| Civil Engineering Technology | 308 |
| Lowest-cost departments | |
| Psychology and Human Services | 94 |
| English | 87 |
| Human Development | 87 |
| History, Philosophy, and Sociology | 74 |
| Foreign Languages, English as a Second Language, and Speech | 72 |

Note. Source: Romano et al. (2011).

easily each semester or year. Direct instructional costs, for instance, will differ each semester as faculty move between departments, more adjuncts are hired, or release time is adjusted.

## Degree Costs: Catalog and Transcript Methods

Once the cost per credit hour is determined, the cost per degree can be calculated. Johnson (2009) presents interesting alternatives. One calculates degree costs based on catalog requirements. Another method is to base degree costs on the actual transcripts of students completing degrees.

**Catalog method.** This is the easiest way to calculate degree costs and the easiest for the public to understand. The catalog costs of a degree are calculated by looking at the course credit requirement for each degree program and multiplying the credits taken from each department by the instructional (direct) cost per credit hour calculated for that department.

If a dental hygiene degree requires six credits in English, multiply six times the cost per credit hour for the English department, which for Upstate was $87, and continue that process until all courses are accounted for. The dental hygiene curriculum requires 48 credits of dental courses, so the high cost of the courses taught by dental hygiene faculty ($454 per credit hour) makes that degree one of the most expensive at the college. Likewise, courses taught by the mechanical technology faculty would generally only be taken by students pursuing that degree, thus that department's high cost per credit hour by itself would only impact the degree cost of mechanical technology.

Table 6.2 provides an illustration of the degree costs for the 1,073 graduates from Upstate Community College in 2008–2009 using the catalog method. It shows the wide range of costs when degree costs are calculated using the catalog method. The highest-cost program is about four times more expensive than the lowest-cost program. Some high-cost programs are influenced by a high number of credit hours required for the degree. But most of the cost difference between programs is a function of the mix of courses needed for the degree.

The program with the largest number of degree completers, the Liberal Arts Associate of Arts degree, shows a full catalog cost of $12,719, because it includes a larger number of low-cost courses than vocational-technical degree programs. A complete list of the degree costs for the 37 degree and two certificate programs analyzed in the earlier version of this study can be found in Romano et al. (2011).

The catalog method is less accurate than the transcript method in calculating degree costs, because it has little to do with student behavior as they enter college and move toward a degree. For example, only twenty-five of

Table 6.2    Catalog Method: Direct Instructional and Full Cost of an Associate's Degree at Upstate Community College Using 2008–2009 Costs per Credit Hour

|  | Direct instructional cost ($) | Full cost ($) (direct + indirect) |
|---|---|---|
| College-wide average (unweighted)[a] | 10,247 | 19,859 |
| College-wide average (weighted)[a] | 9,576 | 18,558 |
| Program |  |  |
| Highest-cost program | 24,751 | 47,968 |
| Lowest-cost program | 6,102 | 11,826 |

Note. Source: Romano et al. (2011).
[a]Weighted or unweighted by enrollment.

all 2008–2009 Upstate graduates (2.6 percent of the cohort) had taken the exact number of credits prescribed by the catalog. Most had taken more, and a few had taken less than the required number of credits. Tracking the actual course-taking pattern of students in degree programs provides a more accurate measure of the costs of producing a degree.

Upstate found a practical use for the catalog method because it is the easiest number to explain to the public. It is routinely used as part of a fund-raising strategy in seeking local or foundation support for high-cost programs that are valued in the community. In a presentation to the local dental society, for instance, the full catalog costs of the dental hygiene degree ($47,968) were compared with the revenue brought in by the program from student tuition and fees, and state and local sources ($16,626). The deficit of $31,342 per student (or $940,249 for all thirty graduates in 2008–2009) was highlighted to show the dollars that had to be raised to ensure a continuing supply of graduates for the local labor market.

**Transcript method.** This method of calculating degree costs requires the examination of student transcripts so that all of the courses taken by graduates can be accounted for. In all but four cases at Upstate the average cost per degree program for the 2008–2009 graduates—as determined by an analysis of transcripts—was higher than the catalog cost because, on average, students took more credits than required. Transcript credits include all failed, withdrawn, incomplete, repeated, and remedial courses that did not count toward the degree but were supported by college expenditures, minus courses credited toward the degree that were not taken at the college (mainly transfer, advanced placement, and waived courses).

Table 6.3 provides a snapshot of average degree costs for the 2008–2009 graduates in the Upstate case study using the transcript method. It is important to note that the full degree costs presented in the Upstate case study do not account for all college expenditures but only for costs associated with educating students who graduated in 2008–2009.

Table 6.3  Transcript Method: Direct Instructional and Full Cost of an Associate's Degree at Upstate Community College Using 2008–2009 Costs per Credit Hour

|  | Direct instructional cost ($) | Full cost ($) (direct + indirect) |
|---|---|---|
| College-wide average (weighted)[a] | 10,395 | 20,146 |
| Program |  |  |
| Highest-cost program | 25,712 | 49,829 |
| Lowest-cost program | 6,503 | 12,602 |

*Note.* Source: Romano et al. (2011).
[a]Weighted based on the number of graduates in each program in 2008–2009.

Upstate's average full transcript cost of a degree was $20,146 (see Table 6.3). Multiplying that figure by the roughly 1,000 degrees produced in 2008–2009 yields an aggregate cost of $20.2 million. Total college expenditures for 2008–2009 were $42.9 million. The remaining $22.7 million was spent educating students who were still enrolled and might or might not graduate in future years, or who left the college. If 2008–2009 expenditures were divided by the number of graduates, as is sometimes done, an average cost per degree of $39,981 ($42.9 million/1,073 graduates) would be generated in contrast to the $20,146 figure generated by the transcript method.

## Excess Credits

Comparing results of the transcript method with the results of the catalog method provides important insight into student course-taking behavior. The Upstate study showed that, on average, 2008–2009 graduates took 11.6 course credits more than the catalog degree requirements for their degree. The issue of excess credits has come under close examination nationwide because taking more credits than required inflates the cost of obtaining a degree from both the students' and the states' perspective.

This concern was evident, for example, when the Florida state legislature commissioned a study of excess credits in community colleges (Office of Program Policy Analysis and Government Accountability [OPPAGA], 2005). Examining a cohort of 14,015 students in Florida's twenty-eight community colleges who received associate's degrees in 2001–2002, the study determined that "on average students accumulated 21.7 more credit hours than they needed to graduate" (p. 2).[3]

Based on the OPPAGA study, Florida recommended setting a standard of allowing about twelve credit hours over the required amount and charging students a surcharge for excess credits beyond that standard. Florida is in the process of incorporating that standard into its system of performance-based funding. Some states have taken other measures to reduce student costs and to restrict choice.

In New York, for example, the State University trustees passed a resolution that required all of its colleges to reduce their credit hour degree requirements to 126 credits for the baccalaureate degree and 64 credits for the associate degree. The directive contained no direct threat to withdraw funding for excess credits, but the message was clear that colleges should worry more about degree costs in the future. For students, the days of exploring what interests them in college may not be over, but states are not as willing to pay for exploration as they were in the past.

## Capital Costs

In calculating the degree cost of a program, it would be desirable to include a more complete picture of the capital costs per year, per credit hour, or per full-time-equivalent (FTE) student. But calculating the cost of land, buildings, and equipment for each graduate would be difficult (as well as expensive) and is rarely included in studies of this nature.

Winston (1998) has outlined conceptual and practical problems involved in estimating yearly capital costs and has shown that they might typically account for 25–40 percent of the total cost of educating a student at a four-year college. In another study, Vernez, Krop, and Rydell (1999), using the Rand Corporation's Education Simulation Model, estimated that annualized capital costs were about 23 percent of the total cost per FTE student at the California community colleges.

Because the Upstate Community College case study only included expenditures from the operating budget, almost all capital costs were excluded. It must therefore be recognized that the case study underestimates the total cost of a degree, especially in space- and equipment-rich vocational-technical programs and in fine and performing arts departments. In calculating our cost per credit hour, departments that require more equipment such as computers, microscopes, and dental equipment would have higher costs as long as those purchases are included in the operating budget. We recommend against including other capital and space costs in calculating degree costs because of the difficulty involved in calculating them and the political capital that would be expended in explaining them. However, a crude estimate of capital and space costs should be part of decisions involving resource reallocation.

## Warnings and Considerations

All colleges sell their product (services) for less than it costs to produce them and must cover the difference with public- and private-sector subsidies. In chapter 2 we illustrated how lower-division undergraduates typically subsidize more expensive upper-division classes. Data from the Upstate case study show that within a college, the production of different degrees requires cross-subsidies.

For example, at Upstate the most expensive degree cost $49,829, using the full-cost transcript method. But this cost was not covered by public and private revenue brought in by the students enrolled in that program (i.e., by the tuition and fees they paid or by the state and local funding their enrollment generated) and therefore needed to be subsidized by lower-cost programs. Expensive health and technical programs were subsidized by the cash cows in the liberal arts area.

Although knowing the cost of what it produces is important for any college and must be given considerable weight in an environment where resources are scarce, colleges should be cautious when interpreting cost data or making this data public before checking for anomalies or developing logical explanations for high-cost programs.

Lay persons will not understand what the data mean or why cost data vary across programs. It will be important, therefore, for college leaders to frame the data in an appropriate context. When carefully reported, data can help college leaders communicate with constituencies about fiscal decision-making. For example, Dellow and Losinger (2004) have argued that the yearly release of trend data on departmental costs and enrollment helps prepare instructors for resource reallocations that tight budgets generally necessitate.

Another danger in calculating degree costs, and the cross-subsidies and excess credits that are generated, is the focus on a single output produced by a college—degrees. A degree might be a more reasonable outcome measure at the four-year college than at the community college where not all students enter with an associate degree in mind. A criticism of the Upstate Community College case study is that it might devalue other goals that students may be pursuing.

For instance, it would be inaccurate to consider the credits earned by non-graduates, and their associated expenditures, as a total loss. As Kane and Rouse (1999) have shown, community college credits earned by students, short of a degree, also have an economic payoff. Placing a precise dollar value on the non-monetary goals that are part of the mission of community colleges would be an impossible task. In the end, policy makers are forced to make decisions that are based not only on the program costs, but also on imperfect information about the monetary and non-monetary benefits that accrue to students and the community served by the college.

## ACTIVITY-BASED COSTING

Another lesser-known experiment in cost control is activity-based costing (ABC), which has been imported into higher education from the business world (Kaplan & Anderson, 2003) and is a standard part of managerial accounting taught to introductory accounting students. ABC "assigns costs to activities and then to goods and services based on how much each good or service uses the activities" (Hilton, Maher, & Selto, 2006, p. 141). According to Mahoney (1997), some businesses under financial pressure in the 1980s began to use the ABC approach as a way to increase productivity and decrease costs. These are exactly the conditions now faced by community colleges.

College budgets typically break down costs (expenditures) into departmental or cost-center units. We have shown in this chapter that one way to look at costs is to calculate the cost of one of the major outputs of education—degrees. In calculating degree costs, the indirect costs associated with operations such as management, maintenance, and student support services, are usually proportioned equally across departments or per departmental FTE student. In actuality, indirect costs are used unevenly across departments, and it would be more accurate to apportion them according to their actual use. This method of assigning indirect costs is often, but not always, used in the ABC method of accounting (Szatmary, 2011).

As it is being used in higher education, activity-based costing prices out the functions or activities that are part of a college's mission. A college advises and registers students, teaches and tutors them, and provides student and career services. Many of these functions are done across cost centers. By assigning time and costs to each activity, a college can explain more accurately the cost of carrying out these functions. Looking at costs in this way helps managers identify cost drivers and non-value-adding activities, which in turn assists in the reallocation of resources to activities that provide the greatest value.

In higher education, ABC is seen as "a . . . management-oriented information system" and seems to be in greater use at universities in Europe and Australia than in the United States (Granof, Platt, & Vaysman, 2000, p. 6). In the United States a few universities have adopted it at the campus, departmental, or course levels. As an example, Cox, Smith, and Downey (2000) describe how Kansas State University used it at the campus level to help tie college budgets to institutional mission and to help explain to external constituents how "specific activities [and what they cost] contributed to the overall performance of the university" (p. 1).

By defining the activities of instructors, for example, the university was able to explain how much time and money was devoted to teaching, advising, committee work, research, and public service. These activities and their costs were then aggregated into broader categories at the departmental, college, and university levels. This exercise not only gave the university a new perspective on how it was spending money, but also helped to align mission with spending decisions. In addition to its use as an internal accounting device, expenditure data was also used in presentations to external audiences such as the state legislature.

Support for the wider use of ABC in colleges and universities can be found in a recent book by higher education policy analyst Robert Zemsky (2013). Reflecting on more than three decades of policy research and analysis, Zemsky laments that colleges "are pretty much stuck where they were in the 1980's," that "those who matter the most are not listening," and that real "reform will not come . . . until and unless the federal government becomes an active sponsor of change" (pp. 16–17). One of Zemsky's most radical suggestions for linking activity-based costing to college funding

> is to end federal student aid altogether and replace it with a reimbursement program much like the reimbursement system that pays hospitals for the care they provide. Colleges would submit invoices detailing the actual costs of instruction at the unit level and what proportion of those costs could be reasonably assigned to the instruction received by students qualifying for federal assistance. [In order to accomplish this] colleges must develop an activity-based cost accounting system of sufficient robustness to allow for the detailed segregation of costs by specific instructional activity. [Along with this] the government would have to establish acceptable costs criteria [that] reflect minimum necessary costs [and should provide] bonuses for moving disadvantaged students [along]. (p. 211)

As a way to reduce instructional costs, Zemsky cites an example of how the use of ABC at the course level allowed Rensselaer Polytechnic Institute in New York, to radically modify a physics course to achieve both lower costs and better learning outcomes. By costing out the various instructional activities involved in teaching the traditional course, the department came to see that some of the activities could be computerized and faculty could be more effectively used as "resource experts" rather than as "chalk and talk" purveyors of material (p. 183).

## ABC at Community Colleges

Although ABC does not appear to be used at community colleges, the Gates Foundation is pushing the idea as a possible accounting device and/ or benchmarking tool for community colleges. It has funded various projects to explore ABC at community colleges, including an initiative by the Institute for Higher Education Policy (IHEP) to develop an ABC method for costing out various strategies to increase college completion. This IHEP project involves a detailed qualitative study to realign expenditures in ways that enhance student completion. The Institute has undertaken a "Redefining Access for the 21st Century" initiative aimed at "aligning research, policy, and practice to assure greater attainment for all" (IHEP, 2014, para. 1).

In another Gates-funded effort, the American Institutes for Research (AIR), in partnership with the National Higher Education Benchmarking Institute (NHEBI) at Johnson County Community College, has developed an ABC method to analyze what instructional and student services activities cost across departments. By benchmarking costs for course development, tutoring, and advising against peer institutions, colleges can better identify cost drivers and make informed judgments about the connection between these expenditures and student outcomes (NHEBI, 2014).

Community colleges might use the ABC method in other ways as well. For example, if educating remedial students was considered a separate and distinct output, the teaching, tutoring, counseling, and advising activities that are needed to produce successful outcomes for remedial students could be calculated. These activity costs could then be compared to costs incurred in teaching well-prepared students in credit courses. If the full costs of teaching remedial students is higher, as many contend, this information can be used to advocate for additional funding for remediation. A crude version of the ABC method could also be used to cost out departmental activities undertaken to support institutional goals detailed in strategic plans. Calculating the costs of each activity could inform decisions and promote the least costly alternatives, or it could help isolate goals and activities that are not worth the cost of achieving.

## COST-CONSCIOUS POLICY MAKING

It is too early to tell if any of the initiatives described above will come into widespread use and lead to the desired result of controlling costs and improving student outcomes. In terms of revenue, community college leaders will be faced with a plethora of ideas, ranging from a total overhaul of existing systems (e.g., getting rid of the Pell program or making college "tuition free") to more modest revisions (e.g., simplifying the FAFSA form and implementing income-contingent loan repayment programs). The latter are more likely to materialize over time than the former, if only because of the daunting political and fiscal cost of wholesale change.

But college leaders will need to scrutinize all proposals for potential unintended consequences, especially those that sacrifice opportunities for low-income, at-risk students—a key equity goal—in the blind pursuit of efficiency. Examples include (but are not limited to) redefining full-time study from twelve to fifteen hours for the purposes of Pell eligibility; repurposing the Pell program from access to other goals; implementing differential tuition without fully considering the impact on the enrollment of low-income students in high-cost programs, particularly in STEM fields; and instituting voucher programs that, like the FAFSA form, are so confusing that they impede rather than encourage college attendance. Distinguishing the sound from the unsound in the numerous policy proposals now in the wind will, in addition to careful enrollment management, be essential features of fiscal management.

Caution is also warranted on the expenditure (cost) side of the budget. Just as cost control in the health care industry has become an increasingly urgent focus of policy makers struggling with the goal of expanding affordable access to health care services, so too has cost control in higher education become a pressing concern for policy makers as they seek to expand access and increase completion rates within the limits of severely restricted state budgets. At the very least, college leaders will be pressed to augment requests for additional funding with timely and accurate information on what degree programs cost and how institutions are attempting to reduce costs where possible.

But in the push to do more with less, college leaders will also need to remind policy makers that quality has a cost and that the expectations they have of community colleges will require resources. Providing high-tech vocational programming, for example, is inherently costly. Improvement in remedial education—for which community colleges bear primary responsibility—will also have a steep price tag; after all, "the cost [of remediation] is high because of the high-risk nature of the students" (Cohen, Brawer, & Kisker, 2013, p. 173). Leaders can do much to put the results of sound cost analyses not only into the service of a college's efficiency goals, but also into the service of a college's equity goals as well.

## NOTES

1. Informed readers might point out that we have ignored other sources of revenue that could be important, such as building on-campus housing (maybe), building endowment income, developing more partnerships with industry, engaging in profit-making entrepreneurial activities, intensifying lobbying for federal and state earmarks, and outsourcing campus services (for examples see Cohen, Brawer, & Kisker, 2014, pp. 169–72, and Brown, 2012, pp. 54–60). We have not discussed these due to space limitations and because it is assumed that readers are familiar with these ideas, which flood the titles of conference sessions at the annual meetings of the American Association of Community Colleges.

2. Subsequent studies from the Community College Research Center have attempted to cost out varying student pathways, including both students who compete credentials and those who do not. See Belfield, Crosta, and Jenkins (2013) and Manning and Crosta (2014).

3. The difference between the excess credits at Upstate (11.6 percent) and Florida (21.7 percent) is even greater than it looks, because the Florida study excluded all remedial courses and the Upstate case study did not.

## Chapter 7

# Future Scenarios

Final chapters are often the place where authors summarize their views and attempt to look to the future. This chapter is no exception. It reviews and extends a few of the key trends that have been highlighted throughout the book and the related policy issues.

While we feel that we have taken a balanced approach to the issues we have examined, we have not been reluctant to take controversial policy positions, some of which would require changes in state or federal legislation while others would not. Some are more likely to be undertaken; others are not, at least right away.

Certainly, some readers will not agree with our observations or projections, and we expect no less. The book was not intended to be a pep talk that would inspire the movement, but, rather, an honest assessment of where we stand and where we might be going with regard to the issues that influence the way community colleges are, or might be, funded.

Our framework for looking at the future has two dimensions. First, we will look at the next ten years or so, staying within the domain of higher education. Here our projections are mostly based on the trends found in the previous chapters and are seen as bringing about gradual changes in the nature of the community college. Next, we will take a broader view. At times venturing outside the realm of higher education, we will speculate on the longer-run societal forces that we believe could impact what we now call the community college. Here the focus will be on potentially disruptive changes that could affect the landscape of higher education.

Looking toward the future reminds us of the importance of the past. As Cohen, Brawer, and Kisker (2013) have said about the future of the community college, "we don't stride boldly into the future; we back into it, dragging our history with us" (p. 435). This suggests that community colleges will

153

evolve differently depending on the state in which they are located. But even within states, some colleges will become more attached to the transfer mission, others to occupational training, and still others to community service. Some colleges will embrace the challenge of responding to the demands of a global workplace, others will not. However, from a national perspective, some discernible patterns will emerge and we will concentrate on those and their possible impact on the way community colleges are funded.

## THE NEXT TEN YEARS

Over the next ten years or so, barring any disruptive events in the political or economic landscape, we do not see any dramatic or sudden changes in the mission and financing of community colleges. Changes will surely come, though slowly, giving colleges sufficient time to adapt and providing them with the opportunity to influence the direction of those changes and the impact they ultimately have. Here are the five major trends that we see in the near future, each followed by related policy positions that we advocate on the basis of the evidence and arguments presented in previous chapters.

### Trend 1: Increased Credentialing and Growing Enrollments

Credentialing has never been the most important function for the community college, but that role will increase over time. Whether or not the optimistic projections of the need for postsecondary education are accurate, all indications are that students will continue to value a college credential and that employers will continue to use them to screen for workers. The policy agenda of the private sector, including the Lumina and Gates Foundations, as well as pressure from state and federal governments, will help push the goal of increasing the proportion of the population that earns a postsecondary credential.

This bodes well for the secular trend of community college enrollments. Nationally enrollments at these institutions will grow at a steady but uneven rate (declining in some years but rising in others) and will continue to outpace the growth at both public research universities and public master's-level colleges. The increasing income inequality and flat or declining incomes of the bottom 40 percent of the population will continue to draw more students into the relatively inexpensive local community college. As history shows, business cycles will periodically thrust waves of displaced workers into the community colleges in addition to younger students.

As the middle class becomes shallower, students will increasingly be diverted from four-year colleges, which will further expand community college enrollments. Among the public four-year colleges, tight budgets, rising sticker prices, the drive for increased prestige (being more selective), and the fear of quality erosion, will work to restrict the entry of recent high school graduates and will drive more of them, with better preparation, into the community college. In addition, if the community college is allowed to expand along with student demand, enrollments from the discredited parts of the for-profit sector will seek refuge in the community college. Losers in the battles over shifting enrollments can be expected to fight back.

The increased enrollment and demand for credentials have also spurred a renewed movement to award credit for prior learning gained through experience (on the job, in the military, etc.) as well as for participation in alternative educational formats such as massive open online courses (Fain, 2013a; Ohio Board of Regents, n.d.). The former will affect older students rather more than younger ones, but all alternative paths to credentials will decouple degrees, or parts of them, from credit hours and seat time.

There is nothing sacred about the connection between seat time and learning, but a significant movement away from credit hours as the basis for funding could present a challenge; the push to decouple degrees from credit hours has not yet been met with corresponding proposals for replacing credit hour production as a fiscal accounting measure. However, we are convinced that over the next ten years this movement will advance slowly enough to allow states and colleges time to adjust.

Another major challenge will be to keep the community college an open-access institution that not only provides a place where all students can prepare for occupations or transfer to the university, but that also serves as a "safe port in a storm" when needed, especially during economic downturns. What is needed is a financing arrangement that moves community college revenues in tandem with fluctuations in enrollments caused by ups and downs in the business cycle and that does not require discretionary action on the part of the political system to do so.

Current funding policies in many states do not do this, resulting in the conditions described in chapters 1 and 2. When recessions swell enrollments, state revenue and funding for higher education fall. A better designed policy would do the opposite. But, history does not show that state funding follows this pattern, thus depriving colleges of revenue when they need it the most. Without shifts in policy, we do not see this changing.

## Trend 1: Policy Issues

As described in chapter 6, money should follow the student, preferably through some kind of stipend, or supply-side voucher, given to the college as enrollments expand, even if it comes at a reduced rate during recessions.

Colleges will need to make up the difference by raising tuition for the students who can afford it, while pressuring states and the federal government to increase need-based aid, supplementing it, when available, with more of their own institutional aid.

In support of these ideas we have argued for a high-tuition, high-aid strategy (see chapters 1 and 2). But, of course, a necessary condition for this to work is that colleges must be able to retain their tuition revenue and, in many states, must also have greater control over the shifting of funds within their budgets. Colleges should also be allowed to carry over funds from year to year if we expect them to efficiently use the resources that are given to them.

In addition, the increased demand for alternative forms of credentialing will spur demands for some type of expanded funding arrangement, possibly in the form of demand-side vouchers given directly to students to use *for* approved modes of learning (e.g., industrial training, apprentice arrangements, and credit by exam) and not only *at* a particular college. But again, this movement will emerge only slowly over the next ten years. In the long run, however, it may enter the list of potentially positive or negative disruptive forces impacting the community college.

These are not new ideas, but given the alternatives and the political climate, they are the way to go, offering plausible ways of addressing the misalignment between enrollment surges and funding while at the same time providing the flexibility needed in an educational environment characterized by ever more diverse credentialing paths. However necessary they may be, additional efforts will be needed to meet growing demand. No magic bullet to increase revenues by any significant amount is on the horizon. Even if performance funding were to work, it would most likely just replace current state funding based on enrollments; indeed, the latest PBF experiments (those dubbed "PBF 2.0") have largely abandoned the strategy of providing performance-based monies in the form of add-on bonuses, tying portions of base funding to performance instead (see chapter 5).

To help students pay the bills, greater use of federal student loans should be promoted, but only if the loans are based on an income-contingent repayment plan. Increased emphasis on this type of lending is in the political wind; but taking things a step further toward the most desirable situation in which payments are collected by the IRS in much the same way as federal income and social security taxes will be more difficult to achieve (see chapter 6).

## Trend 2: Shifting Missions

In their seminal book on community college finance, Breneman and Nelson (1981) wondered whether the community college would evolve into "community-based learning centers" focused on adult learners and noncredit programs (p. 207), or would develop into full-fledged members of the higher education community, concentrating its resources on "traditional collegiate functions" (p. 214). This question has clearly been answered in favor of the latter, and as a consequence, more and more of the community-based, noncredit activities will become self-funded and less of a draw on the operating budget. Such a movement is supported by our twin goals of equity and efficiency outlined in chapter 1.

This is not to say that the comprehensive community college we are familiar with will be abandoned in favor of a single collegiate focus. Looking back over the history of the community college, we can see that although most of its multiple missions—transfer, occupational education, remedial education, and community service—have been there from the beginning, each has expanded and contracted as needed during different time periods.

The current tilt toward the collegiate function is part of this ongoing historical process, demonstrating yet again that the community college has proven to be a flexible and innovative institution. In fact, Sydow and Alfred (2012) argue that it has been the most flexible sector of higher education and will only thrive if it continues to be so. While its interchangeable nature has made some wonder if the community college was confused about its mission, others would claim that it was just responding to the needs of the communities it served.

While the curriculum will change with market demand, albeit slowly, the community college can also be expected—in light of this emphasis on the collegiate function—to expand its reach vertically. It can seek a greater connection with the K-12 system and can also reach up into the territory of the four-year colleges by offering bachelor's degrees. Both of these movements are currently underway but the latter is the strongest.

In the near future, we expect more colleges to adapt to the growing demand for more credentialing by expanding their role as a partner in the bachelor's degree pipeline. This will come from both a greater emphasis on transfer and from the increased production of four-year degrees themselves. As of 2014, seventeen states have allowed at least some of their community colleges to offer bachelor's degrees (Community College Baccalaureate Association, n.d.). The speed of this drift in mission will depend, in part, on the overall health of the economy, the rate of unemployment, and the political pressure in some states to cut the cost of obtaining a four-year degree.

It is likely that political pressure within some states will be exerted to reverse the diversion of students from four-year colleges to the community college. For instance, the Iowa Board of Regents recently changed the funding formula for its public universities to encourage them to enroll more in-state students. This set off an aggressive marketing campaign at the University of

Iowa to recruit these students. Some private colleges and community colleges saw this as serious threat to their enrollments.

The president of Kirkwood Community College was quoted as saying that the change in the funding formula could "dramatically" affect "the balance of power" within the state's system of higher education (Rivard, 2014, para. 10). The director of the Board of Regents expressed no alarm over this possibility, citing the poor graduation rates of the community colleges. While Iowa may prove to be an exception, it does illustrate that public policy shifts can impact enrollments and missions in unpredictable ways.

But it is unlikely that this backlash will reverse the drift in mission, on a national level, that we have described above. As the local colleges look more and more like four-year colleges with on-campus housing and four-year degree programs, students will rationalize their diversion from their preferred four-year colleges and become more comfortable with the idea of completing at least the first two years of undergraduate study, and perhaps even all four, at their local college.

The diverted students will mostly come from public master's-level colleges; research universities, sought out by the best-prepared students and supported by states and the federal government as engines of economic development and innovation, especially through their graduate programs in the sciences, will be not be affected as much.

Ultimately, though, community colleges can expect to enroll greater numbers of younger and better-prepared students. Improved completion rates will be highlighted by college public relations offices and the media, reinforcing a new image of the community college, and many colleges, as in Florida, may drop the word "community" from their names.

As the mission of the community college moves toward greater emphasis on transfer and—in many states—on the increased production of its own bachelor's degrees, tight budgets and increased pressure for better completion rates will squeeze out the least prepared, disadvantaged students. Again, this will be a slow process.

What will happen to the disadvantaged students who are squeezed out? This is a matter of speculation and depends on the health of the economy. Trends visible right now lead us to believe that a few of these displaced students will find satisfying jobs. But others will not be as lucky. Some will enroll at colleges in the for-profit sector where they are less likely to achieve their goals. Others will find low-wage jobs that do not fully utilize their potential. And still others will find employment in the underground or shadow economy, which is the safety net of last resort.

Workers in the shadow economy may engage in illegal activities that impose high social costs upon society. But most in the underground economy will engage in legal but unmeasured, unregulated, and untaxed activities, working as part-time workers and traders in what is largely a cash economy that operates "off the books." The growth of the shadow economy would further erode the tax base and the ability of the public sector to support higher education. A recent estimate of the size of the underground economy in the United States suggests that it entails "$2 trillion in unreported income [and] . . . results in unpaid taxes of as much as $500 billion a year" (Zumbrun, 2013, p. 2).

## Trend 2: Policy Issues

If we don't want to lose the underrepresented populations that community colleges were designed to help, two-year colleges will need more funding per student. If the states will allow it, some of this will come from higher tuition rates and differential program pricing or possibly from higher subsidies for high-cost, high-demand programs (see chapter 6). But the states must also increase their support through higher need-based financial aid for low-income students. This should have the highest priority, and the federal government can help.

We think it is worth increasing the political pressure on congressional representatives to renew efforts to set up a federal state partnership that provides states with incentives to increase need-based financial aid. The Leveraging Educational Assistance Partnership (LEAP) program, which provided federal matching grants to states, should be revived and expanded. The program has worked well in the past and can be expected to do so again in the future (Zumeta et al., 2012). Some guarantee of modest but predictable tuition increases could be tied to these matching funds.

Modifying and expanding the role of Pell grants in financing the education of lower-income students will also be critical to meeting the needs of underrepresented students. Simplifying the application process is within reach and will further stimulate enrollments throughout higher education (see chapter 6). The community college will get its share of these new students, but with more students qualifying for Pell grants, appropriations will run short and college leaders will need to pressure Congress to keep increasing the funds for this program. While linking Pell funds to the performance of students is a welcome idea, it should not come at the expense of funds devoted purely to access (see chapter 6).

## Trend 3: Declining State Support and Rising Tuition

Tuition as a percentage of the operating budget will increase during the next ten years following its historical path. As we explained in chapters 1 and 2, we do not view this as necessarily undesirable, as the benefits obtained for most students, even if they don't graduate, are greater than their out-of-pocket costs. In 1950, on a national level, revenue from tuition and fees contributed about 10 percent to the operating budget (Cohen & Brawer, 1982).

In 2011 it was 28.4 percent, with Pell and state need-based grants paying about one-third of this, and potentially more, for lower-income students. This makes the community college a relatively affordable option for an increasing number of students, including those who can pay the full sticker price.

The increase in the contribution of tuition and fees as a percentage of total revenue could level off if the state substantially increased its contribution. But the need for more support from the public sector will come up against the resistance of a nineteenth-century ideology that seeks a smaller government and lower taxes (Johnstone & Marcucci, 2010).

In an environment where a high percentage of the working population has seen their incomes stagnate, one sure way to increase their disposal income is to cut taxes. The resulting reduction in the ability and willingness of the population to support public spending reduces state support for higher education. While state funding will continue to vary with the business cycle, we believe that it will most likely decline as a percentage of the operating budget.

The pleas of colleges for differential funding for expensive vocational programs will go largely unanswered, but where proportionately higher funds are provided for costly programs, they are likely to be offset by declines in support for other areas. And, although state and local funds may continue to decline, the proportion of community college revenues per student accounted for by these funds will continue to be relatively high, exceeding the proportion of total revenues per student accounted for by state and local monies in other sectors of public higher education. This will take place at the same time states are demanding more accountability.

In return, most states will further integrate the community college into their systems of higher education, improving pathways toward transfer, reducing the number of excess credits students take, and taking other measures that minimize the cost of obtaining a bachelor's degree.

While many of these reforms will increase the efficiency of the system of higher education, none of them will provide enough additional revenue to stem the tide of decreasing state and local support for community colleges. As Noah Brown, the president of the Association of Community College Trustees (ACCT), has said, the importance of community colleges "ought to be sufficient to sway policymakers to increase investment in community colleges. But the reality could not be more different, and the likelihood of continued scarcity remains squarely on the horizon" (Brown, 2012, p. 60).

As community colleges in many states remake themselves into public four-year public colleges, however, they face the possibility that their changing role will be used by policy makers as a justification for treating them more like other sectors of public higher education. This would mean reduced support and perhaps the emergence of another, less-expensive pathway for vocational training. Such a possibility thrusts us into the longer-term view found at the end of this chapter.

## Trend 3: Policy Issues

In the wake of declining state support, state and federal lobbying efforts will need to increase. The American Association of Community Colleges (AACC) and the ACCT can be relied on to do most of this at the federal level but colleges will need to contribute and will need to do more at the state level. The faculty can help, but college leaders will need to step up to the task. In particular, boards of trustees will need to become more active in advocacy at the state level. Funds for this activity will not be able to come from college operating budgets.

In addition, community colleges can step up private fund-raising efforts. These efforts, though growing and yielding isolated cases of highly publicized success, remain a nascent feature of community college finance that has, as yet, an uncertain future. This is borne out by the Delta Cost Project revenue data we cited in chapter 2 and by the huge gap between private funds received by four-year colleges and universities on the one hand and community colleges on the other (Bellafante, 2014).

Yet, community colleges might be able to use their newcomer status in the world of fund-raising to their advantage, because a gift, particularly from a local donor, that might be considered small and relatively insignificant at four-year colleges would most likely be seen as highly significant and impactful at the local community college. The "power of giving local" could be very appealing to potential donors.

A small amount of excess revenue might also be generated from entrepreneurial activities operated through the college auxiliaries. The restaurant and organic farm at Tompkins Cortland Community College (n.d.) in Ithaca, NY are examples of what some colleges are already doing in this area, tying career programs to commercial ventures that offer students real-world experience while at the same time generating revenue streams that support those programs.

Another example can be seen in the Enology and Viticulture Program at Walla Walla Community College (2015) in Washington; wine produced by the students is sold, and the proceeds are used to support the program and its students. More research on these entrepreneurial efforts is needed to understand how and under what circumstances they offer sound fiscal support.

Besides fund-raising, entrepreneurship, and the lobbying efforts directed at increasing revenue, colleges will need to continue to keep a close eye on costs. But as we have noted earlier in this chapter and elsewhere, the cost cutting efforts of the past may be a self-defeating process that lowers quality. When high-cost, but popular, programs are dropped, colleges will suffer from some public backlash. Brave leaders and boards will have to admit that they cannot be all things to all people as tight budgets will continue to force difficult choices about campus missions.

## Trend 4: Low Productivity and Lower Quality

Despite all of the speculation about how disruptive technologies will transform higher education, we do not see any change in the ability of colleges to increase productivity enough to lower the cost of educating students at the community college level (see chapter 3). Nor do we see a large number of these students abandoning the traditional campus in favor of an exclusive online experience. Most need more support than online instruction can currently give them (In the last section of this chapter, we will have more to say on the potentially disruptive change of technology).

This means that community colleges, with their high-touch approach, will continue to attract students to their campuses but will also continue to feel the pressure to cut costs as long as revenues are restricted. This cost-cutting will likely reduce the quality of instruction and learning, and the proof of this will begin to show up more often in studies of the proxy measures of quality such as degree production and scores on standardized tests of student learning, as flawed as these tests may be. Much of this decline in quality will be masked by the slow influx of better-prepared students that have been diverted from four-year colleges.

On the surface all will seem well, but many marginalized students, and others who will not even apply, will abandon their efforts to find their way through the maze of higher education. Another, related threat to quality could come from the widespread use of performance-based funding. In particular, the pressure on part-time faculty to reduce standards in order to move students along and improve completion rates will need to be closely monitored.

Over the last twenty years, community colleges have faced a cost-quality trade-off, and as we have stated earlier, we expect this to continue. More full-time faculty and better student services will be needed to improve quality. But administrators will need to keep a cushion of part-time faculty as a buffer against the fluctuations in enrollments caused by the business cycle and to keep costs and tuition down. As chapters 2 and 3 suggest, in the race between quality and the necessity for cost-cutting, the latter has been winning out.

## Trend 4: Policy Issues

To offset the decline in quality, more funding per student will be needed. A more comprehensive student support system and more full-time faculty will be needed. If community colleges can learn anything from the best colleges in the for-profit sector, it is that aside from improved student advisement, career and placement services must be greatly expanded for the students in vocational programs.

This issue has been studied extensively, and as one study concluded, "advisory boards, career services, and job placement are weak, not active, and poorly connected to the labor market" at the community college (Rosenbaum, Deil-Amen, & Person, 2006, p. 159). Students in vocational programs need an active career and placement service that helps prepare them with the soft skills needed in the workplace and that arranges internships and other connections with related area labor markets. If students see that such a program is working, they are more likely to persist and move toward their goals.

Additionally, investing in educating the disadvantaged students who use the community college as their entry to higher education produces a high rate of return. Studies have shown that the students "with relatively disadvantaged social backgrounds and low levels of early achievement—or those with the lowest probability of completing college—benefit the most from completing college" (Brand & Xie, 2010, p. 293). Regrettably, we think that this message is unlikely to influence policy makers in the near future.

Documenting their inability to help lower-income, first-generation, underrepresented students to succeed due to a lack of funding might be an option for colleges to follow. This would require careful study and documentation about what it would cost to increase the completion rates of these students and how those costs exceed current subsidies. These arguments would be strengthened if it could be shown than even though per-student costs will increase, the cost per completion will fall.

Quietly presenting these results to the right audiences might work to increase state and local government funding as well as private support for continuing this effort. But, these increases are unlikely unless greater economic growth allows the public sector to raise the taxes on some sectors of the society. On balance, we do not expect that many state or local policymakers will respond to these equity arguments because they view the community college as a low-cost provider and intend to keep it that way. Even if it is believed that quality has been compromised, they will respond, quietly, that it is "good enough."

## Trend 5: Experiments with Performance-Based Funding

Despite its checkered history, states continue to experiment with PBF, a trend that will undoubtedly persist given the intense policymaker concern for student persistence and completion. As in the past, these experiments will vary, with a handful of states committing 50 percent to 100 percent of base funding to PBF metrics, a larger number cautiously tying considerably smaller proportions to performance, and a significant number opting out of PBF programming altogether.

The PBF approach undoubtedly has strong advocates and deep roots in a long history of pay-for-performance mechanisms in the public and private sectors. But given the considerable political effort needed to alter long-standing state funding formulas, the need in many cases for state leaders to focus their political capital on other pressing concerns, and the powerful inertia that keeps existing funding systems in place, we do not anticipate that large-scale PBF programs will become the norm across the country over the next ten years.

It is worth emphasizing that state PBF schemes are still experimental and will continue to be for the foreseeable future. The efforts now underway in Tennessee, Ohio, and the Texas State Technical College System (described in chapter 5) to tie up to 100 percent of state funding to performance have not been around long enough for researchers to glean a strong sense of their impact on student outcomes. And even when studies factor in long-standing programs, results are mixed.

The analysis prepared for this volume by Donna Desrochers of the Delta Cost Project, for example, found that states with wide-scale and well-established PBF programs did not consistently outperform states with smaller or recently implemented programs, or states with no PBF programs at all, on measures of completion or retention (see chapter 5).

In-depth research conducted by Kevin Dougherty and his colleagues at Columbia University's Community College Research Center (CCRC) has also identified gaps in our understanding of the impact of PBF programs, emphasizing that more needs to be done to determine if these programs affect student persistence and attainment in ways that policymakers intend (Dougherty et al., 2014).

In addition, these studies have raised serious concerns about unintended and untoward consequences (Lahr et al., 2014), providing evidence of actual or potential instances in which the pressure to perform well on PBF metrics may lead community colleges to tighten admissions criteria and cause faculty members, particularly the growing numbers of adjuncts, to lower academic standards in an attempt to raise course completion rates.

All of these concerns align with what the history of pay-for-performance schemes suggests: that they work better in some industries than in others and are particularly problematic in industries where cognitive rather than physical skills are required (Stecher et al., 2010). We would also add an additional concern—that the focus of PBF programs on persistence and credential completion ignores the benefits accrued to students who may simply use the community college as a way of experimenting with potential career interests or determining whether the pursuit of a postsecondary credential is something they want to commit to at any given point in their lives.

Jones (2013) aptly notes that "too narrow a focus will inevitably lead to unwanted institutional behaviors" (p. 4). In the case of community colleges, PBF programs that focus solely on persistence and completion may cause the institutions to turn away those who are experimenting, as well as those pursuing ad hoc learning goals, focusing instead only on those with clear degree goals or who exhibit behaviors that are indicative of this degree focus. The novel design of the recently established Guttman Community College, which requires full-time study for at least the first year, may be a sign of things to come under narrowly structured PBF programs that undervalue the benefits of relatively open systems that allow students to come and go as their situations require.[1]

## Trend 5: Policy Issues

Given the uncertain and experimental nature of these programs, a cautious approach to performance-based funding seems wise until more is known about the impact—both positive and negative—of these fiscal incentives. We have recommended (in chapter 5) that, for now, a flat rate of 25 percent of state appropriations be tied to performance, a figure that is large enough to communicate the state's concern for student persistence and attainment, but perhaps not so large that it inadvertently leads to lowered academic standards or turns institutions away from valuable community college functions, such as admitting at-risk students or providing students with opportunities to explore educational options, consider alternative career possibilities, or test their aptitudes.

We recognize that because institutions vary in terms of the proportion of total revenues that are derived from the state, this flat rate will result in correspondingly wide variations in the proportion of total revenue derived from PBF funding, ranging, for example, from 2.5 percent at colleges that receive 10 percent of total revenues from the state to 12.5 percent at colleges that receive 50 percent of revenues from the state. Yet, as we noted in chapter 5, the flat rate is relatively easy to explain to constituents and avoids the technical and political difficulties of applying varied rates of PBF across institutions in an attempt to assure that the proportion of total revenues tied to performance remains the same for all colleges.

Past experience with PBF programs leads to three other policy recommendations. First, PBF systems should support the community college's equity mission, providing incentives for college work on the recruitment, retention, and completion of low-income and minority students. Second, in light of mounting concerns about the detrimental impacts on educational quality,

PBF formulas should include quality indicators, such as threshold levels for the proportion of faculty members who are employed on a full-time basis and who may be less vulnerable to pressures to increase course completion rates at the expense of academic standards. Third, given the costly data-reporting demands that PBF programs potentially place on institutional research offices, every effort should be made to limit PBF formulas to data that are already collected or can be collected at the system rather the campus level.

As states continue with their PBF experiments, it will be important for community college leaders and educators to be involved, both as key players in assessments of the impact of these programs on student outcomes as well as helpful critics who can guard against the inclusion of inappropriate metrics that will do more harm than good. State policymakers may have a good sense of what they want—increased student completion, for instance, or greater evidence of student learning—but only a vague sense of what data might best gauge success in achieving those goals, what it will cost to collect and report those data, what unintended consequences might ensue through the policy mandates (in this case, PBF) imposed as a way of achieving desired outcomes.

The inclusion of scores on standardized tests in PBF metrics, for example, might—from the top-down vantage point of the state level—have great appeal and seem an inherently logical approach to understanding what students gain through their college studies. But the naïve inclusion of these test scores without a ground-level understanding of the questionable validity of indicators based on aggregated test-score data (Banta, 2007) will be counterproductive. The insights of campus-based community college educators will be critical.

## POTENTIALLY DISRUPTIVE CHANGES IN THE LONG TERM

Over the long run, the nature of the community college will be more influenced by factors outside the realm of higher education than inside. Interrelated technological, economic, political, and social forces could generate disruptive changes over which the community college would have little or no control and that could shape the destiny of all sectors of higher education. It is how institutions adjust to these changes that will make a difference and possibly be a force in influencing their direction.

When the phrase *disruptive change* is used within the context of higher education, it always seems to refer to the impact of technology on the delivery of learning. We will address that force below, but generally we use the word *disruptive* to mean something broader: big challenges of any kind that are not easily anticipated, that are not localized, and that cause discontinuity and upheaval in an industry. In looking at the big picture, the impact of global pandemics, large-scale war, and environmental disasters on the future of the community college could be considered, but that would lead us too far astray.

At any rate, these kinds of disruptive changes are impossible to predict, so we will restrict our broader view to possible changes that are a little closer to home.[2] Some of the potentially disruptive forces faced by community colleges are generated by economic factors, while others emerge from the growth in alternative learning and training options, and from potential changes in attitudes toward the value of higher education. All could reduce the optimistic enrollment projections upon which many of our short-run trends are based.

## Greater Number of Options

Future student transcripts or employment application forms will reflect a greater diversity of learning environments and greater competition for the community college. This will mirror the greater number of options for learning and for documenting that learning. As we suggested previously, online learning; credit for learning gained through employment, military, or other non-collegiate experiences; competency-based learning; and the growth of internships and apprenticeships are all part of the current education landscape and could expand enough to have a significant impact on traditional college enrollments. Whether colleges might be able to capture a slice of this market is open to question.

Within this realm, most of the discussion in the United States is about alternative forms of credentialing and just how the higher education system and accrediting standards will adapt to the separation of the credential from credit hours and seat time. *Inside Higher ED*, for instance, reports that, to date, the U.S. Department of Education has only approved four institutions to award degrees using the direct assessment of learning, rather than class time.

The University of Southern New Hampshire is most often cited in this regard, but recently the competency-based education movement has gained some credibility by the establishment of a limited number of competency-based degree programs at the University of Michigan, Purdue University, and the University of Wisconsin system (Fain, 2014b). Most view the approval process for this type of credentialing as slow, but the current log jam is likely to be broken, making competency-based approaches a competitive alternative to traditional learning.

The same could be said about apprenticeship programs where quality issues are not as much of a problem. Apprenticeships are not very popular in the United States but over time might prove to be a better value for the dollar, both for the government and the student, than paying for certain training programs at the community college. These training programs are often offered by industries, trade associations, and unions, sometimes in cooperation with community colleges or technical schools. Learners in these on-the-job training programs, unlike learners in internships, are paid, and classroom instruction is directly tied to the training.

Apprenticeships are often cited as a major contributor to the development of a skilled workforce in Europe, especially in Germany, Switzerland, and England. While the number of U.S. apprenticeships was significantly reduced during the last recession as employers cut back spending on training, they have thrived in some areas where skill shortages were apparent.

For example, the South Carolina apprenticeship program, Apprenticeship Carolina, has been led by German manufacturing industries (BMW and Bosch) that have built plants in the state (Berliner, 2014). The South Carolina apprenticeship model has carried over into fields such as nursing, pharmacy, and information technology and operates under a small state tax credit of $1,000 per year per apprentice for four years. While state tax credits could help increase the attractiveness of apprenticeships nationwide, they would also get a major push if the federal government were to offer the type of demand-side voucher discussed in chapter 6.

Under such a potentially disruptive plan, vouchers would be given directly to students to use for any approved program offered at industrial sites or through other providers of on-the-job training programs. Providers might take an interest in these programs as a way of generating revenue and as a way of ensuring a continued supply of skilled workers where the supply is short.

One can imagine that a paid apprenticeship at a Microsoft-like company would have more applicants than spaces available and would develop rather competitive entry standards. Providers would have the advantage of directly observing the skills and work habits of students in the program over an extended period of time. Community colleges might have a role to play in this process by leasing facilities to providers but apprenticeships funded through vouchers could divert current noncredit workforce and vocational training away from the community college.

In this book we have stressed the idea that funding must follow the shifting mission of the community college. Of course, we also recognize that shifts in public policy impact college missions and the way that they are funded. A policy shift to demand-side vouchers for technical training, for instance, would be an example of a shift in funding that would drive the mission. Widespread adoption of this method of training might signal a shift in the attitude toward the value of higher education in general.

## Changing Attitudes about Risk and the Value of Higher Education

At the present time it is clear that, on average, education pays dividends. But, from the standpoint of the investor (student/parent), the rate of return is not guaranteed. Indeed, in financial markets, the higher the rate of return, the higher the risk, other things being equal. From this perspective, going to college is a risky proposition, especially for low-income students for whom tuition and forgone income represent a higher proportion of personal wealth/income than for the more affluent. This risk is increased by the instability of the job market, complex pathways toward a degree, and the uncertainty involved in overcoming past academic deficiencies.

Many of the recommendations in this volume may be seen as steps designed to reduce this risk. Smoother pathways, higher need-based financial aid, and income-based repayment of loans are examples. Even with some risks, students are willing to enroll in colleges if the rates of return are high enough and they have some level of risk tolerance. But what if a generation of students becomes more risk-averse? Then, even high rates of return will reduce enrollments. Students could become more risk averse if employment becomes more unstable and skills learned are quickly outdated. Thus, even if the immediate costs and benefits of going to college do not change, the decision to attend for students on the margin will be altered.

Alternatively, the cost/benefit calculation of going to college can change. If the costs of education and training (particularly the out-of-pocket ones) exceed the benefits, fewer students would enroll, even if their risk tolerance did not change. When the supply of certain kinds of workers exceeds demand, the market adjusts the balance. If few jobs for English majors or lawyers persist for long enough, students get the message and change fields. We know that certain fields and degrees are more "profitable" for students than others and that this causes some shifts in enrollments toward occupations and credentials in greater demand.

All of this rebalancing of supply and demand is part of the normal process of adjustment, and it usually occurs slowly enough for colleges to shift program offerings accordingly. But what if unexpected changes occur and large numbers of students have a change in attitude about the value of higher education? This change in attitude could come about if employers find another way of screening for workers, such as the widespread use of apprenticeships for vocational programs, as mentioned above. This would divert students away from the community college and make the optimistic enrollment projections, assumed throughout this book, to be dramatically wrong.

This change in attitude might also be precipitated by the recognition, on the part of students, that the overall supply of educated workers is likely to outstrip demand for as far into the future as can be seen. Here it is useful to remember that an uncharacteristic slowdown in enrollments occurred following the recession in the early 1970s, though enrollments quickly recovered as the economy grew. This could happen again, but even on a larger scale. Consider the following two contradictory projections.

Anthony Carnevale and his colleagues at the Georgetown University Center on Education and the Workforce have produced a series of reports that show a large unmet demand for more educated workers. These projections have been greeted enthusiastically by the community college movement, and the media have often cited predictions from these reports, such as the statement that "by the year 2018, nearly two-thirds of the 46.8 million [new] jobs—some 63 percent—will require workers with at least some college education . . . and only 36 percent will require workers with just a high school diploma or less" (Carnevale, Smith, & Strohl, 2010, p. 13).

But official projections from the U.S. Department of Labor (DOL) provide a much less optimistic outlook for jobs requiring postsecondary education. DOL economists predict that over this same period occupations requiring the kind of credentials that community colleges award will increase faster than those requiring a bachelor's degree but that approximately 70 percent of all job openings will not require any postsecondary education (Sommers, 2009).

The long-term employment outlook has been clouded by the depth of the recent recession, and the media play up stories of college graduates (especially those with non-STEM degrees) working as baristas instead of in higher paying jobs. Continued demand for higher education, however, indicates that students feel that this underemployment must be temporary and that a college degree still provides the best opportunity to attain a middle-class lifestyle. This is certainly true, but the gap between those with a college degree and those without one has grown mostly because the incomes of those without a postsecondary credential are dropping faster than increases in the income enjoyed by graduates.

It is also worth noting that during recessions and periods of high unemployment, fears of underemployment always catch the attention of the media. In the 1970s, media reports about the erosion of the workforce referenced taxi drivers with bachelor's degrees and scholars who wrote about the deskilling of the American workforce (Braverman, 1974; Freeman, 1976). While these reports were wrong, community colleges did see a temporary surge in vocational enrollments while those in transfer programs fell.

As always, some claim that "it is different this time around." But if underemployment and slow economic growth continue for an extended length of time, young Americans may become discouraged about their long-range prospects and feel that attending college is no longer worthwhile. That would be a disruptive force that would affect all institutions of higher education as most colleges would shrink in size and some would go out of business.

Whether this would leave the community college in a more or less advantageous position than it now enjoys is as impossible to predict as the likelihood of this disruption itself. What is likely, however, is that the underground economy, mentioned above, will expand and possibly become a politically disruptive force.

For now, however, the consensus of most economists is that "there are not too many students going to college" (Autor, 2014, p. 849) and that "both American companies and foreign companies investing in the United States report that the skills of the U.S. workforce are comparatively weak" (Baily & Bosworth, 2014, p. 23). If students do not continue to get this message or are unwilling to take on the risk of enrolling in college, it could cause a disruptive change within the higher education industry, and possibly the society as a whole.

## Economic Factors

Business cycles—booms and busts—will continue, and if the intensity and frequency of these fluctuations increase it could be very disruptive. We have already argued that business cycles impact the community college and its funding. Economic downturns expand enrollments but contract state support. Recessions also have a negative impact on outcomes as students enter a weak job market.

While it would be desirable if we could smooth out these cycles, colleges have little control over this, except that their leaders, especially the faculty, can be influential voices in advocating for programs that promote full employment on a national level. A healthy economy promotes a healthy college and good student outcomes. As far as the short-run swings in funding are concerned, we have suggested (in chapter 2) that we can do something about that, at least when economic downturns are not too destructive, through the high-tuition, high-aid approach that allows colleges to capture tuition revenue during good economic times (without denying opportunity to low-income students) and through policies that allow colleges to keep tuition revenues and use them to offset declines in state funding during recessions.

On a more positive note, most western economists have an optimistic outlook for the future of the economy as a whole. A few years ago some leading economists, including Nobel Prize winners, were asked to predict the future of the world economy. Looking 100 years out, all seemed optimistic about the world our children would inherit, save for some reservations about the possible disruptive impact of climate change (Palacios-Huerta, 2013).

In addition to the ups and downs of the business cycle, income and wealth inequality will also exert an influence. The Occupy Movement and the political debate generated during the 2012 presidential campaign about the top 1 percent versus the 99 percent called attention to the issue of income and wealth inequality in the United States. Income and wealth are different but connected. Income is a flow concept while wealth is a stock concept. So, when discussing the distribution of wealth, a certain percent of the population or of families who own a certain percent of the market value of assets are examined.

Wealth has always been more concentrated than income but between 1970 and 2013, the percentage of wealth held by the top 10 percent of the population has increased to 75 percent, with almost all of it going to the top 0.1 percent. This is the highest concentration of wealth in the industrialized world and was labeled by *BusinessWeek* as "The New Gilded Age" (Coy, 2014; Saez & Zucman, 2014). In fact, the concentration of wealth in the U.S. is above that of many less-developed countries (in India 73.8 percent of everything is owned by the top 10 percent). Inequalities in wealth are one of the factors that generate inequalities in income.

As income becomes much more unequally distributed, as it has, it reduces the ability of the public sector to support higher education and it affects the ability of families to pay for college, impacting the choices that students make about where to attend. But as Figure 7.1 below shows, this is not a recent phenomenon. A widening of the income gap between the top and the bottom has been pronounced since the early 1970s.

Thomas Piketty (2014), in one of the best-selling economics books in recent times, argues that "it is quite possible that inequality will keep getting worse for many more years" (p. 22). But history does show that increases in this gap are not inevitable. Educators would argue that they can help close this gap by expanding educational opportunity and outcomes. This is an enabling factor but it would not be sufficient enough to close the gap between the top and the bottom. Certainly education and training promote economic growth and help to supply skilled workers when shortages exist in specific markets. However, colleges don't directly increase the demand for the educated workers that they produce. As economists are known to say, supply doesn't create demand from a national perspective.

As Figure 7.1 shows, since about 1970 the proportion of national income, in real terms, going to the lowest 40 percent of the population has been relatively flat (falling for the lowest 20 percent but rising slightly for the next 20 percent). This is one factor that has driven students from families in these income brackets into the community colleges. This trend has led to the increased stratification within institutions of higher education by socioeconomic status (SES). Research cited by Carnevale and Strohl (2010) shows that in 1982 community colleges drew 48 percent of their students from the bottom two SES quartiles, but in 2006 this rose to 58 percent. In the same time period, more selective colleges drew their students from the top two SES quartiles.

Oddly enough, this increasing stratification within higher education could reverse itself if income inequality continues to grow. In this scenario, students

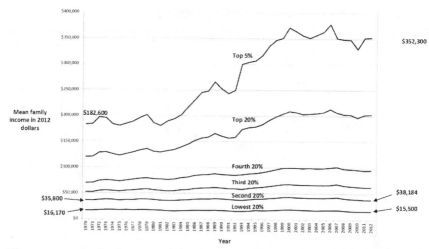

**Figure 7.1   Mean family income by quintiles, 1970 to 2012, in 2012 dollars.** *Source*: United States Census Bureau (2014).

from the middle 40 percent of the distribution will increasingly use the community college, but even greater numbers from the bottom shares, as we have suggested before, could get discouraged and drop out of the pipeline altogether. Over the longer run, this could lead to a crisis of confidence in higher education and potentially disruptive declines in enrollments.

## Technology as a Disruptive Force

In chapter 3 we stressed that in the long run, the most disruptive force reshaping industries are increases in productivity, which are most often driven by changes in technology. This increase in productivity has been the major factor in raising the standard of living and in shifting jobs from agriculture to manufacturing and then to service industries such as education and health care. This process of economic development has taken place in all industrialized countries of the world and the forces that generated such change can be expected to continue. Consider the following historical examples.

**Agriculture.** At the beginning of the twentieth century, the United States was a much poorer country than it is today. Almost half of the U.S. labor force worked in agriculture producing food in small farms at a price that consumed 40 percent of the typical family's income. The price of food, it was argued, was "strangling the country"; families had nothing left to spend on other goods and other sectors of the economy could not grow (Gawande, 2009, para. 7).

Spurred on by the founding and work of the U.S. Cooperative Extension Service, modern farming techniques spread throughout the country, greatly increasing productivity and reducing food prices by one half by 1930 while "absorbing just twenty-four percent of family spending and twenty percent of the workforce" (Gawande, 2009, para. 19). Since that time agricultural productivity has increased efficiency to the point that we produce more food on the same amount of land using only 2 percent of the labor force. The greatly increased production level has reduced prices to the point where it now absorbs only 8 percent of the average family's income (Gawande, 2009). The increase in agricultural productivity also allowed the United States to become a net exporter of its farm products.

Where did all of these released workers go? Over the long run they educated themselves or their children, moved to the cities and went to work in manufacturing at a higher average wage than they had earned as farmers. It was not always a smooth transition but it did result in an overall higher standard of living. During this process, the distribution of income at first widened but then narrowed.

**Manufacturing.** The same sort of transition can be seen in manufacturing. Today the United States produces more manufactured goods than it did in 1900 and manufacturing's share of real GDP is the same as it was 50 years ago (about 12 percent). Although in 2010 China surpassed the United States as the world's leading manufacturer (on a value-added basis), the United States is still a major manufacturing hub, even though it presently has an unfavorable balance of trade with the rest of the world in these goods. This increase in output was accomplished by increases in output per worker or productivity.

Manufacturing employment, on the other hand, declined as a share of total U.S. employment from about 25 percent in 1960 to less than 10 percent today. The displacement of workers out of manufacturing has been particularly sharp since the 1990s as manufacturing employment, which held "steady at around 17 million jobs through the 1990s, . . . dropped by 5.7 million from 2000 to 2010" (Baily & Bosworth, 2014, p. 4).

As with the transition out of agriculture, many displaced workers educated or retrained themselves and their children and moved into service sectors like health care, education, and finance—industries that enjoy a favorable balance of trade with the rest of the world. During this process, the distribution of income and wealth has become much more unequal, as the discussion above shows. Since the transition out of manufacturing into services is still taking place it is unclear where these trends will lead, but it is expected that manufacturing will continue to play a strong role in the U.S. economy, albeit with fewer workers, and that higher education has an important role to play in training the labor needed and in smoothing the transition for both the displaced workers and the economy.

**Services.** Today many observers sound the alarm that education and health care are taking up increasing shares of families' spending, which threatens to restrict growth in the economy. If prices are really too high, history would lead us to conclude that some disruptive force will change that in an attempt to increase productivity. Observers of the rising cost of health care, for instance, warn that over the next ten years or so health care insurance costs, alone, will absorb "more than a fifth of every dollar people earn and that . . . health care spending will essentially devour all of our future wage increases and economic growth" (Gawande, 2009, para. 4).

Similar claims have been made for the cost of higher education, but history suggests that some disruptive change will occur in either or both of these industries ("Creative Destruction," 2014). Once again, technology will be the most likely catalyst. In higher education, the development of massive open online courses (MOOCs) is viewed by many as a way to significantly reduce costs without sacrificing quality. To date, however, technology appears to have increased costs in both health care and higher education rather than deliver cost savings.

## Technology in Higher Education

Will advancing technology transform higher education in the same way that it changed agriculture and manufacturing? It certainly will continue to change the way that education is delivered, but will it reduce the cost? Colleges have used technology to reduce some administrative costs and it appears to make positive contributions to traditional classroom instruction. The use of social media holds the promise of helping students navigate the complexity of the college process and perhaps provides some of the high-touch support that seems to be so important for first-generation, low-income students. As we look out into the future, many hope that technology, in the form of online instruction, will also greatly lower instructional costs.

An article in *The Economist* ("Creative Destruction," 2014) describes Brazil's success in using technology to reduce costs. The Brazilian model combines online and satellite instruction, taught by stellar teachers, along with hundreds of local teaching centers staffed by inexpensive mentors. Quality is monitored through national exams in all subjects, and government-subsidized loans are only available for courses of study that have high pass rates.

This market is controlled by a few private, for-profit firms that enroll about three-quarters of higher education students in the country. Such market power allows for great bargaining power over labor and other inputs, and the spreading of costs over large numbers of students results in lower costs to the student. In other words, great increases in labor productivity have reduced prices. In Brazil, technology seems to be combined with a high-touch environment to produce high completion rates, even though critics claim that colleges have an incentive to admit only those who are most likely to succeed.

Would such a program work in the United States and, more specifically, community colleges? A stringent federally mandated exit test may work in Brazil but is inconsistent with our history (even the common core is a state option). State exams are the norm in the United States and are used in licensing in some professions as a check on quality.

Of course, a standardized workplace readiness test could be developed and used by employers to screen applicants. Such exit tests are used more in Europe and Asia than in the United States but both ACT and ETS have already developed a suite of assessment tests to "help employers select, hire, train and retain" workers (Fain, 2014c, para. 3). The widespread adoption of such a system could bypass the current credentialing system and be a very disruptive force.

As for the broader college student population, we do not see national standardized tests on the horizon but we do see some of the Brazilian elements at work in places like the community college system in Vermont. Here programs are developed from a central office located in the state capital and instruction is carried out by part-time faculty in twelve centers scattered around the state.

The Community College of Vermont lists no full-time teaching faculty and offers an extensive variety of online courses and student support services. Vermont has passed most of the cost on to the students (84.8 percent of education and related expenditures are covered by tuition and fees) and it has one of the highest sticker prices in the nation at $6,923 (2011–2012). In spite of the lower-than-average labor costs, the small, mostly rural population of the state keeps enrollments low (3,114 FTE students in 2011) and an average cost per FTE student that is higher than the national average (Delta Cost Project, 2012).

The decentralized approach to higher education in the United States has resulted in a cornucopia of choices and a number of possibilities for the potential use of disruptive technologies in promoting different agendas. For instance, the movement for competency-based education, which measures outcomes rather than counting contact hours, argues that technology will not only "enable student-driven instruction, assessment and student support" but will also provide a means of documenting learning at a lower cost (Soares, 2012, p. 5).

The lower cost comes with the economies of teaching large numbers of students, using the same knowledge platform and expected outcomes. The Western Governors University and the Carnegie Mellon Open Learning Initiative are examples of promising initiatives.

Once competency-based education is combined with online learning, it could easily bypass the existing system of higher education altogether if employers were to accept it as a substitute for screening workers. Clayton Christensen, at the Harvard Business School, has been a vocal proponent of this approach. Information from his Institute for Disruptive Innovation argues that

> online competency-based education stands out as the innovation most likely to disrupt higher education . . . by breaking down learning into competencies—not courses or even subject matter—providers [not colleges] can cost-effectively combine modules of learning into pathways that are agile and adaptable to the changing labor market. (Weise & Christensen, 2014, p. iv)

Social scientists have not been very successful in predicting the future but sometimes find threads that become magnified by reality. Two of the best thinkers about the future of higher education have been optimistic, but not very specific, about the potentially disruptive impact of technology.

Ronald Ehrenberg (2011) highlights the potential for using technology to "help improve learning outcomes and . . . reduce the costs of instruction" (p. 115). Citing the programs of the National Center for Academic Transformation and the Open Learning Initiative at Carnegie Mellon University, he argues that the coming revolution in technology will change the traditional college structure and its professoriate in fundamental ways.

William Bowen looks at the prospects of an "online fix" for the college cost problem. On balance, he finds the prospects "promising but also challenging" (Bowen, 2012, p. 25). But even his tinkering with the current system to improve productivity does not result in much of a decline in costs. Nevertheless, Bowen remains optimistic that, in the future, online learning can "reduce costs without adversely affecting educational outcomes" (Bowen, 2012, p. 34).

Whether technology in a disruptive form would be adopted by community colleges is another question. Sydow and Alfred (2012) give a number of examples of colleges that have used technology and redesigned courses to lower costs but none of these has as yet been widely adapted. One would hope that online courses taught by outstanding teachers could produce a "heating up" effect that would spur interest in pursuing new ideas and interests. The results to date, however, have not been encouraging (Garza Mitchell, 2010).

The current versions of MOOCs (e.g., those offered through Coursera, Udacity, and edX) are impersonal and not well designed for the community college. They are directed at self-motivated, high-functioning learners around the world. A recent survey summarized in the University of Pennsylvania's alumni magazine, found that of "34,000 MOOC users in 200 countries . . . most were highly educated" and that "MOOCs seem to be reinforcing the advantages of the 'haves' rather than educating the 'have-nots'" ("Course Evaluation: MOOC Edition," 2014, p. 28).

To date, as a tool for educating the masses, the current version of MOOCs has been a failure and lacks the high-touch approach that many community college students need. In addition, MOOCs start and end using a traditional semester format. As stand-alone courses they don't seem to fit the flexible requirements of community college learners. However, they do have some promise as a supplement to traditional courses and newer versions may show even more promise.

Studies do show that hybrid or blended courses (with some face-to-face interaction) can improve learning among students from diverse backgrounds (Bowen, 2012). This may be good for learning, but it is not disruptive in terms of lowering college costs. Nevertheless, newer, more flexible MOOC-like courses, and the structures that are developed to support them, such as social media, are bound to emerge and may suit the part-time and occasional learner better.

To really penetrate the low-income and first-generation student market, the United States will need to improve access to broad-band internet to poor rural and urban homes. The community college, perhaps in conjunction with public libraries and social service agencies, could help here by becoming a hub for such access. As far as lowering instructional costs, however, some say that a technological "tsunami is coming . . . [but they] can't tell how it's going to break" (Bowen, 2012, p. 26).

One factor that is missing from the current MOOC-like courses is some parallel movement toward an open digital credentialing system that could dramatically lower the costs of documenting learning. Open credentialing has the potential of by-passing the current credit hour system controlled by colleges and accreditation agencies and would have a very disruptive impact on the higher education industry.

The software firm Mozilla has created an electronic credentialing system called "Open Badges" that is a step in that direction (Carey, 2015). For such a system to work, however, it would need to be accepted by employers as evidence of skills and knowledge held by students and it would have to build a track record of success in screening for workers. The open badge system of documenting learning, along with the unbundling of degrees, is more likely to take hold in continuing education, but cracking the undergraduate market will be much more difficult and possibly not as desirable.

If the path to a disruptive technology that will lower college costs is not clear, perhaps one does not exist, or perhaps we will need to look toward advances in brain science or genetics as outside forces that will change the nature of learning. Or perhaps "democracy's colleges" will give way to the democratization of postsecondary education: Students, with easy access to knowledge, would design their own learning experiences from a large array of alternatives, thus lowering the cost of education and training and hastening the development of a low-cost way of using technology for credentialing. As we often advise our students, most of the jobs they will hold have yet to be invented. Similarly, the disruptive technologies of the future that will lower costs without sacrificing quality are not yet clearly visible.

\* \* \* \* \*

Our journey exploring how community colleges are, or might be funded, has taken us through a host of issues faced by community colleges and through a tangle of public policy issues, leading directly to a consideration of the community college mission itself. That these issues are connected to finance should not be a surprise. Colleges need revenue to operate—so money matters. In return, college mangers need to use resources in a responsible manner, so costs matter. Many faculty members will insist that higher education should not be treated like a business and that what they are doing in the classroom or in other interactions with students cannot be quantified in terms of costs and benefits and the management of resources. We are sympathetic to the passion behind this view, but resources are not unlimited and have alternative uses.

Colleges will struggle to find a balance in the curriculum between cultivating the mind and teaching the practical skills necessary for labor market success. This balance will differ depending on the state and the leadership in particular colleges. The way that managers use their resources signals their priorities, and those priorities are influenced by the values of the stakeholders they answer to—federal, state, and local policy makers; students and parents who provide an increasing share of college revenue; and faculty members who, rightfully so, have learning and quality goals in mind.

In spite of our focus on the financial side of the enterprise, we should not forget that the ultimate goal of the community college is student access and success. Here, financial matters and jobs are clearly important; but we are also reminded, again, of what Mike Rose said in his study of the educational lives of community college students: Sure, people go to college for economic reasons, but "people also go to college to feel their minds working and learn new things, to help their kids, to feel competent, to remedy a poor education, to redefine who they are, to start over" (Rose, 2012, pp. 141–42). We hope that the perspectives presented in this book will help give college leaders a firmer grip on the financial wheel that can turn the ship toward these loftier goals as well.

# NOTES

1. We recognize that Guttman Community College is not the product of performance-based funding schemes per se and that it is situated within a larger system, the City University of New York, which includes other, more traditionally oriented community colleges that provide opportunities for experimenters or other students who may have an uncertain commitment to a particular degree program. But its structure is a formidable redesign of open access, prioritizing the admission of students who are more probably committed to degree completion than others. Instituting this redesign within single-college districts might be unwise and impractical. In addition, it is easier to design an innovative curriculum from scratch, as Guttman did, than to change a whole structure within an established college.

2. Readers interested in a broader view of the future might consider Al Gore's (2013) book, *The Future: Six Drivers of Global Change*. It is very much in the tradition of Toffler's (1972) *Future Shock* and Naisbitt's (1984) *Megatrends*. A little closer to home, the final chapter of Johnstone and Marcucci's (2010) book on *Financing Higher Education Worldwide* can be read with profit. For the community college, Cohen, Brawer, and Kisker (2014) have a chapter on the future of the community college where they offer some speculations on the institution's various functions, and Sydow and Alfred (2012) conclude their book on *Re-Visioning Community Colleges* with a final chapter on the "Shape of the Future."

# References

Abel, J. R., Deitz, R., & Su, Y. (2014). Are recent college graduates finding good jobs? *Current issues in economics and finance, 20*(1). Retrieved from http://www. newyorkfed.org/research/current_issues/ci20-1.pdf.

Adelman, C. (2005). *Moving into town—and moving on: Community college in the lives of traditional-age students.* Washington, DC: U.S. Department of Education. Retrieved from ERIC database (ED496111).

Adelman, C. (2008, July). *Learning accountability from Bologna: A higher education policy primer.* Retrieved from Institute for Higher Education Policy website: http://www.ihep.org/sites/default/files/uploads/docs/pubs/learning_accountability_from_bologna.pdf.

Adelman, C. (2009). *The spaces between the numbers: Getting international data on higher education straight.* Retrieved from Institute for Higher Education Policy website: http://www.ihep.org/sites/default/files/uploads/docs/pubs/report_the_spaces_between_numbers-getting_international_data_on_higher_education_straight.pdf.

Adelman, C. (2011, June 6). Re: Redefining community college success [Online reader comment]. *Inside Higher Ed.* Retrieved from http://app3.insidehighered.com/news/2011/06/06/u_s_panel_drafts_and_debates_measures_to_gauge_community_college_success.

Aims Community College. (n.d). *Tuition and fees.* Retrieved from http://www.aims.edu/student/cashier/tuition.

Alexander, K., Bozick, R., & Entwisle, D. (2008). Warming up, cooling out, or holding steady? Persistence and change in educational expectations after high school. *Sociology of Education, 81,* 371–96. doi:10.1177/003804070808100403.

Alexander, L., & Bennet, M. (2014, June 18). An answer on a postcard. *New York Times.* Retrieved from http://www.nytimes.com/2014/06/19/opinion/simplifying-fafsa-will-get-more-kids-into-college.html?_r=0.

Alfred, R. (Ed.). (1978). *Coping with reduced resources* (New Directions for Community Colleges, No. 22). San Francisco: Jossey-Bass.

Alva, J. K., & Schneider, M. (2013). *What's the value of an associate's degree?* Retrieved from American Institutes for Research website: http://www.air.org/sites/default/files/Value_of_an_Associate_Degree_10.13.pdf.

American Association of Community Colleges. (2006). *Competencies for community college leaders.* Washington, DC: American Association of Community Colleges. Retrieved from ERIC database. (ED493948).

Amherst Colege. (n.d.). *Transferring from a community college.* Retrieved from https://www.amherst.edu/admission/apply/transfer/community_collegeapp.

Archibald, R. B., & Feldman, D. H. (2011). *Why does college cost so much?* New York, NY: Oxford University Press.

Arkansas Department of Higher Education. (2014). *Performance funding - Definitions and technical specifications.* Retrieved from http:// www.adhe.edu/divisions/researchandplanning/Pages/rp_Perform_C.aspx.

Ashford, E. (2013, October 11). Hiring more full-time faculty to improve student success. *Community College Daily.* Retrieved from http://www.ccdaily.com/Pages/Campus-Issues/Maricopa-Colleges-to-hire-more-full-time-faculty,-fewer-adjuncts.aspx.

Aspen Institute. (2013). *Crisis and opportunity: Aligning the community college presidency with student success.* Retrieved from http://www.aspeninstitute.org/sites/default/files/content/docs/pubs/CEP_Final_Report.pdf.

Astin, A. (2013, April 29). College outcomes depend largely on who enrolls. *Chronicle of Higher Education* [Letter to the editor]. Retrieved from http://chronicle.com/blogs/letters/college-outcomes-depend-largely-on-who-enrolls/.

Attewell, P., & Lavin, D. E. (2007). *Passing the torch.* New York: Russell Sage Foundation.

Autor, D. H. (2014, May 23). Skills, education, and the rise of earnings inequality among the "other 99 percent." *Science, 344* (6186), 843–51. doi: 10.1126/science.1251868.

Bahr, P. R. (2010). The bird's eye view of community colleges: A behavioral typology of first-time students based on cluster analytic classification. *Research in Higher Education, 51,* 724–49.

Bahr, P. R. (2013). The deconstructive approach to understanding community college students' pathways and outcomes. *Community College Review, 41,* 137–53. doi:10.1177/0091552113486341.

Bailey, T. (2012). Can community colleges achieve ambitious graduation goals? In A. P. Kelly & M. Schneider (Eds.). *Getting to graduation: The completion agenda in higher education* (pp. 73–101). Baltimore, MD: Johns Hopkins University Press.

Bailey, T., Jaggars, S. S., & Jenkins, D. (2015). *Redesigning America's community colleges: A clearer path to student success.* Cambridge, MA: Harvard University Press.

Bailey, T., Jenkins, D., & Leinbach, T. (2005). *Graduation rates, student goals, and measuring community college effectiveness* (CCRC Brief No. 28). New York: Community College Research Center, Columbia University. Retrieved from ERIC database. (ED489098).

Bailey, T., Jeong, D. W., & Cho, S.-W. (2010). Referral, enrollment, and completion in developmental education sequences in community colleges. *Economics of Education Review, 29,* 255–70.

Baily, M. N., & Bosworth, B. P. (2014). US manufacturing: Understanding its past and its potential future. *The Journal of Economic Perspectives, 28*, 3–26.

Baime, D. S., & Mullin, C. M. (2011, July). *Promoting educational opportunity: The Pell Grant program at community colleges* (Policy Brief 2011-03PBL). Retrieved from American Association of Community Colleges website: http://www.aacc.nche.edu/Publications/Briefs/Documents/PolicyBrief_Pell%20Grant.pdf.

Banta, T. W. (2007, January 26). A warning on measuring learning outcomes. *Inside Higher Ed.* Retrieved from https://www.insidehighered.com/views/2007/01/26/banta.

Barrow, L., Richburg-Hayes, L., Rouse, C. E., & Brock, T. (2014). Paying for performance: The education impacts of a community college scholarship program for low-income adults. *Journal of Labor Economics, 32*, 563–99.

Baum, S., Conklin, K., & Johnson, N. (2013, November 13). Stop penalizing poor college students. *New York Times*, p. A-31.

Baum, S., & Kurose, C. (2013). Community colleges in context: Exploring financing of two- and four-year institutions. In Century Foundation Task Force, *Bridging the higher education divide. Strengthening community colleges and restoring the American dream* (pp. 73–108). New York: Century Foundation Press. Retrieved from http://tcf.org/assets/downloads/20130523-Bridging_the_Higher_Education_Divide-Baum_Kurose.pdf.

Baum, S., Little, K., & Payea, K. (2011). *Trends in community college education: Enrollment, prices, student aid, and debt levels.* Retrieved from College Board website: http://trends.collegeboard.org/sites/default/files/trends-2011-community-colleges-ed-enrollment-debt-brief.pdf.

Baum, S., & Ma, J. (2011). *Trends in college pricing 2011.* Washington, DC: The College Board.

Baum, S., & Ma, J. (2014a). *College affordability:What is it and how can we measure it?* Washington, DC: The College Board.

Baum, S., & Ma, J. (2014b). *Trends in college pricing, 2014.* Washington, DC: The College Board.

Baum, S., Ma, J., & Payea, K. (2013). *Education Pays, 2013.* Washington, DC: The College Board.

Baum, S., & Scott-Clayton, J. (2013, October 21). *Redesigning the Pell grant program for the twenty-first century.* Retrieved from Brookings Institution website: http://www.brookings.edu/research/papers/2013/10/21-redesigning-pell-grants-baum-scott-clayton.

Baum, S., & Scott-Clayton, J. (2015, January 20). Comments by Sandy Baum and Judith Scott-Clayton on White House announcement on new community college initiatives [web blog post]. Retrieved from The Hamilton Project website: http://www.hamiltonproject.org/blog/comments_by_sandy_baum_and_judith_scott-clayton/.

Baumol, W. J. (1967). Macroeconomics of unbalanced growth: The anatomy of urban crisis. *American Economic Review, 57*, 415–26.

Baumol, W. J., & Blackman, S. A. (1995). How to think about rising college costs. *Planning for Higher Education, 23*, 1–7.

Baumol, W. J., & Bowen, W. G. (1966). *Performing arts: The economic dilemma.* New York: Twentieth Century Fund.

Belfield, C. R., & Bailey, T. R. (2011). The benefits of attending community college: A review of the evidence. *Community College Review, 39*, 46–68.

Belfield, C., Crosta, P. M., & Jenkins, D. (2013). *Can community colleges afford to improve completion? Measuring the costs and efficiency effects of college reforms* (CCRC Working Paper No. 55). Retrieved from Community College Research Center website: http://ccrc.tc.columbia.edu/media/k2/attachments/can-community-colleges-afford-to-improve-completion.pdf.

Bellafante, G. (2014, November 14). How can community colleges get a piece of the billions that donors give to higher education? *New York Times*. Retrieved from http://www.nytimes.com/2014/11/16/nyregion/at-college-where-alumni-pockets-are-shallow-a-struggle-to-raise-money.html?_r=0.

Bensimon, E. M., & Malcom, L. E. (2012). *Confronting equity issues on campus.* Sterling, VA: Stylus.

Berliner, U. (2014, November 6). *In South Carolina, a program that makes apprenticeships work* [National Public Radio broadcast]. Retrieved from http://www.npr.org/2014/11/06/361136336/in-south-carolina-a-program-that-makes-apprenticeships-work.

Bers, T. H., Head, R. B., & Palmer, J. C. (Eds.). (2014). *Budget and finance in the American community college* (New Directions for Community Colleges, No. 168). San Francisco: Jossey-Bass.

Bettinger, E. P., & Long, B. T. (2010). Does cheaper mean better? The impact of using adjunct instructors on student outcomes. *Review of Economics and Statistics, 90*, 598–613.

Bettinger, E. P., Long, B. T., Oreopoulos, P., & Sanbonmatsu, L. (2009). *The role of simplification and information in college decisions: Results from the H&R Block FAFSA experiment* (NBER Working Paper No. 15361). Retrieved from National Bureau of Economic Research website: http://www.nber.org/papers/w15361.

Betts, J. R., & McFarland, L. L. (1995). Safe port in a storm: The impact of labor market conditions on community college enrollments. *The Journal of Human Resources, 30*, 741–65.

Birnbaum, R. (2000). *Management fads in higher education: Where they come from, what they do, why they fail.* San Francisco: Jossey-Bass.

Bogue, E. G., Johnson, B. D. (2010). Performance incentives and public college accountability in the United States: A quarter century policy audit. *Higher Education Management and Policy, 22*(2), 9–30.

Bound, J., Lovenheim, M. F., & Turner, S. (2010). Why have college completion rates declined? An analysis of changing student preparation and collegiate resources. *American Economic Journal: Applied Economics, 2*, 129–57.

Bosworth, B. (2012). Certificate pathways to post-secondary success and good jobs. In A. P. Kelly, & M. Schneider (Eds.), *Getting to graduation: The completion agenda in higher education* (pp. 102–25). Baltimore, MD: The Johns Hopkins University Press.

Bowen, H. R. (1980). *The costs of higher education: How much do colleges and universities spend per student and how much should they spend?* San Francisco: Jossey-Bass.

Bowen, W. G. (2012, October). *The "cost disease" in higher education: Is technology the answer?* Retrieved from http://www.ithaka.org/sites/default/files/files/ITHAKA-TheCostDiseaseinHigherEducation.pdf.

Boylan, R. T. (2010). *States' responses to fiscal droughts and riches.* Retrieved from Social Science Research Network website: http://papers.ssrn.com/sol3/papers.cfm?abstract_id=1641360.

Bradburn, E., Hurst, D., & Peng, S. (2001). *Community college transfer rates to 4-year institutions using alternative definitions of transfer.* Washington, DC: U.S. Department of Education. Retrieved from ERIC database. (ED454301).

Bragg, D. D., & Durham, B. (2012). Perspectives on access and equity in the era of (community) college completion. *Community College Review, 40,* 106–25.

Brand, J. E., Pfeffer, F. T., & Goldrick-Rab, S. (2014, October). The community college effect revisited: The importance of attending to heterogeneity and complex counterfactuals. *Sociological Science, 1,* 448–65. doi: 10.15195/v1.a25.

Brand, J. E., & Xie, Y. (2010). Who benefits most from college? Evidence for negative selection in heterogeneous economic returns to higher education. *American Sociological Review, 75,* 273–302.

Braverman, H. (1974). *Labor and monopoly capital: The degradation of work in the twentieth century.* New York: Monthly Review Press.

Breneman, D. W., & Nelson, S. C. (1981). *Financing community colleges: An economic perspective.* Washington, DC: Brookings Institution.

Brown, J. N. (2012). *First in the world: Community colleges and America's future.* Lanham, MD: Rowman & Littlefield.

Burd, S. (2013). *Undermining Pell: How colleges compete for wealthy students and leave the low-income behind.* Retrieved from New America Foundation website: http://education.newamerica.net/sites/newamerica.net/files/policydocs/Merit_Aid%20Final.pdf.

Bureau of Labor Statistics. (2014). *Labor productivity and costs.* Retrieved from http://www.bls.gov/lpc/lpcover.htm

Burke, J. C. (2005). Reinventing accountability. In J. C. Burke (Ed.), *Achieving accountability in higher education* (pp. 216–45). San Francisco: Jossey-Bass.

Butler, S. M. (2015, January, 20). *Obama's SOTU free college plan is bad for poor Americans.* Retrieved from Brookings Institution website: http://www.brookings.edu/research/opinions/2015/01/20-obama-free-community-college-bad-idea-sotu-butler.

Calcagno, J. C., Bailey, T., Jenkins, D., Kienzl, G., & Leinbach, T. (2008). Community college student success: What institutional characteristics make a difference? *Economics of Education Review, 27,* 632–45.

California Community Colleges Chancellor's Office. (2014). *California Community Colleges Chancellor's Office releases updates student success scorecard for all 112 colleges* [Press release]. Retrieved from http://californiacommunitycolleges.cccco.edu/Portals/0/DocDownloads/PressReleases/APR2014/PRApril_2014_Student_Success_Scorecard_Release_FINAL_w_%20Info_Graphic_4-15-14.pdf.

Carey, K. (2015, March 5). Here's what will truly change higher education: Online degrees that are seen as official. *New York Times.* Retrieved from http://www.

nytimes.com/2015/03/08/upshot/true-reform-in-higher-education-when-online-degrees-are-seen-as-official.html?ref=topics&_r=0.

Carnevale, A. P., Hanson, A. R., & Gulish, A. (2013, September). *Failure to launch: Structural shift and the new lost generation.* Retrieved from Georgetown Public Policy Institute website: https://georgetown.app.box.com/s/8tchnjo0wq9meamwwn5f.

Carnevale, A. P., Smith, N., & Strohl, J. (2010). *Help wanted: Projections of jobs and education requirements through 2018.* Retrieved from Georgetown University Center on Education and the Workforce website: http://cew.georgetown.edu/jobs2018/.

Carnevale, A. P., & Strohl, J. (2010). How increasing college access is increasing inequality, and what to do about it. In R. D. Kahlenberg (Ed.), *Rewarding strivers: Helping low-income students succeed in college* (pp. 71–190). New York: Century Foundation Press.

Carnevale, A. P., Strohl, J., & Smith, N. (2009). Help wanted: Postsecondary education and training required. In R. M. Romano & H. Kasper (Eds.), *Occupational outlook for community college students* (New Directions for Community Colleges, No. 146, pp. 21–32). San Francisco, CA: Jossey-Bass.

Castleman, B. L., & Long, B. T. (2013, December). *Looking beyond enrollment: The causal effect of need-based grants on college access, persistence and graduation.* Retrieved from National Center for Postsecondary Research website: http://www.postsecondaryresearch.org/i/a/document/NCPR_Castleman_Long_FSAG.pdf.

Century Foundation Task Force on Preventing Community Colleges from Becoming Separate and Unequal. (2013). *Bridging the higher education divide. Strengthening community colleges and restoring the American dream.* New York: Century Foundation Press.

Christensen, C. M., Horn, M. B., Caldera, L., & Soares, L. (2011). *Disrupting college: How disruptive innovation can deliver quality and affordability to postsecondary education.* Retrieved from Center for American Progress website: https://www.americanprogress.org/issues/labor/report/2011/02/08/9034/disrupting-college/.

Clotfelter, C., Ladd, H., Muschkin, C., & Vigdor, J. (2013). Success in community college: Do institutions differ? *Research in Higher Education, 54,* 805–24.

Cochrane, D., & Szabo-Kubitz, L. (2014, July). *At what cost? How community colleges that do not offer federal loans put students at risk.* Retrieved from Institute for College Access and Success website: http://projectonstudentdebt.org/files/pub/At_What_Cost.pdf.

Cohen, A. M. (1991). Deriving a valid transfer rate. In. E. B. Jones (Ed.), *A model for deriving the transfer rate: Report of the Transfer Assembly Project* (pp. 1–15). Washington, DC: American Association of Community and Junior Colleges. Retrieved from ERIC database (ED340430).

Cohen, A. M., & Brawer, F. B. (1982). *The American Community College* (1st Ed.). San Francisco, CA: Jossey-Bass.

Cohen, A. M., Brawer, F. B., & Kisker, C. B. (2013) *The American Community College* (6th Ed.). San Francisco, CA: Jossey-Bass.

College Board. (2011). *Trends in student aid, 2011.* Retrieved from http://trends.collegeboard.org/sites/default/files/Student_Aid_2011.pdf.

College Board. (2014). *Trends in student aid 2014*. Retrieved from https://secure-media.collegeboard.org/digitalServices/misc/trends/2014-trends-student-aid-report-final.pdf.

Committee on Measures of Student Success. (2011). *A report to Secretary of Education Arne Duncan*. Washington, DC: U.S. Department of Education. Retrieved from http://www2.ed.gov/about/bdscomm/list/cmss-committee-report-final.pdf.

Community College Baccalaureate Association. (n.d.). *Baccalaureate conferring locations*. Retrieved from http://www.accbd.org/resources/baccalaureate-conferring-locations/.

Complete College Tennessee Act. (2010). Retrieved from http://www.tn.gov/thec/complete_college_tn/ccta_files/ccta/Pub%20Chap%203%20-%201st%20Ex%20Sess.PDF.

Consortium for Higher Education Grants and Work-Study Reform. (2014). *Beyond Pell: A next-generation design for federal financial aid*. Retrieved from The Education Trust website: http://www.edtrust.org/sites/edtrust.org/files/BeyondPell_FINAL.pdf.

Cornell transfer program expands to community colleges. (2014, July 25). *Cornell Chronicle*. Retrieved from http://www.news.cornell.edu/stories/2008/07/three-community-colleges-join-cornell-transfer-program.

Course evaluation: MOOC edition. (2014, August 21). *The Pennsylvania Gazette*. Retrieved from http://thepenngazette.com/course-evaluation-mooc-edition/.

Cox, K. S., Smith, L. G., & Downey, R. G. (2000). *ABCs of higher education-getting back to the basics: An activity-based costing approach to planning and financial decision* (AIR Professional File No. 77). Retrieved from Association for Institutional Research website: http://airweb3.org/airpubs/77.pdf.

Coy, P. (2014, April, 3). The richest rich are in a class by themselves. *Businessweek*. Retrieved from http://www.businessweek.com/articles/2014-04-03/top-tenth-of-1-percenters-reaps-all-the-riches.

Creative destruction. (2014, June 28). *The Economist*. Retrieved from http://www.economist.com/news/leaders/21605906-cost-crisis-changing-labour-markets-and-new-technology-will-turn-old-institution-its.

Dadayan, L. (2012, July). *The impact of the Great Recession on local property taxes* (Rockefeller Institute Brief). Retrieved from Nelson A. Rockefeller Institute of Government website: http://www.rockinst.org/pdf/government_finance/2012-07-16-Recession_Local_%20Property_Tax.pdf.

Delaney, J. A. (2014). The role of state policy in promoting college affordability. *The Annals of the American Academy of Political and Social Science, 655*, 56–78.

Delaney, J. A., & Doyle, W. R. (2011). State spending on higher education: Testing the balance wheel over time. *Journal of Education Finance, 36*, 343–68.

Dellow, D., & Losinger, R. (2004). A management tool for reallocating college resources. *Community College Journal of Research and Practice, 28*, 677–88.

Dellow, D. A., & Romano, R. M. (2002). Measuring outcomes: Is the first-time, full-time cohort appropriate for the community college? *Community College Review, 30*(2), 42–54.

Delta Cost Project. (2012). *TCS online*. Retrieved from http://www.tcs-online.org/Home.aspx.

DesJardins, S. L., & Flaster, A. (2013). Non-experimental designs and causal analyses of college access, persistence, and completion. In L. Perna & A. Jones (Eds.), *The state of college access and completion: Improving college success for students from underrepresented groups* (pp. 190–207). New York: Routledge.

Desrochers, D. M., & Hurlburt, S. (2014). *Trends in college spending: 2001–2011.* Retrieved from Delta Cost Project website: http://www.air.org/sites/default/files/downloads/report/AIR_Delta%20Cost_Trends%20College%20Spending%20 2001-2011_072014.pdf.

Desrochers, D. M., & Kirshstein, R. (2014, February). *Labor intensive or labor expensive?* Retrieved from Delta Cost Project website: http://www.deltacostproject.org/sites/default/files/products/DeltaCostAIR_Staffing_Brief_2_3_14.pdf.

Desrochers, D. M., Lenihan, C. L., & Wellman, J. V. (2010). *Trends in college spending 1998–2008.* Retrieved from Delta Cost Project website: http://www.deltacostproject.org/sites/default/files/products/Trends-in-College-Spending-98-08.pdf.

Desrochers, D. M., & Wellman, J. V. (2011). *Trends in college spending, 1999–2009.* Retrieved from Delta Cost Project web site: http://www.deltacostproject.org/sites/default/files/products/Trends2011_Final_090711.pdf.

Desrochers, D. M, & Wellman, J. (2012, April). *Performance/outcomes-based budgeting. What are the experiments? What is the evidence of effectiveness?* (NASH Issue Brief). Retrieved from National Association of System Heads website: http://www.nashonline.org/.

Differential tuition. (2013, June/July). *Community College Journal, 83*(6), p. 37.

Dougherty, K., Jones, S. M., Lahr, H., Natow, R. S., Pheatt, L., & Reddy, V. (2014). Performance funding for higher education: Forms, origins, impacts, and futures. *Annals of the American Academy of Political and Social Science, 655,* 163–84.

Dougherty, K. J., Natow, R. S., Hare, R. J., Jones, S. M., & Vega, B. E. (2011). *The politics of performance funding in eight states: Origins, demise, and change.* Retrieved from the Community College Research Center website: http://ccrc.tc.columbia.edu/media/k2/attachments/performance-funding-8-states.pdf.

Dougherty, K. J., Natow, R., Hare, R. J., & Vega, B. E. (2010). *The political origins of state-level performance funding for higher education: The cases of Florida, Illinois, Missouri, South Carolina, Tennessee, and Washington* (CCRC Working Paper No. 22). Retrieved from Community College Research Center website: http://ccrc.tc.columbia.edu/media/k2/attachments/state-level-performance-funding-cases.pdf.

Dougherty, K. J., & Reddy, V. (2013). *Performance funding for higher education: What are the mechanisms? What are the Impacts?* (ASHE Higher Education Report, Vol. 39, No. 2). Hoboken, NJ: Wiley.

Dowd, A. C. (2008). Community colleges as gateways and gatekeepers: Moving beyond the access "saga" toward outcome equity. *Harvard Educational Review, 77,* 407–16.

Dowd, A. C., & Grant, J. L. (2006). Equity and efficiency of community college appropriations: The role of local financing. *Review of Higher Education, 29,* 167–94.

Dowd, A. C., & Shieh, L. T. (2013). Community college financing: Equity, efficiency, and accountability. In M. F. Smith (Ed.), *The 2013 Almanac of Higher Education* (pp. 37–65). Washington, DC: National Education Association.

Dunlop, E. (2011, March). *The importance of college choice: A study of community college transfer students in Virginia.* Paper presented at the annual conference of the Association for Education Finance and Policy, Seattle, WA. Retrieved from http://www.aefpweb.org/sites/default/files/webform/cc%20students%20 college%20quality%20AEFP%20Dunlop.pdf.

Duree, C. A. (2007). *The challenges of the community college presidency in the new millennium: Pathways, preparation, competencies, and leadership programs needed to survive* (Unpublished doctoral dissertation). Iowa State University, Ames.

Dynarski, S., & Kreisman, D. (2013). *Loans for educational opportunity: Making borrowing work for today's students.* Washington, DC: The Brookings Institution.

Dynarski, S., & Scott-Clayton, J. (2013). Financial aid policy: Lessons from research. *Future of children. 23*(1), 67–91.

Eagan, M. K., & Jaeger, A. J. (2009). Effects of exposure to part-time faculty on community college transfer. *Research in Higher Education, 50,* 168–88.

Ehrenberg, R. G. (2000). *Tuition rising: Why college costs so much.* Cambridge, MA: Harvard University Press.

Ehrenberg, R. G. (2011). Rethinking the professoriate. In B. Wildovaky, A. P. Kelly, & K. Carey (Eds.), *Reinventing higher education: The promise of innovation* (pp. 101–28). Cambridge, MA: Harvard Education Press.

Ehrenberg, R. G. (2012). *Survey of differential tuition at public higher education institutions.* Retrieved from Cornell Higher Education Research Institute website: http:// www.ilr.cornell.edu/cheri/surveys/upload/2011CHERISurveyFinal0212-3.pdf.

Ehrenberg, R. G., & Rizzo, M. A. (2004, July/August). Financial forces and the future of American higher education. *Academe, 90*(4), 28–31. Retrieved from http://www. aaup.org/AAUP/pubsres/academe/2004/JA/Feat/ehre.htm.

Ehrenberg, R. G., & Smith, R. S. (1997). *Modern Labor Economics.* New York: Addison-Wesley.

Ehrenberg, R. G., & Zhang, L. (2004). *Do tenured and tenure-track faculty matter?* (NBER Working Paper No. 10695). Retrieved from National Bureau of Economic Research website: http://www.nber.org/papers/w10695.

Fain, P. (2012a, April 25). Different course, different price. *Inside HigherEd.* Retrieved from https://www.insidehighered.com/news/2012/04/25/lone-star-college-adopts-differential-tuition.

Fain, P. (2012b, April 9). Tuition model quietly spreading. *Inside Higher Ed.* Retrieved from https://www.insidehighered.com/news/2012/04/09/differential-tuition-grows-popularity-even-community-colleges.

Fain, P. (2013a, March 4). Change from within. *Inside Higher Ed.* Retrieved from https://www.insidehighered.com/news/2013/03/04/ace-doubles-down-prior-learning-assessment.

Fain, P. (2013b, April 5). One price in California. *Inside Higher Ed.* Retrieved from https://www.insidehighered.com/news/2013/04/05/california-community-college-chancellor-opposes-differential-tuition.

Fain, P. (2013c, October 11). Two-tiered tuition is back. *Inside Higher Ed.* Retrieved from https://www.insidehighered.com/news/2013/10/11/californias-governor-signs-two-tier-tuition-law.

Fain, P. (2014a, October 16). Benefits of free. *Inside Higher Ed*. Retrieved from https://www.insidehighered.com/news/2014/10/16/chicago-joins-tennessee-tuition-free-community-college-plan.

Fain, P. (2014b, October 28). Big ten and the next big thing. *Inside Higher Ed*. Retrieved from https://www.insidehighered.com/news/2014/10/28/competency-based-education-arrives-three-major-public-institutions.

Fain, P. (2014c, November 14). Standardized tests for the job market. *Inside Higher Ed*. Retrieved from https://m.insidehighered.com/news/2014/11/14/indian-companys-skills-test-college-graduates.

Fain, P. (2014d, December 3). State-related community colleges. *Inside Higher Ed*. Retrieved from https://www.insidehighered.com/news/2014/12/03/two-year-colleges-illinois-and-other-states-lean-local-government-funding.

Fain, P. (2015a, January 9). Two years of free community college. *Inside Higher Ed*. Retrieved from https://www.insidehighered.com/news/2015/01/09/white-house-plans-take-tennessee-promise-national.

Fain, P. (2015b, February, 26). Accelerated associate degree track at CUNY pays off and earns fans. *Inside Higher Ed*. Retrieved from https://www.insidehighered.com/news/2015/02/26/accelerated-associate-degree-track-cuny-pays-and-earns-fans.

Fain, P. (2015c, March 5). Free community college: It works. *Inside Higher Ed*. Retrieved from https://www.insidehighered.com/news/2015/03/05/tulsa-community-colleges-free-tuition-program-has-paid-while-inspiring-others.

Field, K. (2014, November 3). Lamar Alexander wants to simplify, simplify, simplify. *Chronicle of Higher Education*. Retrieved from http://chronicle.com/article/Lamar-Alexander-Wants-to/149807/.

Finney, J. E., Riso, C., Orosz, K., & Boland, W. C. (2014). *From master plan to mediocrity: Higher education performance & policy in California*. Retrieved from Institute for Research on Higher Education website: http://www.gse.upenn.edu/pdf/irhe/California_Report.pdf.

Foderaro, L. W. (2011, April 10). Admission to college, with a catch: Year's wait. *New York Times*. Retrieved from http://www.nytimes.com/2011/04/11/education/11accept.html?pagewanted=all&_r=0.

Freeman, R. B. (1976). *The overeducated American*. New York: Academic Press.

Friedman, M. (1962). *Capitalism and freedom*. Chicago: University of Chicago Press.

Fuchs, V. R. (1974). *Who shall live?* New York: Basic Books.

Garms, W. I. (1977). *Financing community colleges*. New York: Teachers College Press.

Garza Mitchell, R. L. (2010). Approaching common ground: Defining quality in online education. In R. L. Garza Mitchell (Ed.), *Online education* (New Directions for Community Colleges, No. 150, pp. 89–94). San Francisco: Jossey-Bass.

Gawande, A. (2009, December 14). Testing, testing. *The New Yorker*. Retrieved from http://search.proquest.com/docview/233149546?accountid=10267.

Goldrick-Rab, S., & Kendall, N. (2014). *F2CO Redefining college affordability: Securing America's future with a free two year college option*. Retrieved from Lumina Foundation website: http://www.luminafoundation.org/publications/ideas_summit/Redefining_College_Affordability.pdf.

Goldrick-Rab, S., Schudde, L., & Stampen, J. (2015, in press). Making college affordable: The case for an institution-focused approach to federal student aid.

In A. Kelly & S. Goldrick-Rab (Eds.), *Reinventing Student Aid for the 21st Century*. Cambridge, MA: Harvard Education Press.

Goodman, J., Hurwitz, M., & Smith, J. (2015). *College access, initial college choice and degree completion* (NBER Working Paper 20996). Retrieved from National Bureau of Economic Research website: http://www.nber.org/papers/w20996.

Gore, A. (2013). *The Future: Six drivers of global change*. New York: Random House.

Granof, M. H., Platt, D. E., & Vaysman, I. (2000). *Using activity-based costing to manage more effectively*. Arlington, VA: The PricewaterhouseCoopers Endowment for the Business of Government. Retrieved from http://costkiller.net/tribune/Tribu-PDF/Using-Activity-Based-Costing-to-Manage-More-Effectively.pdf.

Harbour, C. P., Davies, T. G., & Lewis, C. W. (2006). Colorado's voucher legislation and the consequences for community colleges. *Community College Review*, *33*(3–4), 1–18.

Harbour, C. P., & Jaquette, O. (2007). Advancing an equity agenda at the community college in an age of privatization, performance accountability, and marketing. *Equity and Excellence in Education*, *40*, 197–207.

Harris, D. H., & Goldrick-Rab, S. (2010). *The (un)productivity of American higher education: From cost disease to cost-effectiveness* (Working paper no. 2010-023). Available from La Follette School of Public Affairs website: http://www.lafollette.wisc.edu/publications/workingpapers/harris2010-023.pdf.

Hauptman, A. M. (2012). Increasing higher education attainment in the United States. In A. P. Kelly, & M. Schneider (Eds.), *Getting to graduation: The completion agenda in higher education* (pp. 17–47). Baltimore, MD: Johns Hopkins University Press.

Heller, D. E. (2005). Public subsidies for higher education in California: An exploratory analysis of who pays and who benefits. *Educational Policy*, *19*, 349–70.

Heller, D. E. (2013, October 14). A study to measure value of community colleges falls short. *Chronicle of Higher Education*. Retrieved from http://chronicle.com/article/A-Study-to-Measure-Value-of/142289/.

Higginbottom, G. H., & Romano, R. M. (2006). Appraising the efficacy of civic education at the community college. In B. K. Townsend, & K. J. Dougherty (Eds.), *Community college missions in the 21st century* (New Directions for Community Colleges, No. 136, pp. 23–41). San Francisco: Jossey-Bass.

Hillman, N. W., & Orians, E. L. (2013). Community colleges and labor market conditions: How does enrollment demand change relative to local unemployment rates? *Research in Higher Education*, *54*, 765–80.

Hillman, N. W., Tandberg, D. A., & Fryar, A. H. (2015). Evaluating the impacts of "new" performance funding in higher education. *Educational Evaluation and Policy Analysis*. Advance online publication. doi: 10.3102/0162373714560224.

Hilton, R. W., Maher, M. W., & Selto, F. H. (2006). *Cost Management* (3rd Ed.). New York: McGraw-Hill.

Hodel, R., Laffey, M., & Lingenfelter, P. (2006). *Recession, retrenchment, and recovery: State higher education funding and financial aid*. Boulder, CO: State Higher Education Executive Officers. Retrieved from ERIC database. (ED502180).

Hom, W. (2009). The denominator as the "target." *Community College Review*, *37*, 136–52.

Horn, L., & Lew, S. (2008). *California community college transfer rates* (MPR Research Brief). Retrieved from RTI International website: https://www.rti.org/pubs/horn_ccc.pdf.

Horn, L., Li, X., & Weko, T. (2009). *Changes in postsecondary awards below the bachelor's degree: 1997 to 2007* (NCES 2010-167).Washington, DC: National Center for Education Statistics. Retrieved from http://nces.ed.gov/pubs2010/2010167.pdf.

Horn L., & Skomsvold, P. (2012*). Community college student outcomes 1994–2009 (NCES 2012-253).* Washington, DC: National Center for Education Statistics. Retrieved from http://nces.ed.gov/pubs2012/2012253.pdf.

Hovey, H. A. (1999). *State spending for higher education in the next decade: The battle to sustain current support.* Retrieved from National Center for Public Policy and Higher Education website: http://www.highereducation.org/reports/hovey/hovey.pdf.

Hoxby, C., & Avery, C. (2013). *The missing "one offs": The hidden supply of high-achieving, low-income students.* Retrieved from Brookings Institution website: http://www.brookings.edu/~/media/projects/bpea/spring%202013/2013a_hoxby.pdf.

Hoxby, C., & Turner, S. (2013). *Expanding college opportunities for high-achieving, low-income students* (SIEPR Discussion Paper 12-014). Retrieved from Stanford Institute for Economic Policy Research website: http://siepr.stanford.edu/?q=/system/files/shared/pubs/papers/12-014paper.pdf.

Hudson, D. (2015, January 8). The president proposes to make community college free for responsible students to two years [Web log post]. Retrieved from White House web site: https://www.whitehouse.gov/blog/2015/01/08/president-proposes-make-community-college-free-responsible-students-2-years.

Illinois Board of Higher Education (n.d.). *Current funds revenue by source at Illinois community colleges, FY2010.* Retrieved from http://www.ibhe.org/Data%20Bank/DataBook/2011/Table%20VI-11.pdf.

Illinois Community College Board. (n.d.). *What are the fiscal year 2015 measures for community college performance funding?* Retrieved from http://64.107.108.133/pdf/performance_funding/FY15_PerformanceFunding_FAQ.pdf.

In step with Edwin Massey. (2013, December). Retrieved from http://www.indianrivermag.com/emags/NOV13OnlineEditionWeb/index.html#/0/.

Indiana Commission for Higher Education. (n.d.). *History of IN performance funding.* Retrieved from http://www.in.gov/che/files/PBOF_White_Paper_2-22-13_A.pdf.

Indiana Commission for Higher Education. (2013). *2013–2015 higher education performance funding formula model—Weighting and rates for PFF.* Retrieved from http://www.in.gov/che/files/Weighting_of_Metrics_2013-15_Proposed_F.pdf.

Institute for College Access and Success. (2014, April). *Still denied: How community college shortchange students by not offering federal loans* (Issue Brief). Retrieved from The Project on Student Debt website: http://projectonstudentdebt.org/files/pub/still_denied.pdf.

Institute for Higher Education Policy. (2014). *Degrees of hope: Redefining access for the 21st century student.* Retrieved from http://www.ihep.org/sites/default/files/uploads/docs/pubs/ihep_viewing_guide_web.pdf.

Instructional Technology Council. (2011). *2010 distance education survey results. Trends in elearning: Tracking the impact of elearning at community colleges.*

Retrieved from http://www.itcnetwork.org/images/stories/itcannualsurveymay-2011final.pdf.

Jacoby, D. (2006). Effects of part-time faculty employment on community college graduation rates, *The Journal of Higher Education, 77*, 1081–1103.

Jaegaer, A. J., & Egan, M. K. (2009). Unintended consequences: Examining the effect of part-time faculty members on associate's degree completion. *Community College Review, 36*, 167–94.

Jaggars, S. S. (2011, March). *Online learning: Does it help low-income and under-prepared students?* (CCRC Brief No. 52). Retrieved from Community College Research Center website: http://ccrc.tc.columbia.edu/media/k2/attachments/online-learning-help-students-brief.pdf.

James, E. (1978). Product mix and cost disaggregation: A reinterpretation of the economics of higher education. *Journal of Human Resources, 13*, 157–86.

Jankowski, N., Hutchings, P., Ewell, P., Kinzie, J., & Kuh, G. (2013, November–December). The Degree Qualifications Profile: What it is and why we need it now. *Change*. http://www.changemag.org/Archives/Back Issues/2013/November-December 2013/Degree_full.htm.

Jaquette, O. (2009). Funding for equity and success in English further education colleges, 1998–2003. *Oxford Review of Education, 35*, 57–79.

Jaschik, S. (2013, August 22). Obama's ratings for higher ed. *Inside Higher Ed*. Retrieved from https://www.insidehighered.com/news/2013/08/22/president-obama-proposes-link-student-aid-new-ratings-colleges.

Jenkins, D., & Cho, S-W. (2014). *Get with the program . . . and finish it: Building guided pathways to accelerate student completion* (CCRC Working Paper No. 66). Retrieved from Community College Research Center website: http://ccrc.tc.columbia.edu/media/k2/attachments/get-with-the-program-and-finish-it-2.pdf.

Jenkins, D., & Rodriguez, O. (2013). Access and success with less: Improving productivity in broad-access postsecondary institutions. *The Future of Children, 23*(1), 19–41.

Jencks, C. (1970). *Education vouchers: A report on financing elementary education by grants to parents*. Washington, DC: Center for Policy Studies.

Johnson, N. (2009). *What does a college degree cost? Comparing approaches to measuring "cost per degree"* (Delta Cost Project white paper). Retrieved from Delta Cost Project website: http://www.deltacostproject.org/sites/default/files/products/johnson3-09_WP.pdf.

Johnson, N., & Davies, G. (2014). *Can comprehensive public universities implement large-scale affordability reforms?* Retrieved from HCM Strategists website: http://hcmstrategists.com/maximizingresources/images/Gates_Framing_Paper.pdf.

Johnstone, D. B., & Marcucci, P. N. (2010). *Financing higher education worldwide: Who pays? Who should pay?* Baltimore, MD: The Johns Hopkins University Press.

Jones, D. (2013). *Outcomes-based funding: The wave of implementation*. Retrieved from National Center for Higher Education Management Systems website: http://www.nchems.org/pubs/docs/Outcomes-Based%20Funding%20Paper%20091613.pdf.

Jongblod, B., & Koelman, J. (2000). *Vouchers for higher education. A survey of the literature commissioned by the Hong Kong University Grants Committee*. Enschede, The Netherlands: Center for Higher Education Policy Studies, University of Twente.

Kalogrides, D., & Grodsky, E. (2011). Something to fall back on: Community colleges as a safety net. *Social Forces, 89*, 853–77.

Kane, T. J., & Rouse, C. E. (1995). Labor-market returns to two- and four-year colleges. *American Economic Review, 85*, 600–14.

Kane, T. J., & Rouse, C. E. (1999). The community college: Educating students at the margin between college and work. *Journal of Economic Perspectives, 13*, 63–84.

Kansas Board of Regents. (2014). *Performance agreements: Funding guidelines.* Retrieved from http://www.kansasregents.org/resources/PDF/2441-revisedfundingguidelinesJune182014.pdf.

Kantrowitz, M. (2009). *FAFSA completion by level and control of institution.* Available at FinAid.org website: http://www.finaid.org/educators/20091014fafsa completion.pdf.

Kaplan, R. S., & Anderson, S. R. (2003). *Time-driven activity-based costing.* Retrieved from Social Science Research Network website: http://papers.ssrn.com/sol3/papers.cfm?abstract_id=485443

Katsinas, S. G., & Palmer, J. C. (Eds.). (2005). *Sustaining fiscal support for community colleges* (New Directions for Community Colleges, No. 132). San Francisco: Jossey-Bass.

Kelchen, R. (2014, October 13). The costs of free. *Inside Higher Ed.* Retrieved from https://www.insidehighered.com/views/2014/10/13/essay-questions-free-community-college-policies.

Kelly, A. P., & Schneider, M. (Eds.). (2012). *Getting to graduation: The completion agenda in higher education.* Baltimore: The Johns Hopkins University Press.

Kelly, P. J. (2009). *The dreaded "P" word: An examination of productivity in public postsecondary education.* Retrieved from Delta Cost Project web site: http://knowledgecenter.completionbydesign.org/resource/385.

Kelly, P., & Whitfield, C. (2014, May–June). Playing the numbers: Employment outcomes in the two-year sector: The witch hunt for college programs that don't pay off. *Change, 46*(3), 60–63.

Kiley, K. (2013, July 9). No such thing as "free tuition." *Inside Higher Ed.* Retrieved from https://www.insidehighered.com/news/2013/07/09/oregon-plan-would-shift-tuition-payment-after-graduation.

Kirp, D. L. (2014, January 8). How to help college students graduate. *New York Times,* Retrieved from http://www.nytimes.com/2014/01/09/opinion/how-to-help-college-students-graduate.html?_r=0.

Koseff, A. (2014, September 29). Jerry Brown approves community college bachelor's degrees. *Sacramento Bee.* Retrieved from http://www.sacbee.com/news/politics-government/capitol-alert/article2615016.html.

Krugman, P. (1994). *The age of diminishing expectations.* Cambridge, MA: MIT Press.

Kurz, K., & Scannell, J. (2006, May). Enrollment management grows up. *University Business.* Retrieved from http://www.universitybusiness.com/article/enrollment-management-grows.

Lahr, H., Pheatt, L., Dougherty, K., Jones, S., Natow, R., & Reddy, V. (2014). *Unintended impacts of performance funding on community colleges and universities in three states* (CCRC Working Paper No. 78). Retrieved from

Community College Research Center website: http://ccrc.tc.columbia.edu/media/k2/attachments/unintended-impacts-performance-funding.pdf.

Leigh, D. E., & Gill, A. M. (2004). The effect of community colleges on changing students' educational aspirations. *Economics of Education Review, 23*, 95–102.

Leonhardt, D. (2014, June 10). A case study in lifting college attendance. *New York Times*. Retrieved from http://www.nytimes.com/2014/06/10/upshot/a-case-study-in-lifting-college-attendance.html?_r=0.

Lombardi, J. (Ed.). (1973). *Meeting the fiscal crisis* (New Directions for Community Colleges, No. 2). San Francisco: Jossey-Bass.

Lombardi, J. (1976). *No- or low-tuition: A lost cause* (Topical Paper No. 58). Los Angeles, CA: ERIC Clearinghouse for Junior Colleges. Retrieved from ERIC database. (ED129353).

Long, B. T., & Kurlaender, M. (2009). Do community colleges provide a viable pathway to a baccalaureate degree? *Educational Evaluation and Policy Analysis, 31*, 30–53.

Louisiana Board of Regents. (n.d.). *Grad Act*. Retrieved from http://regents.louisiana.gov/grad-act/.

Louisiana Board of Regents. (2014, July). *Grad Act annual report. Progress towards meeting Louisiana's higher education goals*. Retrieved from http://regents.louisiana.gov/wp-content/uploads/2014/07/GRAD-Act-Annual-Report-Year-4-2014-0715.pdf

Mahoney, R. J. (1997, October 17). "Reinventing" the university: Object lessons from big business. *Chronicle of Higher Education*, p. B4.

Manning, T. M., & Crosta, P. M. (2014). Program costs and student completion. In T. H. Bers, R. B. Head, & J. C. Palmer (Eds.), *Budget and finance in the American community college* (New Directions for Community Colleges, No. 168, pp. 41–51). San Francisco: Jossey-Bass.

Massy, W. F., Sullivan, T. A., & Mackie, C. (2012). Data needed for improving productivity measurement in higher education. *Research & Practice in Assessment, 7*(Winter), 5–15. Retrieved from http://www.rpajournal.com/dev/wp-content/uploads/2012/11/RPA_WinterVOL7.pdf.

Massy, W. F., Sullivan, T. A., & Mackie, C. (2013). Improving measurement of productivity in higher education. *Change, 45*(1), 15–23.

McKeown-Moak, M. P. (2013). The "new" performance funding in higher education. *Educational Considerations, 40*(2), 1–12.

McMahon, W. W. (2009). *Higher learning, greater good: The private and social benefits of higher education*. Baltimore, MD: Johns Hopkins University Press.

Melguizo T., Kienzl G., & Alfonso M. (2011). Comparing the educational attainment of community college transfer students and four-year rising juniors using propensity score matching methods. *Journal of Higher Education, 82*, 265–91.

Mellow, G. O., & Heelan, C. (2008). *Minding the dream: The process and practice of the American community college*. New York: Rowman & Littlefield.

Miao. K. (2012, August). *Performance-based funding of higher education. A detailed look at best practices in 6 states*. Retrieved from Center for American Progress web site: https://cdn.americanprogress.org/wp-content/uploads/issues/2012/08/pdf/performance_funding.pdf.

Milliron, M. D., de los Santos, G. E., & Browning, B. (Eds.). (2003). *Successful approaches to fundraising and development* (New Directions for Community Colleges, No. 124). San Francisco: Jossey-Bass.

Missouri Department of Higher Education. (2014, August 21). *State of Missouri performance funding for higher education.* Retrieved from http://dhe.mo.gov/documents/PerformanceFundingReport.pdf.

Moltz, D. (2010, October 26). The new community college tuition hike. *Inside Higher Ed.* Retrieved from https://www.insidehighered.com/news/2010/10/26/tuition.

Monaghan, D. B., & Attewell, P. (2014). The community college route to the bachelor's degree. *Educational Evaluation and Policy Analysis.* Advance online publication. doi:10.3102/0162373714521865.

Montana University System. (n.d.). *Performance funding metrics.* Retrieved from http://mus.edu/board/meetings/2014/May2014/AdminBudget/163-108-R0514_A1.pdf.

Mullin, C. M. (2012). *Transfer: An indispensable part of the community college mission.* (AACC Policy Brief 2012-03PBL). Retrieved from American Association of Community Colleges website: http://www.aacc.nche.edu/Publications/Briefs/Documents/AACC_Transfer_to_LUMINA_BW.pdf.

Mullin, C. M. (2013). *Postcollege workforce outcomes measures: Issues facing policymakers, analysts, and researchers.* Retrieved from American Association of Community Colleges website: http://www.aacc.nche.edu/Publications/Reports/Documents/WorkforceOutcomes_2013.pdf.

Mullin, C. M., Baime, D. S., & Honeyman, D. S. (2015). *Community college finance: A guide for institutional leaders.* San Francisco: Jossey-Bass.

Naisbitt, J. (1984). *Megatrends: Ten new directions transforming our lives.* New York: Warner Books.

National Association of State Student Grant and Aid Programs. (2012). *43rd annual survey report on state-sponsored students aid, 2011–2012 academic year.* Retrieved from http://www.nassgap.org/viewrepository.aspx?categoryID=3#.

National Conference of State Legislatures. (2015, January 13). *Performance-based funding for higher education.* Retrieved from http://www.ncsl.org/research/education/performance-funding.aspx.

National Higher Education Benchmarking Institute. (2014). *Maximizing resources for student success.* Retrieved from https://maximizingresources.org/.

National Student Clearinghouse Research Center. (2012). *Snapshot report on degree attainment.* Available at http://www.studentclearinghouse.info/snapshot/docs/SnapshotReport8-GradRates2-4Transfers.pdf.

National Student Clearinghouse Research Center. (2013). *Completing college: A national view of student attainment rates—Fall 2007 cohort.* Retrieved from http://nscresearchcenter.org/wp-content/uploads/NSC_Signature_Report_6.pdf.

Neault, L. C. (2012). *Implications of state and local policy on community college transfer in California: A regional case study* (Unpublished doctoral dissertation). San Diego State University, California.

Nelson, S. P., & Keller, J. (2014). *Community college performance-based funding model* [PowerPoint slides]. Retrieved from Massachusetts Department of Higher

Education website: http://www.mass.edu/foradmin/trustees/documents/Funding-FormulaOverviewTrusteesOverviewv3.pptx.

Nevada System of Higher Education. (n.d.). *A new model for funding higher education in Nevada.* Retrieved from http://system.nevada.edu/tasks/sites/Nshe/assets/File/Initiatives/fundingformula/New_NSHE_Funding_Model._dtd_3.12.v9.for_final_distribution.pdf.

New Mexico Department of Higher Education. (2013, December). *Funding for performance in higher education in New Mexico.* Retrieved from http://www.nmlegis.gov/lcs/handouts/ALFC%20120913%20Item%208%20HANDOUT%20-%20Funding%20for%20Performance%20in%20Higher%20Education.pdf.

New Mexico Department of Higher Education. (2014). *NM I&G funding formula FY 16* [Excel file]. Retrieved from http://www.hed.state.nm.us/uploads/files/Institutional%20Finance/Budget%20Information/NM%20IG%20Funding%20Formula%20FY16%20v9%209%20Final%202014-11-17.xlsx.

North Carolina State Board of Community Colleges. (2013). *Performance-based funding: A model for embedding performance into formula allocations.* Retrieved from http://www.ncleg.net/documentsites/committees/JLEOC/Reports%20Received/2013%20Reports%20Received/Performance%20Based%20Funding%20Report%20-%20SBCC.pdf.

Obama, B. (2010, January 27). *Remarks by the President in the State of the Union Address.* Retrieved from The White House website: http://www.whitehouse.gov/the-press-office/remarks-president-state-union-address.

Office of Program Policy Analysis and Government Accountability. (2005). *Excess hours at community colleges warrant attention by the department of education and the legislature* (Report No. 05-30). Retrieved from http://www.oppaga.state.fl.us/MonitorDocs/Reports/pdf/0530rpt.pdf.

Ohio Board of Regents. (n.d.). *Prior learning assessment and Ohio's completion agenda.* Retrieved from https://www.ohiohighered.org/sites/ohiohighered.org/files/uploads/PLA/PLA-with-a-Purpose_Report_FINAL_041614_0.pdf.

Ohio Board of Regents. (2013). *State share of instruction handbook: Providing the methodology for allocating state share of instruction funds for fiscal year 2014. For use by: Community and technical colleges.* Retrieved from: https://www.ohiohighered.org/sites/ohiohighered.org/files/uploads/financial/ssi/College_Handbook_2014%20v2.doc.

Ohio Board of Regents. (2014). *Student success initiative—Success points.* Retrieved from https://www.ohiohighered.org/node/936.

Oklahoma State Regents for Higher Education. (n.d.). *State system overview. Part 3: Other responsibilities and programs.* Retrieved from http://www.okhighered.org/state-system/overview/part3.shtml.

Omnibus higher education appropriations bill, SF 1236, 88th Minnesota Legislature. (2013). Retrieved from https://www.revisor.mn.gov/bills/text.php?version=latest&session=ls88&number=SF1236&session_year=2013&session_number=0.

Oreopoulos, P., Wachter, T., & Heisz, A. (2012). The short- and long-term career effects of graduating in a recession. *American Economic Journal: Applied Economics, 4*(1), 1–29.

Palacios-Huerta, I. (Ed.). *In 100 years: Leading economists predict the future.* Cambridge, MA: MIT Press.

Palmer, J. C. (2000). What do we know about transfer? An overview. *Peer Review* 2(2), 8–11.

Palmer, J. C. (2013). State fiscal support for community colleges. In J. S. Levin & S. T. Kater (Eds.), *Understanding community colleges* (pp. 171–84). New York: Routledge.

Palmer, J. C. (Ed.). (2015). *Summary tables, fiscal year (FY) 2014–15.* Retrieved from Grapevine web site: http://education.illinoisstate.edu/grapevine/tables/.

Pascarella, E. T. (1999). New studies track community college effects on students. *Community College Journal*, 69(6), 8–14.

Pascarella, E., & Terenzini, P. (1999). *How college affects students. Findings and insights from twenty years of research.* San Francisco, CA: Jossey-Bass.

Patel, R., & Richburg-Hayes, L. (2012). *Performance-based scholarships: Emerging findings from a national demonstration* (MDRC Policy Brief ). Retrieved from MDRC website: http://www.mdrc.org/sites/default/files/policybrief_41.pdf.

Perez-Pena, (2012, July 20). The new community college try. *New York Times.* Retrieved from http://www.nytimes.com/2012/07/20/education/edlife/the-new-community-college-cunys-multimillion-dollar-experiment-in-education. html?pagewanted=all&_r=0.

Performance Indicators Task Force. (n.d.). *Proposal and recommendations.* Retrieved from Michigan Senate website: http://www.senate.michigan.gov/sfa/Departments/ DataCharts/DCccl_PerformanceIndicators.pdf.

Piketty, T. (2014). *Capital in the twenty-first century.* Cambridge, MA: Harvard University Press.

Pima Community College. (n.d.). *Differential tuition.* Retrieved from https://www. pima.edu/paying-for-school/costs/differential-tuition.html.

Prescott, B. T. (2010, July/August). Is Colorado's voucher system worth vouching for? *Change*, 32(4), 20–26.

Reeves, R. V., & Howard, K. (2013, September). *The parenting gap.* Retrieved from The Brookings Institution website: http://www.brookings.edu/research/ papers/2013/09/09-parenting-gap-social-mobility-wellbeing-reeves.

Rehberg, R. A., & Rosenthal, E. (1978). *Class and merit in the American high school.* New York: Longmans.

Rivard, R. (2014, October, 8). Iowa's balance of power. *Inside Higher Ed.* Available at https://www.insidehighered.com/news/2014/10/08/iowas-largest-public-university-scrambles-students-private-colleges-worry-they-will.

Romano, R. M. (2003, October). *Financing community colleges across the states: An economic perspective.* Paper prepared for a conference on The Complex Community College, Cornell University, Ithaca, NY. Retrieved from http://www.ilr.cornell.edu/cheri/conferences/upload/2003oct/chericonf2003_08. pdf.

Romano, R. M. (2004). Cooling out revisited: Some evidence from survey research. *Community College Journal of Research and Practice*, 28, 311–20.

Romano, R. M. (2005). Seeking the proper balance between tuition, state support and local revenues: An economic perspective. In S. G. Katsinas & J. C. Palmer (Eds.),

*Sustaining financial support for community colleges* (New Directions for Community Colleges, No.132, pp. 33–42). San Francisco: Jossey-Bass.

Romano, R. M. (2012). Looking behind community college budgets for future policy considerations. *Community College Review, 40,* 165–89.

Romano, R. M., & Djajalaksana, Y. M. (2011). Using the community college to control college costs: How much cheaper is it? *Community College Journal of Research and Practice, 35,* 539–55.

Romano, R. M., Losinger, R., & Millard, T. (2011). Measuring the cost of a college degree: A case study of a SUNY community college. *Community College Review, 39,* 211–34.

Romano, R. M., Townsend, B. K., & Mamiseishvili, K. (2009). Leaders in the making: Profile and perceptions of students in community college doctoral programs. *Community College Journal of Research and Practice, 33,* 309–20.

Rose, M. (2012). *Back to school: Why everyone deserves a second chance at education.* New York: The New Press.

Rosenbaum, J. E., Deil-Amen, R., & Person, A. E. (Eds.). (2006). *After admission: From college access to college success.* New York: Russell Sage Foundation.

Rosenbaum, J. E., & Rosenbaum, J. (2013). Beyond BA blinders: Lessons from occupational colleges and certificate programs for nontraditional students. *Journal of Economic Perspectives, 27*(2), 153–72.

Rothwell, J. (2013). *The hidden STEM economy.* Retrieved from The Brookings Institution website: http://www.brookings.edu/research/reports/2013/06/10-stem-economy-rothwell.

Rouse, C. E. (1994). What to do after high school: The two-year versus four-year college enrollment decision. In R. G. Ehrenberg (Ed.), *Choices and consequences: Contemporary policy issues in education* (pp. 59–88). Ithaca, NY: ILR Press.

Rouse, C. E. (1998). Do two-year colleges increase overall educational attainment? Evidence from the states. *Journal of Policy Analysis and Management, 17,* 595–620.

Saez, E., & Zucman (2014). *The distribution of wealth, capital income and returns since 1913* [PowerPoint slides]. Retrieved from http://gabriel-zucman.eu/files/SaezZucman2014Slides.pdf.

Sallie M. (2014). *How America pays for college.* Washington, DC: Author. Retrieved from http://news.salliemae.com/files/doc_library/file/HowAmericaPaysforCollege2014FNL.pdf.

Salt Lake Community College. (2014). *Electronic portfolios at SLCC.* Retrieved from http://www.slcc.edu/gened/eportfolio/index.aspx.

Schneider, B., & Stevenson, D. (1999). *The ambitious generation: America's teenagers, motivated but directionless.* New Haven: Yale University Press.

Secretary of Education's Commission on the Future of Higher Education. (2006). *A test of leadership. Charting the future of U.S. higher education.* Washington, DC: U.S. Department of Education. Retrieved from http://www2.ed.gov/about/bdscomm/list/hiedfuture/reports/final-report.pdf.

Smith, A. A. (2015, March 12). Zeroed out in Arizona. *Inside Higher Ed.* Retrieved from https://www.insidehighered.com/news/2015/03/12/arizona-unprecedented-defunding-community-colleges.

Snyder, T. D., & Dillow, S. A. (2013). *Digest of Education Statistics 2012.* Washington, DC: National Center for Education Statistics.

Snyder, T. D., & Dillow, S. A. (2015). *Digest of Education Statistics 2013.* Washington, DC: National Center for Education Statistics.

Snyder, T. D., Dillow, S. A., & Hoffman, C. M. (2009). *Digest of Ed Statistics 2008,* Washington, DC.

Soares, L. (2012, June 7). *A "disruptive" look at competency-based education.* Retrieved from Center for American Progress website: http://cdn.american-progress.org/wp-content/uploads/issues/2012/06/pdf/comp_based_education.pdf.

Sommers, D. (2009). National labor market projections for community college students. In R. M. Romano & H. Kasper (Eds.), *Occupational outlook for community college students* (New Directions for Community Colleges, No. 146, pp. 33–52). San Francisco: Jossey-Bass.

Sörlin, S. (2007). Funding diversity: Performance-based funding regimes as drivers of differentiation in higher education systems. *Higher Education Policy, 20,* 413–40.

Stange, K. (2009). *Ability sorting and the importance of college quality to students achievement: Evidence from community colleges.* Unpublished manuscript, Ford School of Public Policy, University of Michigan, Ann Arbor, MI. Retrieved from: http://www-personal.umich.edu/~kstange/papers/StangeCollegeQuality.pdf.

Stange, K. M. (2012). An empirical investigation of the option value of college enrollment. *American Economic Journal: Applied Economics, 4*(1), 49–84.

Stange, K. M. (2013). *Differential pricing in undergraduate education: Effects on degree production by field* (NBER Working Paper No. 19183). Retrieved from National Bureau of Economic Research website: http://www.nber.org/papers/w19183.

State Higher Education Executive Officers. (2015). *SHEF 2014: State higher education finance.* Retrieved from http://www.sheeo.org/sites/default/files/project-files/SHEF%20FY%202014-20150410.pdf.

Stecher, B. M., Camm, F., Damberg, L. S., Mullen, K. J., Nelson, C., Sorenssn, P., Leuschner, K. J. (2010). *Toward a culture of consequences: Performance-based accountability systems for public services.* Santa Monica, CA: Rand Corporation.

Strayer, J. (2004). Colorado's higher education vouchers: A new trend or budgetary desperation? *Spectrum: The Journal of State Government, 77*(3), 27–29.

Sullivan, T. A., Mackie, C., Massy, W. F., & Sinha, E. (Eds.). (2012). *Improving measurement of productivity in higher education.* Washington, DC: National Academies Press.

Sydow, D., & Alfred, R. L. (2012). *Re-visioning community colleges.* New York: Rowman & Littlefield.

Szatmary, D. P. (2011). Activity-based budgeting in higher education. *Continuing Higher Education Review, 75,* 69–85. Retrieved from http://files.eric.ed.gov/fulltext/EJ967809.pdf.

Tennessee Higher Education Commission. (n.d.). *Tennessee's outcomes-based funding formula* [PowerPoint slides]. Retrieved from http://www.tn.gov/thec/Divisions/Fiscal/funding_formula/1-Funding%20Formula%20-%20Updated%20for%20Website.ppt.

Tennessee Higher Education Commission. (2010). *2010–2015 performance funding quality assurance.* Retrieved from http://www.tn.gov/thec/complete_college_tn/

ccta_files/outcomes_based_ff/PF%202010-15%20Guidebook%20Dec%201%20 2010.pdf.

Texas Higher Education Coordinating Board. (2013, July). *Texas State Technical College System returned value funding methodology.* Retrieved from http://www. thecb.state.tx.us/reports/pdf/3207.pdf.

Texas Legislature. (2013). *Conference Committee report, S.B. No. 1 General appropriations bill.* (3rd printing). Retrieved from http://www.lrl.state.tx.us/ scanned/83ccrs/sb0001.pdf#navpanes=0.

Toffler, A. (1972). *Future shock.* New York: Bantam.

Tomkins Cortland Community College. (n. d.). *Farm to bistro.* Retrieved from http:// www.tc3.edu/catalog/ap_farm_to_bistro.asp.

Umbach, P. D. (2007). How effective are they? Exploring the impact of contingent faculty on undergraduate education. *Review of Higher Education, 30*(2), 91–123.

Umbach, P. D. (2008, November). *The effects of part-time faculty appointments on instructional techniques and commitment to teaching.* Paper presented at the Annual Meeting of the Association for the Study of Higher Education, Jacksonville, FL. Retrieved from http://www4.ncsu.edu/~pdumbach/part-time.pdf.

United States Census Bureau. (2014). Table F-3. Mean income received by each fifth and top 5 percent of families [Data table]. Retrieved from http://www.census.gov/ hhes/www/income/data/historical/families/.

University of Hawai'i System, Office of the Vice President for Community Colleges. (2014). *2013 performance funding.* Retrieved from http://uhcc.hawaii.edu/ OVPCC/APAPA/2013_performance.php.

Unterman, R. (2014). *Headed to college: The effects of New York City's small high schools of choice on postsecondary enrollment* (MDRC Policy Brief). Retrieved from MDRC website: http://www.mdrc.org/publication/headed-college.

Utah State Legislature. (2013, May). *2013–2014 Appropriations report.* Retrieved from http://le.utah.gov/interim/2013/pdf/00001950.pdf.

Vernez, G., Krop, R., & Rydell, C. P. (1999). *Costs and benefits of closing the gap for blacks and Hispanics.* Santa Monica, CA: Rand Corporation.

Virginia Higher Ediucation Opportunity Act of 2011. (2011). Retrieved from Virginia's Legislative Information System website: http://lis.virginia.gov/cgi-bin/ legp604.exe?111+ful+CHAP0869.

Voight, M., Long, A. A. Huelsman, M., & Engle, J. (2014). *Mapping the postsecondary data domain: Problems and possibilities.* Retrieved from Institute for Higher Education Policy website: http://www.ihep.org/sites/default/files/uploads/docs/ pubs/mapping_the_postsecondary_data_domain_-_main_report_revised.pdf.

Walla Walla Community College. (2015). *Enology & viticulture.* Retrieved from http://www.wwcc.edu/CMSX/main.php?module=department&collegecode=200& deptcode=EV.

Washington State Board for Community and Technical Colleges. (2012). *Student achievement revised framework.* Retrieved from http://www.sbctc.ctc.edu/college/ education/NewStudentAchievementFrameworkfinal.docx.

Washington State Board for Community and Technical Colleges. (2014). *Student achievement initiative.* Retrieved from http://www.sbctc.ctc.edu/ college/e_studentachievement.aspx.

Webber, D. A. (2011). *Expenditures and postsecondary graduation: An investigation using individual-level data from the state of Ohio* (Working Paper No. 140). Retrieved from Cornell Higher Education Research Institute website: http://www.ilr.cornell.edu/cheri/workingPapers/upload/Ohio_expenditures.pdf.

Webber, D. A., & Ehrenberg, R. G. (2010). Do expenditures other than instructional expenditures affect graduation and persistence rates in American higher education? *Economics of Education Review, 29*, 947–58.

Weisbrod, B. A., Ballou, J. P., & Asch, E. D. (2008). *Mission and money: Understanding the university*. New York: Cambridge University Press.

Weise, M. R., & Christensen, C. M. (2014). *Hire education: Mastery, modularization, and the workforce revolution*. Retrieved from Clayton Christensen Institute for Disruptive Innovation website: http://www.christenseninstitute.org/publications/hire/.

Wellman, J. V. (2006). *Costs, prices and affordability: A background paper for the Secretary's Commission on the Future of Higher Education*. Retrieved from U.S. Department of Education website: http://www2.ed.gov/about/bdscomm/list/hiedfuture/reports/wellman.pdf.

West, E. (1997). Education vouchers in practice and principle: A survey. *The World Bank Research Observer, 12*(1), 83–103.

West, R. (1998). *Learning for life: Review of higher education financing and policy*. Canberra: Australian Government Publishing Service.

Western Interstate Commission on Higher Education. (2008). *An evaluation of Colorado's college opportunity fund and related policies*. Retrieved from http://www.wiche.edu/info/publications/policyCOF.pdf.

Winston, G. C. (1998). *A guide to measuring college costs* (Discussion Paper 46). Retrieved from Williams Project on the Economics of Higher Education website: http://www.williams.edu/wpehe/DPs/DP-46.pdf.

Wisconsin Technical College System. (2015). *Outcomes-based funding*. Retrieved from http://www.wtcsystem.edu/initiatives/performance-funding.

Xu, D., & Jaggars, S. S. (2011). *Online and hybrid course enrollment and performance in Washington state community and technical colleges* (CCRC Working Paper No. 31). Retrieved from Community College Research Center website: http://ccrc.tc.columbia.edu/publications/online-hybrid-courses-washington.html.

Zemsky, R. (2013). *Checklist for change: Making American higher education a sustainable enterprise*. New Brunswick, NJ: Rutgers University Press.

Zumbrun, J. (2013, March 28). More Americans work in the underground economy. *Bloomberg Businessweek*. Retrieved from http://www.businessweek.com/articles/2013-03-28/more-americans-work-in-the-underground-economy.

Zumeta, W. A. (2004). State higher education financing: Demand imperatives meet structural, cyclical, and political constraints. In E. P. St. John & M. D. Parsons (Eds.), *Public funding for higher education: Changing contexts and new rationales* (pp. 79–107). Baltimore, MD: Johns Hopkins University Press.

Zumeta, W. A., Breneman, D. W., Callan, P. M., & Finney, J. E. (2012). *Financing higher education in the era of globalization*. Cambridge, MA: Harvard University Press.

# Index

# About the Authors

**Richard M. Romano** is professor emeritus of economics at Broome Community College/State University of New York and director of the Institute for Community College Research. He is also an affiliated faculty member at the Cornell Higher Education Research Institute at Cornell University. Having served as a faculty member/administrator at the community college level for over forty years, he also has been a visiting professor/scholar at UCLA (1983), the State University of New York at Binghamton (1986), the New School (1995), North Carolina State University (2002), and the University of South Florida (2008). His numerous books, articles, reviews, and monographs have been concentrated in three areas—the history of economic thought, international education, and higher education finance. The recipient of a number of awards and grants, in 2003 he received the Chancellor's Award for Excellence in Scholarship and Creative Activities, the highest award given for research by the State University of New York. More recently he has received the Senior Scholar Award (2013) from the Council for the Study of Community Colleges. He has a BA degree in economics from St. Lawrence University and an MA and PhD in economics from the State University of New York at Binghamton.

**James C. Palmer** is professor of higher education at Illinois State University (ISU). Prior to joining the ISU faculty in 1992, he served as acting director of the Center for Community College Education at George Mason University (Fairfax, VA), vice president for communications at the American Association for Community Colleges (Washington, DC), staff associate at the Center for the Study of Community Colleges (Los Angeles, CA), and assistant director for user services at the ERIC Clearinghouse for Junior Colleges (UCLA). Palmer is a past president of the Council for the Study of

Community Colleges, which is affiliated with the American Association of Community Colleges. He is the editor of *Grapevine*, an online compilation of state fiscal support for higher education (http://www.grapevine.ilstu. edu/). In addition, he served as editor of the *Community College Review* from 2007 through June 2013. He has a BA in English and German from Pacific University as well as a master of library science degree and a PhD in education from the UCLA.